W9-BAX-065

British Poets
of the Great War

British Poets
of the Great War

Fred D. Crawford

SELINSGROVE: Susquehanna University Press
LONDON AND TORONTO: Associated University Presses

Associated University Presses
440 Forsgate Drive
Cranbury, NJ 08512

Associated University Presses
25 Sicilian Avenue
London WC1A 2QH, England

Associated University Presses
2133 Royal Windsor Drive
Unit 1
Mississauga, Ontario
Canada L5J 1K5

The paper used in this publication meets the requirements
of the American National Standard for Permanence of Paper
for Printed Library Materials Z39.48-1984.

Library of Congress Cataloging-in-Publication Data

Crawford, Fred D.
  British poets of the Great War.

  Bibliography: p.
  Includes index.
  1. English poetry—20th century—History and
criticism.   2. World War, 1914–1918—Literature
and the war.   3. War poetry, English—History and
criticism.   I. Title.
PR605.W65C7   1988   821′.912′09358   86-43124
ISBN 0–941664–77–5 (alk. paper)

For my parents,
James B. and Geraldine M. Crawford

Contents

Preface

ALTHOUGH POETRY AND POETS OF THE GREAT WAR HAVE BEEN SUBJECTS OF reviews, articles, monographs, and chapters of books for the past seventy years, the establishment of a war poetry "canon" has been fairly recent. In 1964 John H. Johnston's *English Poetry of the First World War: A Study in the Evolution of Lyric and Narrative Form* provided the first full-length scholarly treatment of the war poets. Johnston's approach was to examine war poetry as literature in the light of rigid generic expectations, leading him to conclude that the war poets erred in confining their poetry to lyrics and narratives instead of placing the war into an epic perspective.

However, many of the war poets did not live long enough to develop the general, sweeping vision of the war that Johnston demanded of them and that only few could attain during the appeals to nationalism that prevailed in wartime. Changes so vast were not always workable in short lyrical or narrative poems, and few actions seemed appropriate for epic treatment. The adventures of T. E. Lawrence (of Arabia), for example, did not attract poets but film producers (such as J. Arthur Rank, who commissioned Siegfried Sassoon in the early 1930s to write a screenplay dramatizing Lawrence's *Seven Pillars of Wisdom*), and Richard Aldington's 1955 biography of Lawrence has deflated the illusion that Lawrence was truly heroic in the epic sense.

Johnston's chapter titles name ten poets: Rupert Brooke, Julian Grenfell, Robert Nichols, Charles Hamilton Sorley, Siegfried Sassoon, Edmund Blunden, Wilfred Owen, Isaac Rosenberg, Herbert Read, and David Jones, half of whom published little or nothing during the war. When Bernard Bergonzi published *Heroes' Twilight: A Study of the Literature of the Great War* in 1965, he discussed poetry, fiction, and prose memoirs that reveal changes in values wrought by the war. Bergonzi challenged Johnston's insistence that the epic is the proper vehicle for presenting the truth of modern warfare. However, his "canon" of war poets is almost identical to Johnston's. He also devotes chapters to ten poets, differing from Johnston by replacing Robert Nichols with Robert Graves and by adding a brief chapter on "Civilian Responses."

Jon Silkin's *Out of Battle: The Poetry of the Great War*, published in 1972, modifies Bergonzi's list. Silkin omits Julian Grenfell and Robert Graves, adding chapters on Thomas Hardy, Rudyard Kipling, Edward Thomas, Ivor

Gurney, Richard Aldington, and Ford Madox Ford. Silkin's study combines Johnston's attention to literary form with Bergonzi's emphasis on changing attitudes expressed in the poetry, but Silkin's study has drawn fire from some critics who resent Silkin's political judgments of the poets' relative merit. In the words of Samuel Hynes, in Silkin's book "the attitudes embodied in the liberal myth of war become standards of literary judgment."[1]

Despite their differences in approach to war poetry as literature, Johnston, Bergonzi, and Silkin reveal a common bias: war poets must also be trench poets. Of the seventeen poets named in the three tables of contents, only two—Hardy and Kipling—were noncombatants. These seventeen (excluding Nichols and Ford) are among the best poets who wrote about the war. However, many of these seventeen, some of whom published no war poetry until well after the Armistice, have become war poets only in retrospect. During the war, many others were writing war poems that directly influenced the public's responses to the war.

Catherine W. Reilly's *English Poetry of the First World War: A Bibliography* (1978), limited to poets who published books of war verse or whose war poems otherwise reached a wide audience, listed no fewer than 2,225 English war poets. By the middle of the war, "there seemed some danger that the serious work of professional poets would be swept from public view by the flood of puerile rhymes from public school subalterns and patriotic effusions from armchair patriots and bloodthirsty old ladies from Bath."[2] For those who read poetry during the war, the patriotic effusions that appeared in the *English Review, To-Day, Poetry Review, Graphic, Contemporary Review, Punch,* and even the London *Times* were the typical wartime responses.

Unlike the Imagists, Vorticists, and Futurists, the war poets were not working as a group to change the direction of modern poetry for the sake of literary interests, although their verse demonstrated many features that have come to distinguish modernists from the prewar Georgians. Although the war poets' literary influence has been comparatively minor, the poets provide a rare glimpse of the relationship between literary expression and reality. Since the novels of the war did not appear, for the most part, until long after the Armistice, the war poems provide the most reliable record of how contemporary responses to the war changed. The war poets shared the failings of other occasional poets, but they did have the advantage of immediacy in their verse, and the literature of the war eventually did much to inform our current conceptions, as Paul Fussell has shown in *The Great War and Modern Memory* (1975). However, much of that literature did not have an audience until the war was over.

As early as December 1914, the *Egoist* printed a satire by "Herbert Blenheim" which ridiculed the quality and quantity of second-rate poets then deluging the magazines:

> At the sound of the drum,
> Out of their dens they come, they come,
> The little poets we hoped were dumb,
> The little poets we thought were dead,
> The poets who certainly haven't been read
> Since heaven knows when, they come, they come,
> At the sound of the drum, of the drum, drum, drum.

In his final stanza, "Blenheim" identifies new "horrors of war":

> At the sound of the drum,
> O Tommy, you know, if we haven't all come
> To stand by your side in the hideous hum,
> It isn't the horrors of war we fear,
> The horrors of war we've got 'em here,
> When the poets come on like waves, and *come*
> At the sound of the drum, of the drum, drum, drum.

These "horrors" pose a major problem in providing a comprehensive survey of how poets responded to the war during the war. On the one hand, if we are to understand how the most widely read poets responded to the war in the popular press, we must consider the traditional responses that characterized early reactions. On the other hand, many of these poems are simply awful and do not really merit literary discussion for their own sake. However, in order to trace the emergence of new techniques and approaches as well as to evaluate better responses, we must begin with the fumbling efforts of the mainstream versifiers, if only to have a standard to apply to the better poems. Since one purpose of this study is to determine how the literature developed in reaction to the war itself, frequently discussion of traditional responses focuses on content more than on poetic technique. At least this background can allow greater appreciation and respect for the better war poets.

This book attempts to provide a comprehensive view of the diverse ways in which British poets responded to the 1914–18 war, both during and after the conflict. Instead of focusing only on the relatively small number whose work has literary value, this study considers as "war poets" those whose verse addressed aspects of the war, whether the poets were soldiers in the trenches, noncombatants, V.A.D. nurses, civilians, or whatever, with or without literary background. Although this approach requires including many writers whose poetry is not very good, it can also provide a better sense of what the public was reading as the war continued, how poetry reinforced pre-1914 conceptions during and even after the war, and how outmoded views of the conflict prevailed to the point of obscuring those poets whose views are more in accord with our own.

The first section focuses on traditional responses, including calls to action, chivalric treatments of the war, pastorals, and elegies. This is the poetry that conformed to pre-1914 values and that prevailed in the popular press during the war. The second section, addressing shifts in technique and attitude, examines verse that reflects the ways poets' views and methods altered as the nature of the war became more clear. The third section, examining innovative responses, discusses the work of four poets who, in striking contrast to the war poets in general, deserve a lasting place in English literature on the merits of their war verses. The final section examines poetry that expressed diverse retrospective views of the war. This book hopes to place the war poetry into a context that reveals its reception by the public when it appeared as well as its literary and philosophical worth in retrospect.

Acknowledgments

I WISH TO THANK THE PEOPLE WHOSE HELP HAS MADE THIS BOOK POSSIBLE. Richard E. Winslow, III, has offered many suggestions, unearthed obscure bibliographical information, and provided copies of several poems from forgotten periodicals. Stanley Weintraub, Research Professor of English at Penn State and Director of the Institute for the Arts and Humanistic Studies, provided many suggestions as well as almost inaccessible materials. Mrs. Margaret Barnes contributed biographical information on her late husband, Leonard Barnes, and provided copies of his books. David Roland Leighton sent a privately printed edition of the poetry of his uncle, Roland Leighton, which includes biographical information. Mrs. Myfanwy Thomas offered helpful comments on the poetry of her father, Edward Thomas. Chet Wolford reviewed part of the manuscript, and Bruce Morton provided bibliographical data. I am also indebted to Kinley E. Roby for suggesting that I undertake this study.

"Bombardment" and "Soliloquy 1" from *The Complete Poems of Richard Aldington* (Allen & Unwin) by Richard Aldington are reprinted by permission of Alister Kershaw; "Nightfall" and "The Volunteer" from *Poems 1912–1933* (Sidgwick & Jackson) by Herbert Asquith are reprinted by permission of Sidgwick & Jackson, Ltd.; selections from *Youth at Arms* (Peter Davies) and *The Glory of the World Sonnets* (Peter Davies) by Leonard Barnes are reprinted by permission of Mrs. Margaret Barnes; "Nox Mortis" from *Bombing of Bruges* (Hodder & Stoughton) by Paul Bewsher is reprinted by permission of Hodder & Stoughton Ltd.; "For the Fallen (September 1914)" from *Laurence Binyon Anthology* (Hodder & Stoughton) by Laurence Binyon is reprinted by permission of Mrs. Nicolete Gray and The Society of Authors on behalf of the Laurence Binyon Estate; "Rural Economy" from *Poems 1914–1930* (Cobden-Sanderson) by Edmund Blunden is reprinted by permission of A. D. Peters & Co., Ltd.; "I. Peace," "III. The Dead," and "V. The Soldier" from *Complete Poems of Rupert Brooke* (Sidgwick & Jackson) by Rupert Brooke are reprinted by permission of Sidgwick & Jackson, Ltd.; "Elegy in a Country Churchyard" from *Collected Poems of G. K. Chesterton* (Dodd, Mead) by G. K. Chesterton is reprinted by permission of the Estate of G. K. Chesterton and Dodd, Mead

& Co., Inc.; "A Dirge of Victory" from *Fifty Poems* (Curtis Brown) by Lord Dunsany is reprinted by permission of Curtis Brown Ltd., London, on behalf of John Child-Villiers and Valentine Lamb as literary executors of Lord Dunsany; "International Conference" from *Mournful Numbers, Verses and Epigrams* (Macmillan) by Colin Ellis is reprinted by permission of Macmillan, London and Basingstoke; "The Deserter" from *The Judgement of Valhalla* (Chatto & Windus) by Gilbert Frankau is reprinted by permission of Mrs. Susan Frankau; "The Bayonet" and "His Father" from *Collected Poems 1905–1925* (Macmillan) by Wilfrid Gibson are reprinted by permission of Mr. Michael Gibson and Macmillan, London and Basingstoke; "A Dead Boche" and "The Trenches" from *Poems 1914–1926* (Heinemann) by Robert Graves are reprinted by permission of Robert Graves; "To His Love" from *War's Embers* (Sidgwick & Jackson) by Ivor Gurney is reprinted by permission of Sidgwick & Jackson, Ltd.; "Prisoners" and "The Sleepers" from *Gloucestershire Friends* (Sidgwick & Jackson) by F. W. Harvey are reprinted by permission of Sidgwick & Jackson, Ltd.; "After the Battle" from *The Bomber Gypsy* (Methuen) by A. P. Herbert is reprinted by permission of the Estate of A. P. Herbert; "Before Action" from *Verse and Prose in Peace and War* (Murray) by W. N. Hodgson is reprinted by permission of John Murray (Publishers); "Batteries Out of Ammunition," "Common Form," and "A Dead Statesman" from *Rudyard Kipling's Verse: The Definitive Edition* (Doubleday) by Rudyard Kipling are reprinted by permission of The National Trust of Great Britain and Doubleday & Company, Inc.; "Bombardment" from *The Complete Poems of D. H. Lawrence* (Viking) by D. H. Lawrence is reprinted by permission of Viking Penguin Inc., the Estate of Mrs. Frieda Lawrence Ravagli, and Lawrence Pollinger Ltd.; "Hédauville" by Roland Leighton is included by permission of David Roland Leighton, his nephew; "The Miners' Response" from *Bull and Other Verses* (Constable) by D. S. MacColl is reprinted by permission of Constable Publishers; "In Flanders Fields" by John McCrae is reprinted by permission of *Punch;* "Another Epitaph on an Army of Mercenaries" from *Collected Poems of Hugh MacDiarmid* (Macmillan) by Hugh MacDiarmid is reprinted by permission of his son, Michael Grieve, Executor for his father; "Before the Charge" from *Soldier Songs* by Patrick MacGill, published by E. P. Dutton in 1918, is reprinted by their permission; "Noon" from *Ardours and Endurances* (Chatto & Windus) by Robert Nichols is reprinted by permission of the author's Literary Estate and Chatto & Windus, Ltd.; "Futility," "Anthem for Doomed Youth," and "Dulce et Decorum Est" from *The Collected Poems of Wilfred Owen* (Chatto & Windus) by Wilfred Owen are reprinted by permission of The Owen Estate, Chatto & Windus Ltd., and New Directions; "How Long, O Lord" from Lord Selbourne's *The Life of Robert Palmer* (Hodder & Stoughton) by Robert Palmer is reprinted by permission of Hodder & Stoughton Limited; "Fear" and "The Happy

Warrior" from *Collected Poems of Herbert Read* (Faber & Faber) by Herbert Read are reprinted by permission of David Higham Associates Limited on behalf of the author's estate; "Trench Poets" from *Collected Poems* (Bodley Head) by Edgell Rickword is reprinted by permission of The Bodley Head; "Winter Warfare" from *Behind the Eyes* (Sidgwick & Jackson) by Edgell Rickword is reprinted by permission of Sidgwick & Jackson, Ltd.; "Break of Day in the Trenches" and "Returning, We Hear the Larks" from *The Collected Works of Isaac Rosenberg* (Oxford University Press) by Isaac Rosenberg are reprinted by permission of Chatto & Windus Ltd.; "Base Details," "Dreamers," "The General," "Glory of Women," "Lamentations," and "Suicide in the Trenches" from *Collected Poems of Siegfried Sassoon*, copyright 1918 by E. P. Dutton Co., copyright renewed 1946 by Siegfried Sassoon, are reprinted by permission of Viking Penguin Inc; "The Soul of a Nation" by Owen Seaman is reprinted by permission of *Punch*; "The Old Soldiers" from *Poems 1912–1932* (Macmillan) by Edward Shanks is reprinted by permission of Macmillan, London and Basingstoke; "Judas and the Profiteer" from *Selected Poems Old and New* (Duckworth) by Osbert Sitwell is reprinted by permission of David Higham Associates Ltd. on behalf of the author's literary estate; "To Germany" and "When You See Millions of the Mouthless Dead" from *Marlborough and Other Poems* (Cambridge University Press) by Charles Hamilton Sorley are reprinted by permission of Cambridge University Press; "Solomon in All His Glory" from *The Unutterable Beauty: Collected Poems* (Hodder & Stoughton) by G. A. Studdert-Kennedy is reprinted by permission of Hodder & Stoughton Limited; "As the Team's Head Brass," "No One Cares Less Than I," and "This Is No Case of Petty Right or Wrong" from *Collected Poems* (Faber & Faber) by Edward Thomas are reprinted by permission of Faber & Faber and Myfanwy Thomas, his only surviving child; "From Albert to Bapaume" from *Resentment: Poems* (Grant Richards) by Alec Waugh is reprinted by permission of A. D. Peters & Co., Ltd.; "Flanders" from *The Star Fields and Other Poems* (Blackwell) by Willoughby Weaving is reprinted by permission of Basil Blackwell, Publisher; "God! How I Hate You" from *Diary of a Dead Officer* (Allen & Unwin) by Arthur Graeme West is reprinted by permission of George Allen & Unwin (Publishers) Ltd.; "France" from *The Fourth of August* (Eyre Methuen) by Humbert Wolfe is reprinted by permission of Associated Book Publishers Ltd.; "On Being Asked for a War Poem" from *Collected Poems* (Macmillan) by W. B. Yeats is reprinted by permission of M. B. Yeats, Anne Yeats, Macmillan London Limited, and Macmillan Publishing Co., Inc.

British Poets
of the Great War

PART I

Traditional Responses

1

Poetry and the Great War

AT THE OUTBREAK OF HOSTILITIES, SIR EDWARD GREY EXPRESSED HIS PRO-
phetic awareness of the far-reaching consequences of the war: "The lamps
are going out all over Europe; we shall not see them lit again in our lifetime."
The cost of the war was catastrophic—Central Powers at least 3.5 million
dead, Allies at least 5 million dead—with untold physical and mental injuries. The reality of the war violated all prewar expectations. War poet Robert
Graves recalled that "continuous shell fire and the lesser nuisances of machine guns, trench mortars, rifle grenades so stimulated our adrenal glands
that, after three months, we became mentally off-center; after six, certifiably
insane."[1] When war correspondent H. M. Tomlinson wrote his war novel
All Our Yesterdays in 1930, he expressed the soldier's newfound abhorrence
of mechanical warfare: " 'As things are,' an officer explained, 'a consumptive
machine-gunner, too scared in an attack to bolt, can sit in a lucky hole in the
ground and scupper a company of the best as they advance. Courage isn't
what it used to be. The machine runs over us and we can't stop it.' "[2]

Since the British Army assigned three or four times as many officers to the
line as did the Germans, the elite class that provided junior officers suffered
disproportionate losses. By 1916, men of the other ranks received field
promotions to fill the gaps left by the "lost generation," permanently
altering England's social structure. Throughout the war, the British soldier
seemed to bear the brunt of the struggle. French *poilus* mutinied and
subsequently held back from the heaviest fighting, Russian troops mutinied
and then pulled back from all fronts early in 1917, and United States soldiers
did not reach France until June 1917 and did not clash with the Germans
until November 1917. Of the major countries involved in the Allied cause,
only the British doggedly endured unremitting fighting for the entire four
years.

Noncombatants as well as soldiers felt the effects of the war. Civilians did
not suffer so much as soldiers, but their anguish was genuine enough, and
they had constant reminders of the war. The Defence of the Realm Act
(DORA), passed by the House of Commons after five minutes' deliberation
on 8 August 1914, abrogated civil liberties and placed England under martial
law. Immediate results included the incarceration of aliens of military age,

censorship, irregular pub hours, restriction on foreign travel, and harassment of suspect individuals (including D. H. Lawrence, whose wife, Frieda, a naturalized British citizen, was related to Baron von Richthofen). During 1915 Germany's submarine blockade of Great Britain intensified existing shortages, and that year the costs of the war drove the British income tax to an unprecedented 15 percent (later it would reach 30 percent). Zeppelins raided England during 1915 and 1916, and on 28 November 1916, within a month of the largest zeppelin raid, the Germans began airplane bombardments. By 1917, food prices in Britain had risen 94 percent above prewar levels.

The beginning of military conscription emphasized the continuing losses of men and outraged many who felt that conscription was demeaningly "continental." Rationing, which began in January 1918, applied to virtually all food except potatoes and bread by the summer. Casualties were so extensive that newspapers printed lists of the fallen in miniscule type to obscure the number of casualties. In England, one could even hear the thunder of artillery from the front, a short channel-crossing away. Although noncombatants did not visit the trenches, they suffered shortages, fatalities, and bereavement. Civilian involvement did not include trench fighting, but it included enough of hardship and loss to enable civilian poets to write as personally of the war, if not of the front, as did many trench poets.

The changes brought by the war coincided with major shifts in British poetry. During the first decade of the century, poets subsequently identified as Georgians realized that British poetry was in a bad way. In December 1908, dramatist John Synge surmised that "before verse can be human again it must learn to be brutal."[3] Georgianism, however, was not a movement but a loose collection of diverse poets whose work appeared in the *Georgian Poetry* anthology in 1912. The existence of Georgianism was less the result of poetic innovation than of the timing of Edward Marsh, Winston Churchill's private secretary, who edited that volume and the four which followed. Poets of the first volume included Lascelles Abercrombie, Gordon Bottomley, Rupert Brooke, G. K. Chesterton, W. H. Davies, Walter de la Mare, John Drinkwater, James Elroy Flecker, W. W. Gibson, D. H. Lawrence, John Masefield, Harold Monro (whose Poetry Bookshop published the anthology), T. Sturge Moore, Ronald Ross, Edmund Beale Sargant, James Stephens, and R. C. Trevelyan. Except for their appearance in the same volume, these poets had little in common other than their identity as post-Victorian writers and their desire to contribute to a poetic tradition. One can appreciate their awareness of the need for changes in poetry, but their response to that need fell considerably short. Perhaps the greatest accomplishment of Marsh and his anthologies was to demonstrate that there was an audience for poetry. The *Georgian Poetry* series was unexpectedly popular, enabling Marsh to pay royalties to the contributors.

Modern critics, in retrospect, have attacked the Georgian poets for failures both of purpose and of technique. According to E. L. Black, Georgian poetry "lacked contact with science and industry, its emotions were gentlemanly and restrained; it enthused about the trivial details of rural life. Its vocabulary was artificially romantic and its metre was tediously orthodox. It lacked the vigour and the social purpose that was being shown in contemporary *prose* by writers such as Conrad, George Bernard Shaw and D. H. Lawrence."[4] John H. Johnston has cited specific failings of the Georgian poets, including "timidity, conservatism, self-consciousness, and lack of originality and genuine imaginative power" as well as "loss of contact with contemporary reality."[5] He views Georgian poetry as "incapable of irony or ambivalence because it could not achieve any critical distance from its subject-matter; avoiding any complexity of attitude, it exercised emotion and sensibility, not the intellect."[6]

Rupert Brooke demonstrated these failings in his prewar poem "A Channel Passage," which attempts to describe seasickness realistically. Trying to retain control of his rising gorge, the poem's speaker "must think hard of something, or be sick," and, to the potential consternation of the addressed lover, the speaker "could think hard of only one thing—*you!*" Despite the speaker's attempt to conquer his stomach with his heart, "Retchings twist and tie me, / Old meat, good meals, brown gobbets, up I throw." In this ludicrous attempt at "brutal" realism, Brooke failed for several reasons, not the least of which is the triviality of the subject itself. The inverted diction ("up I throw") only emphasizes the distance between the poem's expression and the promptings of *mal de mer.*

The Georgians helped create an atmosphere that would enable war poetry to enjoy a large audience, but the vast distance between their literary techniques and actual experience shunted the Georgians onto a literary siding. The Georgians and their followers lacked a "cause" beyond their fondness for poetry. Their absorption in the possibilities of the poetic medium produced little that was new, primarily because they treated poetry as something totally removed from life despite their avowed intention to write poetry that more truly imitated reality. Ironically the war poets, for the most part, are on a similar siding because they went to the opposite extreme. Most of the soldier poets were not conscious innovators of poetic form. They were attempting to communicate their feelings and observations of war to an ignorant public, to tell the truth while their elders were lying. In the process, many subordinated style to subject matter and rejected prescribed romantic paraphernalia and conventions.

Innovation came, however, as Jon Silkin notes:

> The war poets' use of contemporary speech and vocabulary was not in the main the result of any alteration in literary attitudes, but, rather, the

result of new and terrifying circumstances. Because it was the environ-
ment that changed their work (even Rosenberg's, to some extent), the
change was deeper than linguistic and structural. The new circumstances necessitated a new vocabulary and, to a lesser extent, altered
forms and syntax. The traditional forms were tested, not merely by the
new substance they had to express, but by the intensity of response to
it.[7]

When W. B. Yeats excluded the work of the trench poets (except for Herbert
Read's *The End of a War*) from his edition of the *Oxford Book of Modern
Verse* in 1936, he objected not to method but to subject: "passive suffering is
not a theme for poetry." Early critics focused on the illuminating content
rather than on the poetic shortcomings of the trench poets' work. For
Arthur Waugh, "It would seem to be not so much a fact that the war has
made poetry, as that poetry has, now for the first time, made War—made it
in its own image, with all the tinsel and gaud of tradition stripped away from
it; and so made it perhaps that no sincere artist will ever venture again to
represent War in those delusive colours with which Art has been too often
content to disguise it in the past."[8]

The importance of the war poetry for Waugh's contemporaries, and also
for us, lies more in its content than in its technique, more in what the poetry
says than in how the poetry says it. However, the position of Great War
poets between post-Victorian and modernist poetry remains awkward. According to critic Philip Hobsbaum,

> English poetry in the twentieth century has had four atrocious strokes
> of luck. They are worth enumerating. First of all, that the wrong
> emphasis should have been placed on the work of the one great Vic-
> torian who could have had a useful influence—I mean Hardy. Secondly,
> that the Georgians, for the most part, should have chosen to regard
> tradition as a resting-place rather than a spring-board. Third, that three
> of the poets who *were* developing an essentially English modernity
> [Wilfred Owen, Isaac Rosenberg, and Edward Thomas] should have
> been killed in the war—their publication, too, was a delayed and
> incomplete one. And, lastly, that Eliot and Pound should have chosen
> to start an essentially American revolution in verse technique over here
> rather than in the United States, and so filled the gap which the death of
> the war poets left with an alien product whose influence has been a bad
> one.[9]

As a group, the war poets were unable to meet Johnston's expectations of all
poets: "They must live precariously on the frontiers of an expanding consciousness; they must adapt their attitudes and techniques to the rhythms of
modern life; they must discover or invent the forms necessary for the
representation of contemporary experience. If the poetry of World War I has

taught us this, it has justified itself not only in its own terms but also in terms of what it has illustrated for modern literature."[10]

By definition, war poets are occasional poets, responding to an emerging reality that the Georgians largely ignored. The war poet, according to Philip Larkin, "is chained . . . to an historical event, and an abnormal one at that. However well he does it, however much we agree that the war happened and ought to be written about, there is still a tendency for us to withhold our highest praise on the grounds that a poet's choice of subject should seem an action, not a reaction. 'The Wreck of the Deutschland', we feel, would have been markedly inferior if Hopkins had been a survivor from the passenger list."[11] The point, however, is that the war poets did succeed in responding to striking and almost incomprehensible changes in modern life, in communicating their grasp of these changes to a larger public, and in demonstrating the role of poetry in responding to new challenges. Although the Georgians as a group were better poetic technicians, the war poets were more forthright revealers of truth, paving the way for later poets to combine the two.

War poetry followed a pattern that was roughly, but not rigidly, chronological. The poets' responses to the war began with the continuation of prewar expectations, usually in traditional poetic forms. Most calls to action still seem unsatisfying because the poets themselves had little time to formulate their responses. Poet Laureate Robert Bridges wrote "Wake Up, England"—a call to action ending in the demand that "GOD DEFEND THE RIGHT!"—almost immediately. The more thoughtful Thomas Hardy recorded the spirit of volunteers in "Men Who March Away," describing the "faith and fire" within the men rather than interpreting issues beyond the generality of a "just" cause. Soldier poets such as E. A. Mackintosh, after experiencing trench warfare, wrote calls that were ironical without compromising their belief that English victory was essential. In "Recruiting," Mackintosh mocked civilians' armchair patriotism but pleaded in earnest for volunteers to "Come and learn / To live and die with honest men." John McCrae made of "In Flanders Fields" a plea to "Take up our quarrel with the foe" rather than to negotiate peace, and younger men matched the enthusiasm of their elders. Rupert Brooke's *1914* sonnets exulted, "Now, God be thanked Who has matched us with His hour" in all seriousness, and made of a soldier's grave "some corner of a foreign field / That is for ever England" without embarrassment.

Even after the Somme Offensive provided grim evidence that "patriotism is not enough," poets not only supported the war but also tried to ennoble it. In retrospect, it seems odd to regard the war as a continuation of a chivalric tradition, but even those who fought were slow to reject the romance of chivalric combat. Julian Grenfell, a professional soldier, exalted "joy of battle" in "Into Battle." Another soldier-poet, W. N. Hodgson, made "Before Action" a soldier's prayer to prove worthy in the lines: "Make me a man, O Lord" and "Help me to die, O Lord." Although the new technology of warfare inspired soldiers to view the mechanics of modern war in a new light, many persisted in a chivalric view of new machines, particularly of aircraft.

Cecil Lewis, a pilot in the Royal Flying Corps, while recognizing the end of chivalry in the trenches, heralded the continuation of chivalry in the air. In his autobiography *Sagittarius Rising* (1936), he wrote of aerial combat's contrast to the trenches:

> It was like the lists of the Middle Ages, the only sphere in modern warfare where a man saw his enemy and faced him in mortal combat, the only sphere where there was still chivalry and honour. If you won, it was your own bravery and skill; if you lost, it was because you had met a better man.
>
> You did not sit in a muddy trench while someone who had no personal enmity against you loosed off a gun, five miles away, and blew you to smithereens—and did not know he had done it! That was not fighting; it was murder. Senseless, brutal, ignoble. We were spared that.[12]

F. Victor Branford, a flight lieutenant, was also aware of the contrast between flier and infantryman. In "Night-Flying," first published in *To-Day*, the flier, "in the Cathedral of God's brain," looks down to

> mark the inconstant strain
> Of delible ambition wax and wane
> Over the soil, where men and maggots pry,
> While wraiths of vanished ages surge, and sigh
> Forgotten valour and sagas of dead pain.

In the same moment that the impersonal nature of trench slaughter impinged on the awareness of the soldier, possibilities of placing the war into a chivalric perspective suggested themselves. Robert Nichols, despite his moot claim of experience in war, could communicate his rather confused sense that the "new Elizabethans" included himself, Graves, and Sassoon as the Three Musketeers.

War poets also exploited pastoral and elegiac conventions. Pastorals ranged from E. W. Tennant's "Home Thoughts in Laventie"—a nostalgic poem ending with "Home—what a perfect place!"—to Francis Ledwidge's "Soliloquy," which shifts from memories of his home to his wartime circumstances:

> And now I'm drinking wine in France,
> The helpless child of circumstance.
> Tomorrow will be loud with war,
> How will I be accounted for?

Others wrote pastoral descriptions of war scenes, contrasts between scenes of peace and war, and laments on war's destruction of natural order and beauty. Traditional elegies, predictably, were common in the war. The most moving was Laurence Binyon's "For the Fallen (September 1914)," which stressed the immortality of the slain: "Age shall not weary them, nor the years condemn." A. E. Housman took a more direct view of the feelings of the dead: "Life, to be sure, is nothing much to lose; / But young men think it is, and we were young." In some writers, notably Sergeant Leslie Coulson, the pastoral and elegiac suggested the beginnings of antiwar protest, particularly in the poem "Who Made the Law?", which angrily asks, "Who made the Law that men should die in meadows?"

As the war progressed, poets' attitudes toward the war changed, which led them to shift their poetic techniques. Poets who modified form and attitude include the Imagists, those searching for a broader perspective, those adopting a comic stance, those who protested, and several women poets who tried to broaden the relevance of the war. The Imagists, including T. E. Hulme, Ezra Pound, Ford Madox Ford, D. H. Lawrence (nominally), Richard Aldington, and Herbert Read, applied a prewar revolution in poetic expression to their perceptions of a new reality. Aldington's "Soliloquy—1" presents a soldier's reaction to the carnage with stark realism:

> Dead men should be so still, austere,
> And beautiful,
> Not wobbling carrion roped upon a cart. . . .
>
> Well, thank God for rum.

The Imagists' chief contribution, largely due to prewar changes in verse technique, was a clearer depiction of war's reality and thus a harsher impact on the sensibilities of the reader.

However, poets who grasped the place of the war in a larger context usually placed less emphasis on poetic innovation than on content. Charles Hamilton Sorley, for example, favored the sonnet, but in "To Germany" he expressed a view of the war that went beyond simplistic notions of a just cause: "You are blind like us. Your hurt no man designed. . . ." In "A Hundred Thousand Million Mites We Go" he transcended the soldier's usual implication that the universe ended at the trench walls. Arthur Graeme West lashed poets who clung to outmoded attitudes toward the war:

> God! How I hate you, you young cheerful men,
> Whose pious poetry blossoms on your graves
> As soon as you are in them. . . .

W. W. Gibson, using the *persona* of a lower-class recruit comparing present circumstances with civilian life, communicated the shock many similarly displaced soldiers felt.

Two poets, Robert Graves and Edgell Rickword, retreated behind the comic mask in their depictions of war's brutalities. Siegfried Sassoon, who lacked their restraint, became a standard for judging other war poets in expressions of protest against profiteers, politicians, inept generals, and unsympathetic civilians. Other protesters attacked bloodthirsty civilians, economic opportunists, and anyone else who seemed either to prolong the war or to gain from it, but only a few treated war itself as an evil. Most protesters questioned the conduct of the war rather than war's necessity.

The dual allegiance of the Irish, torn between their concern for the soldiers at the front and their desire for national independence, resulted in a mixture of poetic expressions concerning the war, some fiercely anti-German but others questioning Ireland's involvement in an English war after Parliament suspended Home Rule, hard-won and finally on the statute books in September 1914, for the duration of the war. Irish poets of protest objected to English recruiting tactics in Ireland, the complicity of Irish nationalist leaders who supported England's war, and particularly the subordination of Irish concerns in the name of the war effort. Sean O'Casey's "The Grand Oul' Dame Brittania" satirized England's indifference to Irish concerns, while his "If the Germans Came to Ireland in the Morning" ridiculed the favorite scare tactic of the war propagandists. Most of the Irish poets, however, focused less on the war than on the troubles at home that culminated in the Easter Uprising of 1916 and the trial and execution of Roger Casement.

Women poets contributed calls to action, celebrations of the fallen, pastoral contrasts, and protests similar to those of soldier poets, although inevitably the women poets fell short when they tried to depict realistically the trenches they had never seen. They also provided poems arguing that women had their place in the struggle. Vera Brittain, the best of the women war poets, never lost her early enthusiasm for the poetry of Rupert Brooke. She focused on the sacrifices of women during the war and the postwar blight for those who survived their service. Her poem "To My Brother," written a few days before her brother's death, evokes the suffering that war brought to those whose involvement was not military. Many of her later poems communicate the resentment she shared with soldiers and others who learned that their wartime service was exploited or dismissed by those who had stayed at home.

Truly innovative poets of the war were few. Edmund Blunden, a pastoral poet, sought acceptance and harmony in violent surroundings. In his poem "Zero," Blunden wrote, "It's plain we were born for this, naught else," and he refused to subordinate his descriptions and narratives to curative rhetoric.

In "Rural Economy (1917)" he created a metaphor of war as a farmer, letting his comparison speak for itself: "The field and wood, all bone-fed loam, / Shot up a roaring harvest-home." Similarly Edward Thomas strove for acceptance of his quiet patriotism and tried to place the war into a larger, historical perspective. In "This Is No Case of Petty Right or Wrong," he insisted that

> I hate not Germans, nor grow hot
> With love of Englishmen, to please newspapers.
> Beside my hate for one fat patriot
> My hatred of the Kaiser is love true.

Wilfred Owen, who developed the sustained use of pararhyme (rhymes that retain their initial and ending consonant sounds but differ in their vowels, such as *shell* and *shall* or *bleed* and *blade*) and who focused on "the pity of war," moved from overt protest to poems of broader significance. His poetry remains within a tradition of English romanticism but applies itself to modern problems. In "Greater Love," for example, he begins, "Red lips are not so red / As the stained stones kissed by the English dead," and his response to civilian insensitivity also employs romantic diction: "But cursed are dullards whom no cannon stuns, / That they should be as stones." Isaac Rosenberg, whose affinity for Blake and the romantic tradition is unmistakable, also found traditional modes effective to express modern feelings. In "Dead Man's Dump," the brutal depiction of war's horrors reveals Rosenberg's eye for physical detail, his attention to simple descriptive language, and his awareness of the pity of war:

> A man's brains splattered on
> A stretcher-bearer's face;
> His shook shoulders slipped their load,
> But when they bent to look again
> The drowning soul was sunk too deep
> For human tenderness.

Of these four innovative poets, only Blunden survived the war.

When the war ended, retrospective views varied widely. Siegfried Sassoon offered a purely lyrical poem, "Everyone Sang," to celebrate the arrival of peace, while Lord Dunsany, reflecting on the cost, chose to commemorate the Armistice with "A Dirge of Victory." Hugh MacDiarmid, recalling the carnage in 1935 and contemptuous of Housman's tribute to "mercenaries," declared in "Another Epitaph on an Army of Mercenaries" that "It is a God-damned lie to say that these / Saved, or knew, anything worth any man's pride." Leonard Barnes, whose *Youth at Arms* (1933) and *The Glory of the World Sonnets* (1979) placed war experiences into their twentieth-century context, combined private anguish with an historical view. Herbert Read's "To a Conscript of 1940," speaking on behalf of the war dead and of the empty survivors, tells the conscript, "We think we gave in vain. The world was not renewed," but he does offer one sliver of hope:

> But you, my brother and my ghost, if you can go
> Knowing that there is no reward, no certain use
> In all your sacrifice, then honour is reprieved.

David Jones, whose *In Parenthesis* appeared in 1937, came closer than any of the others to writing a Great War epic, including the devices commonly associated with battle epics to depict the 1915–16 phase of the war. However, as Jones commented in his preface, the Battle of the Somme greatly diminished the possibility of taking an heroic view of the war that would remain satisfying.

The hundreds of poets of the Great War expressed viewpoints that covered a vast range. Current views tend to regard the war protesters as superior to those with traditionally patriotic perspectives, reflecting current distaste for chauvinistic fervor. Since most recent discussions of war poets dwell on a minority, one can easily forget that the prevailing voices during the war were those who wanted to continue the struggle, argued in favor of England's cause, and accepted atrocity tales (providing the atrocities were performed by Germans) as unquestionably true. Indicative of the popular attitude during the war was a poem published in the *Athenaeum* in January 1916, "Marching Song of the King's Royal Rifles":

> I've lost my rifle and bayonet,
> I've lost my entrenching tool,
> I've lost my little oil-bottle,
> I've lost my pull-through,
> I've lost the gloves that they gave me
> To see me the whole winter through,
> And, Lord love my brother, if they give me another,
> I'll lose that too.

Poems such as this made it much harder for the public to recognize the horrors that the war had unleashed.

2

Calls to Action and Enthusiastic Replies

THE OUTBREAK OF THE WAR INSPIRED HUNDREDS OF POETS TO ISSUE CALLS TO join the struggle. However, as the critic Edmund Gosse noted in 1920 when he surveyed poetic phenomena associated with the war, "The youngest poets were more completely taken by surprise in August 1914 than their elders. The earliest expressions of lyric military feeling came from veteran voices. It was only proper that the earliest of all should be the Poet Laureate's address to England. . . ."[1] It was also surprising, for Robert Bridges (1844–1930), Poet Laureate since 1913, had frequently refused to write poetry at the government's behest and had become known as the Silent Laureate. His response to the first days of the war, however, surpassed all expectations.

"Wake Up, England" is a direct appeal that "Ye peacemakers, fight!" The first of eight quatrains provided the pattern for the whole, a compelling chant that is *not* lyrical despite Gosse's view:

> Thou careless, awake!
>   Thou peacemaker, fight!
> Stand, England, for honour,
>   And God guard the right!

Bridges is explicit in his appeal to lay mirth aside, to accept the seriousness of the challenge, and to continue an English tradition of upholding justice. He links his appeal to the crusading spirit:

> Much suffering shall cleanse thee;
>   But thou through the flood
> Shall win to Salvation,
>   To Beauty through blood.

Bridges's verse remains detached from reality in its use of chivalric cliché and abstract diction. As a poem, "Wake Up, England" is easily twice as long as it should be.

Another "veteran," Thomas Hardy (1840–1928), wrote an early call to action, but his influence on the poetry of the war differed considerably from that of Bridges. Whereas Bridges's role was to sound the "right note" from the government's point of view, Hardy presented the conflict from an individual's perspective. Hardy had no firsthand experience of warfare, but the years of his maturity included the Franco-Prussian War and the Boer War, and he even remembered men who had fought at Waterloo. He maintained a lifelong abhorrence of war without going to the extreme of pacifism. Hardy had frequently directed public poems to a nonliterary audience in response to public occasions, but he departed from the prevailing mood during the Boer War when he avoided writing jingoistic verse.

Three prewar works were of particular significance to later trench poets. Hardy's three-part verse-epic of the Napoleonic wars, *The Dynasts* (1903, 1906, and 1908) anticipated stances that poets of the Great War would take. "The Man He Killed," written in 1902 and published in 1909, in which a soldier reflects he had killed a man whom he would have befriended in peacetime, was very popular among soldiers at the front. It anticipated the sense of kinship that soldiers on both sides came to feel for each other, as well as the need felt by the postwar soldier to justify his survival. "Channel Firing," the curiously prophetic poem which Hardy published in April 1914, months before the war, introduces other devices which later poets would adopt: pastoral description of the thunder of artillery, voices from the grave commenting on the world's insanity, and man's indifference to Christian values revealed when nations strove to "make / Red war yet redder."

For some critics, notably Jon Silkin, the contrast between the insight of these prewar poems and the call to action of "Men Who March Away" is the basis for an indictment of Hardy, "because we know from Hardy's earlier poetry that he recognized the facts of war. By omitting even a few telling, sensuous details, the verse becomes declamatory propaganda in the pejorative sense of the word."[2] The view of James Hazen seems more reasonable, however: "Hardy's approach in poetry to the subject [of war] is almost exclusively a critical one, full of scepticism about the proclamations and purposes of political leaders, identifying itself most readily with the personal tragedies of average men and women affected by war."[3]

Hardy's approach was to describe the attitude of the soldiers from their viewpoint rather than to extol martial virtues or to glorify death in battle. In "Men Who March Away," first printed in the London *Times* and dated 5 September 1914, Hardy expresses the crusading spirit in traditional meter:

> What of the faith and fire within us
>   Men who march away
>   Ere the barn-cocks say
>   Night is growing gray,
> Leaving all that here can win us;
> What of the faith and fire within us
>   Men who march away?

In a version published in *Poetry Review* in October 1914, the fifth line became more direct—"To hazards whence no tears can win us"—but the variation came too late.

Instead of focusing on war's hazards, Hardy describes the soldiers' sense of conviction:

> Nay. We well see what we are doing,
> Though some may not see—
> Dalliers as they be—
> England's need are we; . . .

He ends by affirming the soldiers' optimism: "Press we to the field ungrieving, / In our heart of hearts believing / Victory crowns the just." "Men Who March Away" became popular as an expression of the public mood during the first weeks of the war, perhaps because the public misinterpreted Hardy's reticence about the realities of war. He was to write several poems during the war, none so direct a call to arms as "Men Who March Away" and only one ("The Pity of It," written in March 1917) even hinting at anti-German feeling. Hardy's immediate response to the English cause later inspired scores of younger poets to voice their own emotional responses to the crusade.

Rudyard Kipling (1865–1936) greeted the outbreak of hostilities with mixed feelings, including some measure of relief. He had long expected a "Teutonic" war and had argued in favor of military conscription and greater preparedness since the Boer War. Kipling's attention to the lot of the soldier and his praise of men in the ranks made him unique among well-known prewar poets. His use of simple rhythms and notions allowed him to reach a vast public audience, while his use of colloquial speech and varied meters inspired several imitators during the war. Kipling received the Nobel Prize for Literature in 1907, and on three occasions he refused the post of Poet Laureate (to which his "Recessional" for Queen Victoria's Diamond Jubilee in 1897 alone would have entitled him). However, approval of Kipling as a man of letters and as an imperialist poet was hardly unanimous. Kipling's poem "The Islanders" appeared in the London *Times* in 1902 as a protest against England's slackness and unwillingness to prepare for war. He infuriated thousands with his slur against English sport: ". . . then ye contented your souls / With the flanelled fools at the wicket or the muddied oafs at the goals." C. F. G. Masterman, who directed England's propaganda effort during the war, once commented to Sir Edward Grey that Kipling should be locked up "as a danger to the State."

Kipling's "For All We Have and Are" begins with his view of the urgency of the struggle:

> For all we have and are,
> For all our children's fate,
> Stand up and take the war.
> The Hun is at the gate!

In forty lines, Kipling reiterates the passing of "Comfort, content, delight" now that the war has begun, argues the need for fortitude, and repeats his assertion that only the sacrifice of body, soul, and will can make England prevail. For Kipling, the issue is the very existence of England as a nation, and he lays it on thick, putting almost every conceivable appeal to nationalism in his verse.

Halfway through the next world war, George Orwell presented a reasonable view of Kipling's perspective, admitting that Kipling

> is accused of glorifying war, and perhaps he does so, but not in the usual manner, by pretending that war is a sort of football match. Like most people capable of writing battle poetry Kipling had never been in battle, but his vision of war is realistic. He knows that bullets hurt, that under fire everyone is terrified, that the ordinary soldier never knows what the war is about or what is happening except in his own corner of the battlefield, and that British troops, like other troops, frequently run away. . . .[4]

When Orwell takes exception to Kipling, he does so, predictably, on political grounds: "It is notable that Kipling does not seem to realize, any more than the average soldier or colonial administrator, that an empire is primarily a money-making concern. Imperialism as he sees it is a sort of forcible evangelising. . . . He could not foresee, therefore, that the same motives which brought the Empire into existence would end by destroying it."[5]

Edward Shanks (1892–1953) was one of Kipling's many imitators among the soldiers in the trenches. Shanks had associated himself with Sir Edward Marsh and Harold Monro of the Georgian movement before enlisting in the 8th South Lancashire Regiment in 1914, from which he was invalided in 1915. After the war Shanks won the Hawthornden Prize (1919), lectured at the University of Liverpool for a year, and became a leader-writer for the *Evening Standard*. His poem "The Old Soldiers" is reminiscent of Kipling's verse more for his depiction of soldiers than for his appeal to imperialist feelings, although the presence of recruits coming from foreign countries and from different walks of life hints unmistakably of empire. Like Kipling's soldiers, Shanks's are often comical in the ranks, and his verse depends on colloquial expressions to convey a sense of realism:

> We come from dock and shipyard, we come from car and train,
> We come from foreign countries to slope our arms again,

And, forming fours by numbers or turning to the right,
We're learning all our drill again and 'tis a pretty sight.

Our names are all unspoken, our regiments forgotten,
For some of us were pretty bad and some of us were rotten;
And some will misremember what once they learnt with pain
And hit a bloody sergeant and go to clink again.

Like Kipling, Shanks presents Tommy Atkins as cheerful, fatalistic, and willing to accept a public-school/military code of conduct. Shanks's appeal is more subtle than the direct calls of Bridges or Kipling, for Shanks merely presents his old soldiers as examples of appropriate patriotic conduct.

Another soldier poet, E. A. Mackintosh (1893–1917), based his call to action on a soldier's irritation with inactive civilians who allowed others to sacrifice for them. Mackintosh left Oxford to enlist in the 5th Seaforth Highlanders, where he earned a commission as second lieutenant. He won the Military Cross and fought in the Battle of the Somme in 1916, where he was gassed and wounded. After an eight months' respite he spent training the Cadet Corps at Cambridge, he returned to the front. He died in action at Cambrai on 21 November 1917. Like Kipling, Mackintosh detested the slackness of civilians. His poem "Recruiting," which appeared in *A Highland Regiment* (1916), examines the motives of civilians who urge others to enlist and recalls Kipling's hostility toward his inactive countrymen.

"Lads, you're wanted, go and help,"
On the railway carriage wall
Stuck the poster, and I thought
Of the hands that penned the call.

Fat civilians wishing they
"Could go out and fight the Hun."
Can't you see them thanking God
That they're over forty-one?

Girls with feathers, vulgar songs—
Washy verse on England's need—
God—and don't we damned well know
How the message ought to read.

"Lads, you're wanted! over there,"
Shiver in the morning dew,
More poor devils like yourselves
Waiting to be killed by you.

Go and help to swell the names
In the casualty lists.

Help to make a column's stuff
For the blasted journalists.

Help to keep them nice and safe
From the wicked German foe.
Don't let him come over here!
"Lads, you're wanted—out you go."

*   *   *   *   *   *   *   *   *   *   *

There's a better word than that,
Lads, and can't you hear it come
From a million men that call
You to share their martyrdom.

Leave the harlots still to sing
Comic songs about the Hun,
Leave the fat old men to say
Now *we've* got them on the run.

Better twenty honest years
Than their dull three score and ten.
Lads, you're wanted. Come and learn
To live and die with honest men.

You shall learn what men can do
If you will but pay the price,
Learn the gaiety and strength
In the gallant sacrifice.

Take your risk of life and death
Underneath the open sky.
Live clean or go out quick—
Lads, you're wanted. Come and die.

As a poem, "Recruiting" has many defects. The meter plods without variation. The poem uses such disparaging adjectives as *vulgar, wicked*, and *blasted* instead of trying to arouse an effect with sensory imagery. The diction is frequently archaic, and the language blatantly appeals to the chivalric spirit *(England's need, German foe, martyrdom, gallant sacrifice)*, despite attempts to imitate colloquial trench speech. The poem seems more realistic than Bridges's, Hardy's, or Kipling's, but it still glorifies death in battle and the call is painfully direct. Despite the superficial differences between his ironical appeal and others' appeals to English empire, Mackintosh's poem emphasizes the same essentials: duty to country, necessity for sacrifice, and purification in the war.

Some calls to action went beyond straightforward appeals intended only to swell the ranks of the English army. Some poets, fearing that England

might stop short of crushing Germany, wrote to forestall attempts to negotiate peace. The most insidious of these, and certainly the most widely known
today, is "In Flanders Fields," which appeared anonymously in *Punch* on 8
December 1915. The author, John McCrae (1872–1918), was Scottish by
birth, Canadian by upbringing, and a surgeon by profession, but he spoke as
an English soldier desiring victory at any cost. McCrae was no stranger to
war, which makes his poem even less commendable than if he had written
from ignorance. He served as Lieutenant of Artillery in the South African
Field Force (1899–1900), winning the Queen's Medal with three clasps, and
during World War I he was surgeon for the First Brigade of Canadian
Artillery. He wrote "In Flanders Fields" during the Second Battle of Ypres
and might have produced pastoral visions of the war to rival those of any of
the trench poets. Instead, in the words of Paul Fussell, he wrote "a recruit-
ing-poster rhetoric apparently applicable to any war."[6]

The poem's first nine lines give no hint of the "argument" to follow.
Combining the voice-from-the-grave device of Hardy's "Channel Firing"
with evocative pastoral imagery, the poem's first two sections might have
introduced any of several sympathetic appeals:

> In Flanders fields the poppies blow
> Between the crosses, row on row,
>   That mark our place; and in the sky
>   The larks, still bravely singing, fly
> Scarce heard amid the guns below.
>
> We are the Dead. Short days ago
> We lived, felt dawn, saw sunset glow,
> Loved and were loved, and now we lie
>   In Flanders fields.

Fussell has identified the sources of these lines' undeniable appeal in

> the red flowers of pastoral elegy; the "crosses" suggestive of calvaries
> and thus of sacrifice; the sky, especially noticeable from the confines of
> a trench; the larks bravely singing in apparent critique of man's folly;
> the binary opposition between the song of the larks and the noise of the
> guns; the special awareness of dawn and sunset at morning and evening
> stand-to's; the conception of soldiers as lovers; and the focus on the
> ironic antithesis between beds and graves where "now we lie."[7]

From this beginning, however, the poem turns to blatant insistence on
continuing the war:

> Take up our quarrel with the foe:
> To you from failing hands we throw

The torch; be yours to hold it high.
If ye break faith with us who die
We shall not sleep, though poppies grow
    In Flanders fields.

That the poem's closing seems unworthy of its beginning results from two abrupt shifts—the change in tone to the demand and threat of the last six lines and the use of chivalric imagery and diction *(foe, failing hands, torch, ye, break faith)* outside the pastoral tradition for which the reader has been prepared.

Other poets continued to express the notion of the living's obligation to the dead. Sir Henry Newbolt (1862–1938), Chairman of the Departmental Committee on the Distribution of Books Abroad as well as Controller of Wireless and Cables during the war, had his greatest influence on poetry of the war sixteen years before Sarajevo. His best known poem, "Vitaï Lampada," literally equated public-school playing fields with British battlefields and applied the urgings of a team captain ("Play up! play up! and play the game!") to soldiers' duties in the line. Although by 1923 Newbolt described "Vitaï Lampada" as a "Frankenstein Monster" which drew attention from his later poetry, during the war Newbolt Man came to represent the ideal British soldier: "honorable, stoic, brave, loyal, courteous—and unaesthetic, un-ironic, unintellectual and devoid of wit."[8] Although Newbolt was a quiet scholar with extensive knowledge of Latin, Greek, and English poetry, he has become a symbol of the vulgar spirit prevalent during the war years.

Newbolt commented that "Owen and the rest of the broken men rail at the Old Men who sent the young to die: they have suffered cruelly, but in the nerves and not the heart—they haven't the experience or the imagination to know the extreme human agony."[9] Newbolt was among those older civilians who *would* have enlisted had they been able. He held what Bernard Bergonzi has called "the implicit and unexamined premise . . . that the military continuation of the struggle was absolutely necessary and unavoidable; the war had to be fought to a finish and any suggestion of a negotiated peace was a 'trap.' "[10] In the light of the postwar conviction that the war had been futile, Newbolt's reputation has suffered considerably, partly because his efforts to support the conduct of the war (under his good friend General Douglas Haig) were unstinting. Newbolt's poem "Hic Jacet Qui in Hoc Saeculo Fideliter Militavit" ("Here Lies One Who Fought Faithfully in This Age") takes McCrae's propagandistic argument against a negotiated peace one step farther. After describing a soldier who fought without fear, New-bolt indicates the source of the soldier's confidence that the enemy can never win: "For he has left in keeping / His sword unto his son." For Newbolt, who lost a son in the war, that promise might have had personal meaning, but the attempt to invest the modern war with the glory of antiquity in the

Latin title and the image of passing the sword to the next generation make the poem uncongenial to an age which believes that one builds for the future instead of expecting the future to validate the past.

Among the many poets who regarded the challenge of the war as an opportunity for a purifying and ennobling experience, none has generated more controversy than Rupert Brooke (1887–1915). Edmund Gosse called Brooke "the finest specimen of a certain type produced at the universities, and then sacrificed to our national necessity."[11] Brooke seemed to represent the best qualities of his generation. The son of a Rugby schoolmaster, Brooke studied at King's College, Cambridge, where he won honors in Classics in 1906 and became a Fellow in 1913. His personal beauty and intellectual prowess affected almost everyone who knew him, and his early poems (notably "The Old Vicarage, Grantchester") received favorable notice. His first volume of poetry, published in 1911, included a bare-shouldered photograph of Brooke as frontispiece, irrevocably linking his appearance with his writing.

Edward Marsh's first volume of *Georgian Poetry* (1912) included Brooke's work. His friends included the eminent writers and political figures of his time—John Masefield, Edward Marsh, Wilfrid Gibson, Winston Churchill, the Asquiths, Lascelles Abercrombie, John Drinkwater, Walter de la Mare— and he had sufficient means to undertake a voyage in 1913 to the South Seas by way of Canada and the United States. After he returned to England in 1914, he collaborated with Abercrombie, Gibson, and Drinkwater on a periodical called *New Numbers*, intended as a vehicle for the work of these four Georgians.

When England declared war, Brooke joined the Artists' Rifles. Through the efforts of Winston Churchill, then First Lord of the Admiralty, Brooke became part of the Anson Battery in September 1914 and was present during Britain's futile attempt to save Antwerp. On Christmas leave, Brooke wrote the five sonnets which form the basis of his current reputation, published in the fourth and final issue of *New Numbers* in December 1914. By 15 February 1915, after a case of influenza, Brooke was on his way to the Dardenelles. At the island of Skyros, however, Brooke developed blood-poisoning (variously reported as the result of the bite of a mosquito, a fly, and a scorpion), and he died there on 23 April 1915.

Brooke's sonnets achieved widespread popularity after Dean Inge praised "V. The Soldier" in his Easter sermon of 5 April 1915, and the legend of Rupert Brooke began to grow immediately after his death. Winston Churchill's encomium of Brooke, published in the London *Times* on 26 April 1915, presented Brooke as a symbol of England's patriotic youth. According to Churchill, "The thoughts to which he gave expression in the very few incomparable war sonnets which he has left behind will be shared by many thousands of young men moving resolutely and blithely forward in this, the hardest, the cruellest, and the least-rewarded of all the wars that men have fought. They are a whole history and revelation of Rupert Brooke himself."[12] Dean Inge's earlier praise of Brooke's sonnet had been only slightly less fulsome: "The enthusiasm of a pure and elevated patriotism, free from hate, bitterness, and fear, had never found a nobler expression. And yet it fell somewhat short of Isaiah's vision and still more of the Christian hope."[13] Brooke, who received a *Times* clipping reporting Inge's statements, revealed in his last recorded remark a capacity for wry comment—he regretted that the Dean had not thought him as good as Isaiah.

Churchill conscripted Brooke as a poet in service to a warring state. That Churchill's eulogy helped to make Brooke an instrument of war propaganda was quite beyond Brooke's control, but it has led many critics to fight nonliterary skirmishes on the field of Brooke's sonnets while purporting to discuss Brooke's merits as a poet. Their conclusions, often contradictory, remain unsatisfying. Johnston does not hesitate to describe Brooke as "the most gifted of the Georgians,"[14] thereby attributing Brooke's widespread popularity to his ability. Bergonzi calls Brooke "very far from being the most talented of the Georgian group"[15] without nominating a successor. Fussell shifts emphasis from the verse to Brooke's almost mythical beauty: "The equation of blondness with special beauty and value helps explain the frantic popularity of Rupert Brooke, whose flagrant good looks seemed an inseparable element of his poetic achievement."[16] Edmund Blunden, an impressive war poet in his own right, described both the immediate impact of Brooke's sonnets and the bitter aftertaste of the postwar years: "Few of these [Brooke's contemporaries] who were in the early phase of war service as Brooke was in 1914 and 1915 and heard his 'music' will ever have forgotten it, even though they might survive into years of deepening despair and horror which for them made its graces unsuitable." Blunden does not hesitate to mention the abstract nature of Brooke's poems, the appeal of which "is unconnected with the particulars of war experience."[17] The soldier poet whose criticism of the *1914* sonnets has been most damning was Charles Hamilton Sorley, himself among the tragic losses of literature to the war. In his view, the sonnets revealed that Brooke was "far too obsessed with his own sacrifice. . . . He has clothed his attitude in fine words: but he has taken the sentimental attitude."[18]

Several criticisms of Brooke's war sonnets dwell on their detachment from reality. For critic Geoffrey Matthews, the sonnets "are not war poems at all, except in the most accidental sense, but—to put it crudely—poems celebrating the export of English goods. . . ."[19] Jon Silkin has called the sonnets "vehicles for imperialist attitudes,"[20] and Brooke's recent biographer, John Lehmann, has expressed the same general feeling: "The weakness of the war sonnets lies not merely in their even more fulsome use of such insubstantial rhetoric, but in the fundamental shallowness and inadequacy of the sentiments expressed in relation to the grimness of the challenge which faced the young men on the German as well as the British side."[21] Lehmann suggests, as others have before him, that had Brooke only lived to witness the later years of the war, his poetry would have been significantly different: "It was one of Rupert's many misfortunes at this time to die before the appalling carnage on the Western Front utterly changed the mood in which the young soldiers could write of the war."[22]

However, there are at least two reasons to doubt that further knowledge of the war would have drastically altered Brooke's war poetry. First, the highly personalized perspective that he shared with other Georgian poets was part of his makeup long before the war. This would have been likely to endure in a writer who, at twenty-eight, had been conscientiously writing poetry for almost a decade and had already developed his style and his poetic stance. It seems unlikely that Brooke's later war poetry would have changed unless he could have forsaken both his commitment to Georgian lyricism and his intensely personalized approach to what he observed. A second reason to doubt that experience of war would have changed Brooke's perspective is that he had already acquired some experience when he wrote the sonnets, for he had witnessed the evacuation of Antwerp. At Churchill's request, he even appeared at Churchill's office to report his observations.

In a letter to Leonard Bacon dated 11 November 1914, Brooke reported enough to belie the common assumption that Brooke had seen nothing of the horrors of modern warfare:

> I marched through Antwerp, deserted, shelled, and burning, one night, and saw ruined houses, dead men and horses: and railway-trains with their lines taken up and twisted and flung down as if a child had been playing with a toy. And the whole heaven and earth was lit up by the glare from the great lakes and rivers of burning petrol, hills and spires of flame. That was like Hell, a Dantesque Hell, terrible. But there—and later—I saw what was a truer Hell. Hundreds of thousands of refugees, their goods on barrows and hand-carts and perambulators and wagons, moving with infinite slowness out into the night, two unending lines of them, the old men mostly weeping, the women with hard white drawn faces, the children playing or crying or sleeping. That's what Belgium is now: the country where three civilians have been killed to every one soldier. That damnable policy of "frightfulness" succeeded for a time. When it was decided to evacuate Antwerp, all of that population of half a million, save a few thousands, fled. . . . Half a million people preferred homelessness and the chance of starvation, to the certainty of German rule. It's queer to think one has been a witness of one of the greatest crimes of history.[23]

This description suggests that Brooke responded to the war by resolving to oppose the instigators of such suffering. Far from shaking his convictions, his observations confirmed his belief that England had to oppose the Germans.

The *1914* sonnets themselves, frequently interpreted according to critics' predisposed attitudes toward the war, become more sympathetic when placed in a context that combines Brooke's experience at Antwerp, his attention to the traditions of English poetry, and his rhetorical stance in the sonnet sequence. W. K. Thomas, in his 1974 article "The War Sonnets of Rupert Brooke," attempts to do this. Thomas finds in the five sonnets one unifying purpose for which generalizations are preferable to specifics:

> They are all written to console. In civilian life, when one writes a letter of condolence to a recent widow, what does one say? Does one dwell on the excruciating agony her husband underwent for six months of cancer pain? Does one describe how ghastly he came to look, how utterly changed he was? Of course not. One writes about how much he meant to the writer of the letter, of what he had to offer to his friends, of the great good he has done, and of the good which he will in effect continue to do because of the example he has set. That is what consoles. And that is what Brooke is doing.[24]

Thomas stresses the role of English poetic tradition in the five sonnets, each of which includes echoes of earlier poets. Thus (although the case for the first sonnet is weak), Thomas establishes the role of Wordsworth's poetry in the first sonnet, Donne's "The Anniversarie" in the second, Tennyson's *The Princess* and "Ode on the Death of the Duke of Wellington" in the third, and Shelley's "Adonais" in the fourth and fifth. The combination of Brooke's observations at Antwerp, deliberate purpose of consolation, and conscientious alignment with poetic tradition places Brooke's sonnet sequence in a more acceptable perspective.

The first sonnet, "Peace," begins with a contrast between the false peace before the war and the true peace which can result for those dying in a just cause:

> Now, God be thanked Who has matched us with His hour,
>   And caught our youth, and wakened us from sleeping,
> With hand made sure, clear eye, and sharpened power,
>   To turn, as swimmers into cleanness leaping,
> Glad from a world grown old and cold and weary,
>   Leave the sick hearts that honour could not move,
> And half-men, and their dirty songs and dreary,
>   And all the little emptiness of love!

Although Brooke had participated in the Fabian movement and had associated with several Bloomsbury figures, his early fumblings with liberalism gave way to a somewhat self-righteous disgust with the rise of feminism and a contempt for the conscientious objection and sexual proclivities connected with Bloomsbury.

Brooke could view the war as an opportunity to turn away from disturbing social changes to uphold a traditional purpose, as he indicates by his rejection of "sick hearts that honour could not move." He offers some consolation in the first sonnet: "we have found release there, / Where there's no ill, no grief, but sleep has mending, / Naught broken save this body, lost but breath." Consolation plays a greater role in "Safety," the second sonnet, which argues that "We have found safety in all things undying," and that

> Safe shall be my going,
> Secretly armed against all death's endeavour;
> Safe though all safety's lost; safe where men fall;
> And if these poor limbs die, safest of all.

In addition to the consolation of release from the stagnation of prewar England, Brooke's third sonnet offers assurance that the soldier's sacrifice was not in vain:

> Blow out, you bugles, over the rich Dead!
>   There's none of these so lonely and poor of old,
>   But, dying, has made us rarer gifts than gold.
> These laid the world away; poured out the red
> Sweet wine of youth; gave up the years to be
>   Of work and joy. . . .

(The pouring of wine, as Thomas points out, is not only the mawkish image of spilled blood but also a reference to "the classical sacrifice of wine made to the gods, as when Achilles poured out shining wine from a goblet onto the earth, in Book XVI of *The Iliad,* in an effort to secure divine favour for his youthful friend Patroklos."[25]) The fourth sonnet offers another facet of consolation—assurance that the dead had experienced the joys of living to the fullest before dying.

The fifth sonnet subsumes the consolations of the first four, including the joyful experiences of life, the purifying effects of war, and the assurance that the soldier is at peace. Even the opening lines offer consolation in their emphasis on "immortality" achieved by soldiers in death:

> If I should die, think only this of me:
>   That there's some corner of a foreign field
>   That is for ever England.

Although Dean Inge felt that this sonnet "fell somewhat short" of the Christian affirmation, consolation of an afterlife is implicit throughout:

And think, this heart, all evil shed away,
  A pulse in the eternal mind, no less
    Gives somewhere back the thoughts by England given;
Her sights and sounds; dreams happy as her day;
  And laughter, learnt of friends; and gentleness,
    In hearts at peace, under an English heaven.

The sonnet sequence stresses the ennobling of the fallen and thus the happiness of their lot, gratitude for the experiences of a full life before the war, belief in the enduring quality of a worthwhile sacrifice, and assurance that the reward of the struggle is an enduring peace. For thousands of young Englishmen, *1914 and Other Poems*, edited by Edward Marsh and published on 6 June 1915, expressed eloquently the soldier's justification for his sacrifice as well as the sentiments which the soldier could expect himself to feel. Sorley deplored the "sentimental attitude," but he also recognized the power of Brooke's "fine words."

Several poets, like Brooke, were quick to regard English opposition to Germany and English defense of Belgium as proofs that the English cause was just. Most contented themselves with tributes to Belgian bravery (such as M. Forrest's "The Heroes," laden with pathos, which describes a Belgian soldier's entry into Valhalla) or heavy-handed ridicule of Kaiser Wilhelm. "Gott Mit Uns!", a five-stanza diatribe by an author identified only as "W. K. C.", castigates Germany for virtually every imaginable offense, but in terms so general that only the writer's hatred is unambiguous. The second stanza merely approaches specifics in its ranting:

GOTT MIT UNS as they tear up the treaties
  They swore to observe in His name!
As they ravage and decimate Belgium
  With cannon and famine and flame!

This appeared on 21 August 1915. Two years later, in the *Graphic* (9 June 1917), "The Hun Within the Gate" by J. Lewis Milligan asks, "Shall we yield on tyrant's terms, / Cower before a Kaiser's threat?" only to respond, lest the reader misunderstand the question, "Not while God's sun shines on high." In addition to continuing McCrae's argument against a negotiated peace, Milligan provides his emphatic view of the justice of England's position:

Bastioned by Eternal Right,
  Nought shall ever make us rue:
Britain has the conqueror's might,
  If she to herself be true.

In Milligan's verse, worn phrases abound.

Some moderate voices managed to present England's position in a more reasonable tone. Such was the approach of John Drinkwater (1882–1937), a

Georgian poet who subsequently won fame as an actor, lyricist, playwright, and stage manager. During the war he worked with Sir Barry Jackson at the famous Birmingham Repertory Theatre. Drinkwater's "We Willed It Not" presents England as a reluctant participant in the war:

> We willed it not. We have not lived in hate,
> Loving too well the shires of England thrown
> From sea to sea to covet your estate,
> Or wish one flight of fortune from your throne.

Drinkwater does not hesitate to ascribe all responsibility for the war to Germany: "You thrust this bitter quarrel to our hand." After accusing the German nation of trading in death, mocking life, and raising a tumult of blasphemy, Drinkwater warns, "We rise, and, by the yet ungathered dead, / Not lightly shall the treason be atoned." Compared with the verse being printed in the *Graphic,* the *Poetry Review,* and even the London *Times,* Drinkwater's poem seems restrained, but he ends the verse with a threat. His assumptions are clear: Germany's part in the war results from overbearing pride and a desire for conquest, whereas England's resistance to Germany results from a love of peace and an abhorrence of barbarism.

Soldier poets were frequently more explicit in their attribution of blame to Germany. R. E. Vernède (1875–1917) was older than many soldier poets. He was thirty-nine when he managed to enlist in the 9th Royal Fusiliers (known as the Public Schools Battalion) in September 1914. He received his commission as second lieutenant in May 1915, was wounded at the Somme, turned down the offer of a safe position in the War Office, and returned to the front in December 1916. On 9 April 1917, he died under machine-gun fire while leading his platoon in an attack at Havrincourt Wood.

Some of his later poems, as Edmund Gosse remarked, "show the vigour of moral experience," but poet and critic T. Sturge Moore had noticed another side of Vernède's poetry: "I cannot help feeling that the Kaiser has done for the word 'God' very much what 'über alles' has done for professions of patriotism. Yet Vernède raps it out with all the assurance of a bishop."[26] In "A Listening Post," Vernède combines pastoral imagery with an argument for prosecuting the war. After describing a blackbird who "didn't know the world's askew" and two English soldiers lying in wait "To shoot the first man that goes by," Vernède muses on the blackbird's innocence:

> How could he know that if we fail
>   The world may lie in chains for years
> And England be a bygone tale
>   And right be wrong, and laughter tears?

He does not hesitate to suggest a purpose which transcends the need for "murder of our fellow man," lest some question whether the end actually does justify the means.

Brooke's conviction that the experiences of war could purify the soldier became a popular theme of contemporary poets. Fred G. Penney's "War the Physician," published in the *Poetry Review* early in 1917, explicitly attributes healing powers to war in dreadful lines:

> Through him the dullest ear begins
> To catch the magic spell
> Of heaven, though only heard within
> The fragment of a shell.

Members of the clergy were not above extolling the virtues of war. Geoffrey Anketell Studdert-Kennedy (1883–1929), an Anglican chaplain popularly known as "Woodbine Willie," compared the biblical "lilies of the field" and Tommy Atkins in "Solomon in All His Glory." After declaring that no lily ever was "clothed in royal beauty / Such as decks the least" of the English soldiers, Studdert-Kennedy takes his comparison further:

> Tattered, torn, and bloody khaki,
>   Gleams of white flesh in the sun,
> Raiments worthy of their beauty,
>   And the great things they have done.
>
> Purple robes and snowy linen
>   Have for earthly kings sufficed,
> But these bloody sweaty tatters
>   Were the robes of Jesus Christ.

One suspects that the chaplain has missed the point of the biblical image.

More popular than Penney's graceless verse or Studdert-Kennedy's overblown comparison was the practice of narrating the transfiguration of prewar nondescripts into heroes. Although evidence is scant, "E. Preston" may have been Lieutenant-Colonel Sir Edward Hulton Preston, 5th baronet (1888–1963), who won the DSO (Distinguished Service Order) and MC (Military Cross) in 1918, the year he succeeded his father to the title. Preston's "Then and Now," which appeared in the *Poetry Review* late in 1916, tried to describe the effect of the just war on upper-class youth in pedestrian meter, chivalric cliché, and generalities:

> At home he was an idle soul
> Living upon his fine estate:
> He shot the game on heathered hill,
> And thought the world a dreary waste.
>
> But he signed on for bigger things,
> When England rose to right the wrong,
> And marched through English fields and lanes,
> A sun-burnt soldier, keen and strong.

> Heirs waste not time on battle-fields,
> "Last, he was seen," in that rough race,
> Leading a lost hope to its grave,
> With the high glory in his face.

Another poetical treatment of the notion that warfare ennobles the recruit, in the same narrative tradition, came from the pen of a well-connected trench poet. Herbert Asquith (1881–1947), son of the Prime Minister and captain in the Field Artillery, completed his education at Oxford and practiced as a barrister before enlisting. He was among the Georgian fellowship. Wounded in June 1915, he spent some time in England before returning to the front in March 1917. His older brother, Raymond, died at the Battle of the Somme in 1916, and his younger brother, Arthur, who was present at Brooke's burial at Skyros, earned the rank of brigadier general in 1918 at the age of 35. Although Herbert Asquith may have aspired to a place in literary history on his own merits, he will more likely be remembered (with his wife, Cynthia) for his association with D. H. Lawrence, who used the Asquiths as models for the Chatterleys in *Lady Chatterley's Lover.*

Asquith's "The Volunteer" takes the form of an obituary, describing a clerk who spent half his life toiling at ledgers and "Thinking that so his days would drift away / With no lance broken in life's tournament." However, the war has changed that dreary prospect:

> And now those waiting dreams are satisfied;
> From twilight to the halls of dawn he went;
> His lance is broken; but he lies content
> With that high hour, in which he lived and died.
> And falling thus he wants no recompense,
> Who found his battle in the last resort;
> Nor needs he any hearse to bear him hence,
> Who goes to join the men of Agincourt.

Asquith, within a chivalric tradition, describes the war as the means by which the "low" can aspire to ennobling adventure.

Understandably, most of the calls to action were not good poetry despite the sincerity of the poets' patriotic leanings or the validity of their attachment to traditional English values. Most of the poems seemed effective not because they formed public opinion, but because they expressed in an adequate manner precisely what the public already thought, or felt that it should think. The calls to action of Bridges, Hardy, Kipling, and Shanks avoided concrete images of the horrors of war, while the calls of Mackintosh, McCrae, and Newbolt, appearing to emphasize death in battle, appealed to a chivalric sacrifice far removed from the realities of the trenches. Without his consent, Rupert Brooke posthumously became the spokesman for a government that wished to convince its people that the war would somehow ennoble it. Other (and lesser) voices complemented the "message" of Brooke's sonnets with protests of German perfidy, claims of England's enrollment in a just cause, expressions of hope that a benign deity would ensure greater harmony after the war, and claims that participation in war provides a soldier (an *English* soldier) with a clearer view of reality, a closer affinity with Christ's sacrifice, and an opportunity to rise above the idleness of a lusterless civilian existence. Belief in these claims would not survive the Great War.

THE OUTFIT OF AN OFFICER

THE THRESHER CAMPAIGN COAT

FOR the well-equipped officer there is no such indispensable as this. It is the supreme War Coat—the accepted standard recommended at the outset by the British War Office, and since used by 24,000 British and Allied Officers. To the wearer it means absolute security from wet or wind, and it means—comfort.

The Thresher Trench £ s. d.
Coat with detachable
Kamelcott lining ... 7 7 0
With detachable
Lambskin lining 10 10 0
The Thresher Trench
Coat, unlined ... 5 5 0

All sizes in stock. Send size of chest and approximate height when ordering.

KIT IN GENERAL

FAMED for Military Kit since Crimean days, THRESHER & GLENNY have probably to-day the largest clientèle amongst Allied Officers. The skill, the care and the accumulated knowledge which established the Thresher Trench Coat go to the making of Thresher Kit in precisely the same degree. Naval and Military Uniform, Breeches especially, shirts and all manner of Equipment made at 152-3 Strand, represent the best of quality and value.

	£	s.	d.
Field Service Jacket, Whipcord, from	5	15	6
Slacks	2	2	0
Riding Breeches, Bedford Cord and	3 3 0 / 4	4	0
Field Service Caps	0	15	6
Sam Browne Belts with shoulder straps only	1	7	6
Complete with frog, Ho'ster, pouch, &c.	2	15	0

Patterns and prices sent by return to all enquirers

AND— MUFTI

JEALOUSLY guarded is the reputation of the old House of THRESHER & GLENNY in respect to mufti. Top-hole quality at fair (not fancy) prices is the foundation of that repute.

	£	s.	d.
Lounge suits	6	6	0
	and 8	8	0
Overcoats, from	5	5	0
Dress suits, from	10	10	0

Patterns of materials sent to officers requiring suits to wear on leave.

By appointment to H.M. The King

THRESHER & GLENNY
Military Tailors & Outfitters   Established 1755
152 & 153 Strand, LONDON, W.C.2.

By appointment to H.M. The King

A

This advertisement from the November 1918 issue of *The Dagger* shows how little the realities of the war had impinged upon the civilian consciousness two years after the Somme Offensive.

3

The Clash of Chivalry and Modern War

IN RETROSPECT, ANY ASSOCIATION OF THE GREAT WAR WITH KNIGHTHOOD
seems absurdly anachronistic. Eventually soldiers like Raymond Asquith
would describe the war, even before the Somme, as "utter senselessness" and
conclude that "The suggestion that [war] elevates the character is hideous."
As Mark Girouard points out, the chivalric tradition would seem "infinitely
remote from the real world of mud, blood, boredom, fear, endurance,
carnage, and mutilation" in the trenches.[1] However, the appalling conditions of the war did not suddenly end poets' attempts to identify the 1914–18
war with long-standing chivalric, heroic, or warrior traditions. If the nature
of war had changed, there was still a need to identify with traditional values
and expectations.

Medieval figures, such as bands of questing knights on chargers, would
find lances unavailing against a peasant dug in with a machine gun, but poets
could draw from some qualities of the tradition. Far from entirely rejecting
martial traditions that celebrated soldiers in battle, upheld personal courage,
emphasized the heroic nature of self-sacrifice, glorified individual combat,
praised wholehearted commitment to nationalistic ideals, and the like, several war poets did what they could to suggest that, although the trappings
had changed, the chivalric/heroic/warrior spirit continued despite drastically
altered circumstances.

Whenever they could, some poets invited comparison between modern
soldiers and knights of old. They used archaic diction to elevate the contemporary (e.g., the British "Unknown Warrior" as opposed to the "Unknown
Soldier"). They exalted modern acceptance of a soldier's code, argued the
need to prove worthy of a traditional standard, and presented the new roles
of modern soldiers in terms intended to identify modern war with traditional
values. If the images of knighthood would not apply, the chivalric spirit
informing tales of valorous self-sacrifice in a just cause might still apply to
modern warfare in spite of mud, lice, and cold. When modern warfare
refused to conform to tradition, several poets devoted their talent to suggesting that, although external circumstances might have changed, the warrior's
code remained intact.

The early spirit of joyous acceptance, martial fervor, and celebration of battle found its most eloquent spokesman in Julian Grenfell (1888–1915). Like Rupert Brooke, Grenfell regarded the war from a subjective, highly personalized perspective. His background resembles that of Brooke, his almost exact contemporary. Grenfell, eldest son of William Henry Grenfell (later Baron Desborough), graduated from Eton and Oxford, where he excelled in classical studies and sports. He became a professional soldier, joining the Royal Dragoons in India in 1910 and moving with his regiment to South Africa in 1911. When his unit moved to France in 1914, the altered requirements of trench warfare quickly made themselves felt. The cavalry regiment became infantry at the front—a fit emblem for what the new war imposed on the tradition of chivalry.

Grenfell (like Siegfried Sassoon after him) refused to remain a mere cipher. Identifying himself as a warrior, he made a specialty of stalking German snipers behind enemy lines and killing them in hand-to-hand combat. For Grenfell, war did not cease to depend on the initiative of independent soldiers. By the end of 1914, Grenfell had been twice mentioned in dispatches and had received the DSO. Whether awareness of the way the war was shaping might have changed Grenfell's fighting style remains unanswerable, for he received a severe head wound during the Second Battle of Ypres on 12 May 1915 and died two weeks later in a Boulogne hospital.

Grenfell wrote "Into Battle" after hearing of Brooke's death. The poem, published in the London *Times* on 27 May 1915, the day after Grenfell's death, impressed critic Edmund Gosse, who called it "the clearest lyrical expression of the fighting spirit of England in which the war has found words."[2] Rudyard Kipling felt that Grenfell's "lips must have been touched when he wrote it," and other contemporaries responded favorably to Grenfell's expression of a soldier's "proper" feelings. By 1915, poetical reassurance that England's warrior tradition remained intact was doubly welcome from a soldier celebrating "joys" of combat.

Grenfell's strategy is to make the fighting soldier an inherent part of the natural order. The second stanza equates a soldier's death with natural processes and establishes an intrinsic relationship between the soldier and the sources of life:

> The fighting man shall from the sun
>   Take warmth, and life from the glowing earth;
> Speed with the light-foot winds to run,
>   And with the trees to newer birth;
> And find, when fighting shall be done,
>   Great rest, and fullness after dearth.

In the next five stanzas, Grenfell links the fighting man to natural phenomena—the soldier is comrade to the stars, friend to the trees, like the kestrel and owl in hearing and vision, like the blackbird in desire for song, and like the horse in patience and courage. Then, in the battle itself,

> the burning moment breaks,
> And all things else are out of mind,
> And only joy of battle takes
> Him by the throat and makes him blind.

The soldier knows that, should he survive, his death was not "Destined Will." Should he fall, "Day shall clasp him with strong hands, / And Night shall fold him in soft wings."

Most modern readers recoil from Grenfell's predatory view of battle, but T. Sturge Moore helps one understand the overwhelming approval Grenfell's poem received when it appeared by pointing to the contrast between Grenfell's focus on the soldier and others' abstract effusions on the justice of England's fight:

> Throughout the poem no hint is given of the nature of the enemy; he does not proclaim, as so many have done, that he fights for right or against tyranny. He does not himself look forward to tasting the fruits of victory; he accepts death as the natural necessary reward of taking up arms. Even in peace he had chosen to serve by being ready to fight. Yet he does not cry up devotion to England. You will say *his* was obvious. That is just it, true poetry does not say what is unnecessary.[3]

Sharing many of Grenfell's assumptions, Moore (in 1919) did not find their absence from the poem's lines troublesome. He would regard such statements as superfluous, and therefore inimical to the economy of fine verse. Silkin's statement that "In the end Grenfell probably felt he needed some kind of approval—as opposed to sanction—for his behaviour"[4] would surely strike Moore as absurd, primarily because Moore had already granted that approval.

A lesser-known poem by Grenfell, "Prayer for Those on the Staff," suggests that, had Grenfell survived, he might have written satires similar to those of Sassoon and others who resented noncombatants for not doing their full share. Significantly early in the war, Grenfell indicated his resentment of the contrast between line soldiers and staff, but his approach is much more playful than Sassoon's:

> Fighting in mud, we turn to Thee,
> In these dread times of battle, Lord,
> To keep us safe, if so may be,
> From shrapnel, snipers, shell, and sword.

But not on us, for we are men
    Of meaner clay, who fight in clay,
But on the Staff, the Upper Ten,
    Depends the issue of the Day.

The staff is working with its brains,
    While we are sitting in the trench;
The Staff the universe ordains
    (Subject to Thee and General French).

God help the staff—especially
    The young ones, many of them sprung
From our high aristocracy;
    Their task is hard, and they are young.

O Lord, who mad'st all things to be,
    And madest some things very good,
Please keep the extra A.D.C.
    From horrid scenes, and sight of blood.

See that his eggs are newly laid,
    Not tinged as some of them—with green;
And let no nasty draughts invade
    The windows of his Limousine.

When he forgets to buy the bread,
    When there are no more minerals,
Preserve his smooth well-oiled head
    From wrath of caustic Generals.

O Lord, who mad'st all things to be,
    And hatest nothing thou has made,
Please keep the extra A.D.C.
    Out of the sun and in the shade.

"Prayer for Those on the Staff" differs from Sassoon's later heavy-handed protests in several respects: it does not blame the staff for the conditions of the trenches, nor does it lay thousands of deaths at the staff's door, nor does it attempt to inflict injury by crushing its targets. The touch is much lighter. Unlike "Into Battle," this poem introduces some of the realities of trench fighting. However, the poem remains well within the confines of tradition, for the point is that the extra A.D.C. and the rest of the staff do not live up to the warrior's code. They are contemptible because they are not playing the game.

Several soldiers longer-lived than Grenfell saw sufficient carnage to make their views of war less optimistic, but their poems continued to reflect traditional assumptions. Their verse began to emphasize the new conditions of the struggle without questioning the nature or causes of the war. F. W. Harvey (1888–1957) retained the warrior spirit despite his personal misfortunes. A boyhood friend of the poet Ivor Gurney, Harvey was a solicitor when the war began. He went to France as a private, won the DCM (Distinguished Conduct Medal) as a lance-corporal, and in 1915 accepted a field commission as lieutenant in the Gloucestershire Regiment. Captured by the Germans in 1916, Harvey spent the rest of the war in various prison camps. His *Gloucester Friends* (verse) appeared in 1917, and *Comrades in Captivity* (memoirs) appeared in 1920. "Prisoners" addresses the humiliation of the fighting man removed from battle. Instead of representing the rigors and risks of battle, Harvey's poem reflects the frustration of gallant warriors no longer free to fight, "Safe in Stagnation," left to "rot, till something set us free!" The verse ends with a bitter irony that soldiers seeking "Adventure found in gallant company" should

> Laugh like old men with senses atrophied,
> Heeding no Present, to the Future dead,
> Nodding quite foolish by the warm fireside
> And seeing no flame, but only in the red
> And flickering embers, pictures of the past:—
> Life like a cinder fading black at last.

Harvey directs his reader's attention not to the slaughter, but to the soldier's frustration at being left out of the conflict.

Other poets chose to speak of modern warfare more explicitly, yet still within the traditional context. John W. Streets, a sergeant in the 12th York and Lancaster Regiment who died of wounds incurred during the Somme advance on 1 July 1916, wrote a number of sonnets describing modern experience in a medieval perspective. Streets wrote this justification of his war poems:

> They were inspired while I was in the trenches, where I have been so busy I have had little time to polish them. I have tried to picture some thoughts that pass through a man's brain when he dies. I may not see the end of the poems, but hope to live to do so. We soldiers have our views of life to express, though the boom of death is in our ears. We try to convey something of what we feel in this great conflict to those who think of us, and sometimes, alas! mourn our loss. We desire to let them know that in the midst of our keenest sadness for the joy of life we leave behind, we go to meet death grim-lipped, clear-eyed, and resolute-hearted.[5]

Streets's sonnet "A Lark Above the Trenches," originally published in the *Poetry Review* early in 1916, occasionally refers to the rigors of trench warfare without dwelling on them. "Hushed is the shriek of hurtling shells" while somewhere "carols a lark. / I in the trench, he lost in heaven afar; . . ." leads to an explicit contrast that becomes the point of the poem: " 'Tis strange that while you're beating into life / Men here below are plunged in sanguine strife." Beyond mentioning two constant conditions of trench warfare, the unremitting noise of shells and the immobility of men in the trenches, Streets does not suggest a departure from traditional views of war.

Similarly Lord Gorell (Ronald Gorell Barnes, 1884–1963), whose poetry frequently appeared in the *Contemporary Review* during the war and whose *Days of Destiny: War Poems at Home and Abroad* (1917) sold well, does not regard the unpleasant nature of modern war as a challenge to the warrior's code. "Song Before Battle," written in the Somme Valley in August 1916, includes description of battlefield conditions:

> We, who have clung for long, long months
>   To battered lines of knee-deep mud,
> Fixed targets for your slope-set guns
>   To drench the ooze with British blood;
> We who have toiled through winter's rain
>   With sand-bag, shovel, plank, and wire,
> Rivetting marshy parapets,
>   Building protection from your fire—
>   We have weapons now, O Huns!

Although the first lines seem to dwell on the horrors of modern war, the substance of the poem is the vengeful promise that, now that the English have weapons, it is Germany's turn to "dig and wire and quail." The point is that the just will prevail.

Another poet who maintained the heroic nature of war was Fred G. Penney, whose "War the Physician," discussed earlier, argued the curative properties of conflict. He chose to represent the hero not as a patrician officer, but as the stolid peasant who readily accepts his sacrifice. "In Hospital" is a monologue of a common soldier in the tradition of Kipling— fearful at the first sign of combat but mastering his fear, simple in his thoughts and manner of expressing them, and uncomplaining of (even curiously detached from) his war experience. Unfortunately the circumstances of this awful monologue are so untrue to life that they would not mislead a fairly bright child. The speaker describes how he carried a wounded soldier through an artillery bombardment after the soldier and the speaker have each lost an arm:

> I got it into our lines;—'twas the "Cap,"
> And the boys was cheering like sin.
> *I* couldn't cheer, for a splinter of shrap
> Had caught me under the chin.

The soldier's attitude toward his injury becomes unconvincing in its flippancy: "I often laugh in my empty sleeve / When I think of my quivers and qualms." Penney's poem drew more inspiration from clichés such as "laugh up one's sleeve" than from any clarity of vision. The last stanza presents a dramatic inconsistency when the soldier, who apparently speaks to a visitor from his hospital bed, delivers his concluding words:

> Bit of my jaw, too, blown away,
> —The wife'll put up with *that* loss—
> What's that thing on the table? you say!
> Oh!—that's the Victoria Cross.

Apart from making the reader wonder how the soldier managed to speak his twenty-eight line piece without his jaw, the soldier's explicit dismissals of his mutilations and of his VC do not accord with reality. In its clumsy way, the poem tries to describe the proper behavior of the peasant / soldier in a tradition that goes back to Dunner, "a simple peasant," in *The Battle of Maldon* (ll. 254–59).

Since the warrior tradition drew rigid distinctions between those who failed and those who succeeded in achieving the martial ideal, many poets expressed their fervent wish to live up to the traditional standard in the face of horrible challenges. William Noel Hodgson (1893–1916), so deeply influenced by Brooke that he enlisted after reading Brooke's *1914* sonnets, served as a lieutenant in the Devon Regiment. He won the Military Cross in October 1915 but died at the Battle of the Somme on 1 July 1916. His *Verse and Prose in Peace and War* appeared in 1916. Two days before the Somme Offensive, Hodgson wrote "Before Action," a soldier's prayer for courage. The soldier of his poem desires only to fulfill his duty. Like Brooke's sonnets, Hodgson's poem draws heavily upon remembered pleasures of civilian life to prepare the soldier for death. In succeeding stanzas, the soldier prays, "Make me a soldier, Lord," and "Make me a man, O Lord." The final stanza combines Georgian pastoral description with the soldier's dread, culminating in the prayer of traditional knights:

> I, that on my familiar hill
>   Saw with uncomprehending eyes
> A hundred of Thy sunsets spill
>   Their fresh and sanguine sacrifice,
> Ere the sun swings his noonday sword
>   Must say goodbye to all of this;—
> By all delights that I shall miss,
>   Help me to die, O Lord.

For Hodgson, who died two days later, the prayer was prophetic.

The need to attain worthiness also extended to civilians. Sir Henry Newbolt's "The Non-Combatant" describes an Englishman, neither soldier nor leader, "born to fail, / A name without an echo" who nevertheless "Fulfilled the ancestral rites." Newbolt suggests that some who saw "the weakling huddled at his prayers" learned the nature of glory and the sacred spirit of the just cause. Alfred Noyes (1880–1958) directed "The Searchlights" toward the noncombatant population in November 1914 *(Poetry Review):*

> Search for the foe in thine own soul,
>   The sloth, the intellectual pride;
> The trivial mockery of the goal
>   For which our fathers lived and died;
> The lawless dreams, the cynic Art,
> That rend thy nobler self apart.

Like Kipling, Noyes found civilians' slackness detestable.

Sir Owen Seaman (1861–1936), editor of *Punch* from 1906 to 1932, wrote several vigorous invectives during the war. As early as 5 August 1914 he satirized English laggards' supposed attitude toward the war in "Lines Designed to Represent the Views of an Average British Patriot":

> Why should I follow your fighting line
> For a matter that's no concern of mine? . . .
>
> I shall be asked to a general scrap
> All over the European map,
> Dragged into somebody else's war,
> For that's what a double entente is for.

For current readers, Seaman's irony is easy to miss since what he offered as a contemptible view seems reasonable in retrospect.

Seaman's "The Soul of a Nation," appearing in *Punch* on 3 April 1918, appealed to civilians to turn their minds from "little things"—the taxi shortage, meat rationing, buzz-bombs—which are insignificant compared with "the thunder rolling in the West." Seaman appeals to civilians to accept their share of the burden:

> O England, staunch of nerve and strong of sinew,
>   Best when you face the odds and stand at bay,
> Now show a watching world what stuff is in you!
>   Now make your soldiers proud of you to-day!

The standards of heroic conduct did not confine themselves to the battlefield, and several besides Seaman were willing to remind noncombatants of those standards. Like Seaman, they tended to do so by attributing warrior traits to noncombatants in such phrases as "face the odds."

More common, however, were poems expressing a resolve to uphold traditional standards. Sir Cecil Spring-Rice (1859–1918), British Ambassador to the United States during the war, attempted to link loyalty to England with the City of God in "I Vow to Thee, My Country." The first half of the poem expresses Spring-Rice's conception of duty to country:

> I vow to thee, my country—all earthly things above—
> Entire and whole and perfect, the service of my love,
> The love that asks no question: the love that stands the test,
> That lays upon the altar the dearest and the best:
> The love that never falters, the love that pays the price,
> The love that makes undaunted the final sacrifice.

The second half of the poem describes "another country" whose armies are uncountable, whose King we may not see, "And her ways are ways of gentleness, and all her paths are peace." Set to music by Gustav Holst, Spring-Rice's poem has since become a popular hymn.

R. E. Vernède, as befits an active combatant, becomes more specific in "A Petition." Like Brooke and Hodgson, Vernède takes care to specify the gifts by England given—birthright, childhood's ease, love, friends' loyalty, quenchless hope, laughter—before asking "All that a man might ask thou has given me, England, / Yet grant thou one thing more." Vernède's request, recalling Hodgson's prayer, is

> That now when envious foes would spoil thy splendour,
>   Unversed in arms, a dreamer such as I
> May in thy ranks be deemed not all unworthy,
>   England, for thee to die.

For Vernède, the request was entirely without irony.

Major Sydney Oswald, of the King's Rifle Corps, published "Dulce et Decorum Est Pro Patria Mori" in the *Poetry Review* early in 1916, before Wilfred Owen's "Dulce et Decorum Est" imposed an ironical interpretation on Horace's line. Oswald's poem, dedicated to three soldiers who distinguished themselves during the landing at Gallipoli on 25 April 1915, stresses the rewards of proper conduct:

> Full soon they died, yet made
> A name of lasting glory; gained applause
> From all the brave; a fame which cannot fade.

For these examples of martial valor, and for all soldiers, grieving is inappropriate, for

> Glory is theirs; the People's narrative
>   Of fame will tell their deeds of gallantry,

And for all time their memories will live
   Shrined in our hearts.

Like similar verses, Oswald's marshals the tired phrases of the propagandistic pamphlets of the war.

Gilbert Frankau (1884–1952), captain in the 9th East Surrey Regiment of the Royal Field Artillery, recorded the inglorious end of a soldier who refused to follow honor's course. He knew of the soldier's struggle to control fear, for he fought at Loos, Ypres, and the Somme, and he ultimately was invalided out for shell shock in February 1918. An early poem, "The Deserter," describes the military execution of a coward:

"I'm sorry I done it, Major."
We bandaged the livid face;
And led him out, ere the wan sun rose,
To die his death of disgrace.

In the last stanza, "the shameless soul of a nameless man / Went up in the cordite-smoke." The victim acknowledges responsibility for his execution, but apology is not enough—"death of disgrace" sufficiently indicates both the victim's and the others' feelings about the execution. The poem leaves no room for sympathy, presenting the firing squad as a warning for those who might weaken at the crucial moment. Throughout the poem, such phrases as "death of disgrace" and "shameless soul" indicate Frankau's confidence that his readers share his assumptions.

Some changes in the manner of warfare required men to assume dehumanizing roles. A soldier might endure four years' active duty at the front without seeing the face of an enemy because he served a machine. Some poets attempted to elevate such bloodless and unromantic service, with mixed results. Frankau recognized the new dominance of man by machine in "Ammunition Column," which describes a soldier's servitude to artillery:

I am only a cog in a giant machine, a link of an endless chain:—
And the rounds are drawn, and the rounds are fired, and the empties
   return again;
Railroad, lorry, and limber; battery, column, and park;
To the shelf where the set fuse waits the breech, from the quay where
   the shells embark.

Frankau, however, is not complaining. By the third stanza he shifts his opening line to exalt man's new role: "I am only a cog in a giant machine, but a vital link in the chain."

Some poets tried to ennoble modern "warriors" whose functions were hardly inspiring. Rudyard Kipling's "Mine Sweepers" describes a fleet of mine-sweeping trawlers that, in three stanzas, seek, locate, and clear mines.

Despite the devices which worked well for Kipling elsewhere—colloquial speech, vivid description, and dramatic presentation of each stage of the venture—the poem is very dull. At one point there are loud noises which scare jackdaws. Otherwise the mission is routine. E. Hilton Young (1879–1960) was more successful in "Mine-Sweeping Trawlers." A lieutenant-commander in the Royal Naval Volunteer Reserve, Young lost his right arm in 1918. From 1915 to 1935 he was MP for the city of Norwich, and he received the DSO during the war. Young's strategy in his poem was not, like Kipling's, to derive a sense of accomplishment from a routine mission, but to state the case more realistically:

> Not ours the fighter's glow,
>   the glory, and the praise.
> Unnoticed to and fro
>   we pass our dangerous ways.

He describes men as "fishermen of death" who take pride in their knowledge that they have cleared the seas for battle. Since the German fleet spent most of the war withdrawn from the open seas, naval engagements offered little material for the war poets, while the sneaking nature of U-boat attacks made submarine poems inappropriate for celebrations of heroism.

The emergence of the airplane as a military weapon, however, offered a means of restoring the glory of individual combat to the modern soldier. The most explicit comparison of the modern flier with the medieval knight occurs in "The Knight on Wings" by Paul Bewsher (1894–1966). A journalist before the war, Bewsher became a captain in the Royal Air Service, won the DSC (Distinguished Service Cross), survived one crash behind his own lines, and flew several bombing missions. When Bewsher compares the knight with the flier, he emphasizes the quest for adventure, the unexpected nature of each encounter with an adversary, and the advance into enemy territory. After establishing these points in common, Bewsher describes modern fighters in chivalric terms:

> Once more they battle man to man,
>   Alone amidst the watching skies;
> No shouting friends their zeal to fan—
>   They charge and thrust with eager eyes,
> And win . . . and to the Western sun
> Bring back their shield—the battle won;
> Their greatest prize, the work well done.

Bewsher's vision of the pilot's role was not one-sided. In "Searchlights" he describes the "lonely airman" haunted by searchlights and the enemy's attempts to shoot him down, and in "Nox Mortis" he voices an effective ethical protest against the bombing missions he has flown over enemy towns.

Perhaps the most accurate measure of the warrior-tradition's strength was the ease with which a mediocre poet and weak-spirited soldier was able to exploit it. Robert Malise Bowyer Nichols (1893–1944), a Georgian poet and Oxford graduate, received a commission as second lieutenant in the Royal Field Artillery in October 1914. After a few weeks of front-line duty, suffering from shell shock, he spent five months in hospital and was invalided out of the service in 1916. His first book of verse, *Invocation: War Poems and Others* (1915), appeared while he was in hospital. A second volume, *Ardours and Endurances* (1917), edited by Edward Marsh, became overwhelmingly popular, partly because it seemed to combine the heroic tradition with a realistic approach to modern war. Nichols, realizing that he was onto something, embarked on a lecture tour of the United States sponsored by the Ministry of Information. Nichols's poems appealed to a larger audience which, in Fussell's words, "took pleasure in images of the war that featured fated, beautiful soldier boys mourned sentimentally and 'romantically' by their intimate male friends."[6]

Nichols also popularized the work of two poets superior to himself, Robert Graves and Siegfried Sassoon. Graves saw no reason to be grateful. In *Goodbye to All That* (1929), Graves recalled that Nichols "read Siegfried's poetry and mine, and started a legend of Siegfried, himself and me as the new Three Musketeers, though the three of us had never once been together in the same room."[7] In an undated letter written after the publication of Nichols's *Anthology of War Poetry 1914–1918* (1943), Graves presented an even less restrained view to historian Basil Liddell Hart:

> Robert Nichols—I never answered your query about him. He was an unbalanced undergraduate in 1914 who pelted Lloyd George with mangolds and pheasants at the Union—you remember the political context, I expect. Then he went to the war, spent 3 weeks with the Gunners in a quiet part of the line, fell off a roof, went home as shell-shocked, slept with 17 prostitutes in 3 weeks and got a bad dose. As his mother was in the looney-bin and he himself was always pretty unsettled, this did him no good; he recovered, was a terrific comet of success in poetry in 1917, went to the USA to lecture, told frightful lies about his war service and involved me in them. . . . Is now rather living on past glories. . . . I like him but he is too much of an embarrassment to have about.[8]

Who knows what Graves might have said had he *not* liked Nichols?

Edmund Gosse, whose 1920 criticism tended to reflect his sympathy with the war poets, remained dissatisfied with some features of Nichols's work, particularly Nichols's omission of all but highly personal responses: "We might read his poems over and over again without forming the slightest idea of what all the distress was about, or who was guilty, or what was being defended. This is a mark of great artistic sincerity; but it also points to a certain moral narrowness."[9] The "narrowness" of Nichols's poetry is that it has only one subject, the limited awareness of Nichols in the field, particularly as it served a traditional conception of courage. What Moore had praised in Grenfell's verse, Gosse condemned in Nichols's.

For Nichols's audience, "The Assault" seemed to present a shocking contrast to the conventional Georgian lyric. It tries to present the noises of battle onomatopoeically, but with little success. After describing the tension in the trenches as an artillery barrage pounds the enemy line and then lifts, Nichols describes the charge across No Man's Land:

> A wail.
> Lights. Blurr.
> Gone.
> On, on. Lead. Lead. Hail.
> Spatter. Whirr! Whirr!

When the men discover German targets, Nichols combines the rapid movement of thought with the representation of sound:

> Ha! ha! Bunched figures waiting.
> Revolver levelled quick!
> Flick! Flick!
> Red as blood.
> Germans. Germans.
> Good! O good!
> Cool madness.

Douglas Goldring comments on these lines to dismiss them: "It was characteristic of our war-time criticism that this masterpiece of drivel, instead of exciting derision, was hailed as a work of genius and read with avidity."[10] One doubts it was often read aloud. As Arthur Waugh noted, "Unless a poem can bear recitation, its workmanship is condemned. And to read Mr. Nichols's 'Assault' aloud is to be persuaded of a creaking chain of artistic improprieties, which strain vehemently towards effect, only to end in incoherence. . . . This is neither metre nor *vers libre*. It has no form or true proportion; the fever of war has infected it, and left it void."[11]

Although most of Nichols's poems are highly subjective and even self-centered representations, two poems stand apart. "Comrades: An Episode," despite its theatrical pathos, attempts to present an objective narrative. "Noon," Nichols's best war poem, achieves what it attempts—description of a lull in the trenches. However, after the opening stanza has established the atmosphere of the fly-infested and hot midday, when Nichols turns his attention to the men, his inconsistent imagery fails him:

> No sound in all the stagnant trench
> Where forty standing men
> Endure the sweat and grit and stench,
> Like cattle in a pen.
>
> Sometimes a sniper's bullet whirs,
> Or twangs the whining wire.

Nichols ends the poem with a contrast: an airplane passes above,

> And sweating, dizzied, isolate
> In the hot trench beneath,
> We bide the next shrewd move of fate
> Be it of life or death.

Even the deep-rooted ideal of bravery under the worst of conditions could not sustain the popularity of a poet whose chief merit was his appeal to pathos.

Most of the traditional appeals failed as poetry, not only because in retrospect the heroic view jarred with the new realities of warfare, but also because the language of chivalry inhibited the poets' ability to express themselves. Poems such as Julian Grenfell's "Into Battle" or Lord Gorell's "Song Before Battle" or Sir Cecil Spring-Rice's "I Vow to Thee, My Country" could move only those readers predisposed to be moved, could convince only those who were already convinced. The effect of most of these utterances was not to intrude anything new upon the public consciousness, but to reinforce the prewar conceptions of warfare. As a result, the poems themselves are largely unimaginative, choked with cliché, and filled with abstract phrases so vague that they could evoke no real feeling. The wonder is that many contemporary readers found the poems in any way stirring.

4

Pastorals and Elegies

SEVERAL WAR POETS, SEEKING TO DESCRIBE THE STARTLING, UNFORESEEN conditions of the war, turned to classical verse forms. These were not always appropriate. Pastoral poetry, introduced by the Greek poet Theocritus, had originally celebrated country folk and shepherds, but the form evolved to serve other functions. One possibility for the war poets was the pastoral's use to criticize life in a corrupt or sterile city or court by contrast with an innocent and healthful rural life. The tactic of criticism by contrast suggested a strategy for war poets who wished to describe trench warfare and the soldier's miserable lot without moving to strident or explicit protest. Shepherds were as unlikely to be at the front as were medieval knights, but poets might describe contrasts between peace and war, home and front, creation and destruction, to make implicit protests.

However, the imagery of romantic nature poetry could still serve the chivalric/warrior/heroic tradition. Willoughby Weaving, a protégé of Robert Bridges who served as lieutenant in the Royal Irish Rifles until he was invalided from the western front in 1915, kept his personal experience of war's horrors separate from his poetic treatment of an heroic war. "Flanders," which appeared in *The Star Fields and Other Poems* (1916), obscures all traces of carnage by combining the language of the warrior tradition with the imagery of nature:

> Man has the life of butterflies
> In the sunshine of sacrifice;
> Brief and brilliant, but more
> Guerdon than the honeyed flower,
> And more glory than the grace
> Of their gentle floating pace.

Other poets applied the tactic of contrast to emphasize the unheroic aspects of soldiers' lives. Early poems expressed the soldier's homesickness. To fight in the trenches was doubly hard since the troglodyte existence, artillery bombardment, and machine-gun fire occurred a short seventy miles from London. Early in the war, when soldiers refrained from describing actual conditions (partly due to censorship, partly to feelings of decency), expressions of longing for the English countryside conveyed a soldier's unhappiness at the front. Edward Wyndham Tennant (1897–1916) demonstrates not only his ability to express a harsher reality in "The Mad Soldier," but also his conformity to decency's code of reticence in "Home Thoughts in Laventie." Tennant, the son of Baron Glenconner, was at Winchester when war was declared, joined the Grenadier Guards, spent one year of training in England, and then went to France, where he shared a dugout with Osbert Sitwell. He was killed in action at the Somme on 22 September 1916, and he was buried next to his friend Raymond Asquith, a casualty of the same battle. Tennant's "The Mad Soldier" first appeared in Edith Sitwell's *Wheels, 2nd Cycle* after Tennant's death. The poem reveals Tennant's awareness of the bitter realities of trench life, such as rats eating the dead and men huddling in fear during artillery barrages, and explicitly equates the war with hell.

"Home Thoughts in Laventie," first published in the London *Times* in 1916, describes the contrast between scenes of war and the delights of a green garden apparently untouched by the war. Tennant's description of the daffodils and jasmine and daphne of this unexpected garden shifts to thoughts of home:

> I saw green banks of daffodil,
>   Slim poplars in the breeze,
> Great tan-brown hares in gusty March
>   A-courting on the leas;
> And meadows with their glittering streams, and silver scurrying dace,
>   Home—what a perfect place!

Tennant's poem captures a moment of the soul's flight from present to past without explicitly indicting the war.

F. W. Harvey, whose "Prisoners" reflected a prisoner-of-war's frustration at being out of battle, described a soldier's longing for the English countryside in "In Flanders":

> I'm homesick for my hills again—
> My hills again!
> To see above the Severn plain
> Unscabbarded against the sky
> The blue high blade of Cotswold lie. . . .

For Harvey, it is sufficient to identify as the heart's cry "I'm homesick for my hills again" a second time after naming Malvern. The simplicity of the lament is eloquent, despite the regrettable presence of such archaic martial imagery as the "unscabbarded . . . blade."

In "The Sleepers," Harvey contrasts images of the trenches and descriptions of nature to produce a pastoral elegy. The poem's first few lines might have introduced a romantic description of a tumbledown cottage in the peaceful countryside:

> A battered roof where stars went tripping
> With silver feet,
> A broken roof whence rain came dripping,
> Yet rest was sweet.

The next stanza, however, introduces images of the trenches, including the ubiquitous squeaking rats and reeking dead, and the "sweet" rest becomes the sleep of the dead "Within a cell / Of brown and bloody earth." The economy of Harvey's description of the trenches, limited to two references to "dug-out" in addition to the rats and the slain, keeps the emphasis on tranquil images of the aloof stars and of the archaic but consoling "Thrice blessed sleep, the balm of sorrow," which protects the slain.

Patrick MacGill (b. 1890) used nature imagery to intensify the anguish of a soldier who waits for attack. MacGill, an Irish poet and novelist, joined the London Irish Rifles at the outbreak of the war and reached the rank of sergeant. He fought in the Battle of Loos in 1915 and was wounded. His *Soldier Songs* (1916) enjoyed wide popularity. In "Before the Charge," MacGill describes the tension of soldiers awaiting battle, and he conveys the sense of foreboding by presenting a series of images that emphasize the slowness of time passing: "The night is still and the air is keen, / Tense with menace the time crawls by" and "The dead leaves float in the sighing air, / The darkness moves like a curtain drawn." The first hint of battle does not come until the poem's last line: the sun will tear the curtain of darkness "From the face of death.—We charge at dawn." Despite MacGill's personal experience of battle and its consequences, his poem evokes the soldiers' impatience rather than their fear of pain, mutilation, or death.

E. W. Tennant describes the trenches in "Light After Darkness," in which he conveys a sense of horror by describing destructive weaponry with detachment. After nightfall has hidden an ugly scene, lights play above No Man's Land:

> Now the space between,
> Fringed with the eager eyes of men, is racked
> By spark-tailed lights, curvetting far and high
> Swift smoke-flecked coursers, raking the black sky.

Tennant describes this macabre light show without comment until the end of the poem's second stanza, which reveals that the lights illuminate "Pale rigid faces, lying dead, below." In the final stanza the reader learns that the dead, "tainting the innocent air," will remain hidden until the dawn will reveal them, "The broken heralds of a doleful day." "Light After Darkness" is within the pastoral tradition that criticizes man's departure from an earlier, rural innocence, but, like Harvey's "In Flanders," the poem suffers from its chivalric imagery.

Nature's silent criticism of human warfare also appears in "From Albert to Bapaume" by Alec Waugh (1898–1981), son of critic Arthur Waugh and elder brother of satirist Evelyn Waugh. Only sixteen when the war began, Waugh spent a year in the Inns of Court Officers' Training Corps and then went to Sandhurst for Royal Military College. He received his commission as lieutenant in April 1917. In France he served as machine-gun officer in the Dorset Regiment from July 1917 until 28 March 1918, when he was captured during the British retreat from Arras. Waugh spent the rest of the war in an officers' prisoner-of-war camp in Germany. He had fought at Passchendaele and Cambrai, which contributed to his growing anger at the realities of war. His poem "Cannon Fodder," written near the end of the war, bitterly describes the fate of conscripts, and the title of his later volume of war poetry, *Resentment* (1918), further emphasizes his attitude. In "From Albert to Bapaume," the silent battlefield is "half articulate" about what the slain have experienced. Waugh proceeds to provide images to demonstrate this:

> A battered trench, a tree with boughs
> Smutted and black with smoke and fire,
> A solitary ruined house,
> A crumpled mass of rusty wire.

In the final lines, poppies in the field suggest that "the blood of the dead men / Had not been wholly washed away." Earlier poems posed idyllic pictures of rural life as condemnations of urbanization. Waugh's portrait of a wounded battlefield rebukes man's propensity for self-slaughter.

The soldier at the front not only endured privation absurdly near London, but also constantly observed natural phenomena which recalled days of peace. T. P. Cameron Wilson (1878–1918), a captain in the Sherwood Foresters, found such reminders particularly poignant, but not enough to move him to protest. Born in South Devon, Wilson was educated at Oxford and became a schoolmaster. He was killed in action in the Somme Valley by machine-gun fire on 23 March 1918, the day after he had crawled out into No Man's Land to carry back one of his men from the wire entanglements. His poem "Magpies in Picardy," originally published in the *Westminster Gazette*, implies the irony of men marching to war through undisturbed countryside:

> The magpies in Picardy
> Are more than I can tell.
> They flicker down the dusty roads
> And cast a magic spell

On the men who march through Picardy,
Through Picardy to hell.

The magpie imparts a message to the soldier, a fatalistic truth: ". . . two things have altered not / Since first the world began— / The beauty of the wild green earth / And the bravery of man." Wilson can depict the contrast of natural beauty and war, but he still equates war with bravery and tends to ennoble the soldiers.

Two poets who were struck by the contrast of nature's beauty and war's destruction found opposite meanings. Claude H. Dodwell, a private in the Canadian Contingent, whose "Trench Violets" appeared in the *Poetry Review* in 1916, provides an economical description of violets that are in contrast to the war's ugliness, "Lest men forget." For Dodwell, white violets blooming on the parapet show that "God sets His Seal." Hubert Dayne found different import in the spectacle of moonlight shining above German night attacks in Belgium. In "To the Moon," after addressing the "Calm moon" to ask "Where art thou sadly gazing whilst we sleep?", Dayne describes what the moonlight reveals:

> Torn lungs and shell-rent limbs. . . .
> Hard sobs through tight-clenched teeth. . . .
> Bright eyes that death's hand dims. . . .
> A blood-drenched field beneath. . . .

He ends his poem with his dread of nature's heartless indifference: "How can'st thou gaze so calm-eyed, silvery-white, /Whilst, choked with pain and blood, men writhe all night?" Dayne's poem derived inspiration from a newspaper's statement that the Belgians found moonlight beneficial during night attacks, but the poet found the illumination of the carnage more significant than any tactical advantage. The poem suffers from archaic imagery and diction that clash with Dayne's contemporary subject, while his meter often seems almost jaunty, but the emphasis on soldiers' suffering is more compatible with current views of war.

The significance of man's impact on his world during the war occurred to several poets. For Francis Brett Young (1884–1954), man's encroachments on the land return him to the Stone Age. Young, educated at Epsom College, Birmingham University, served as a major in the Royal Army Medical Corps until he was invalided home after malaria and exhaustion overcame him in East Africa. Before the war, Young wrote a critical study of Robert Bridges, and he published *Poems 1916–1918* in 1919. His most ambitious work, *The Island,* a verse history of England up to the Battle of Britain, appeared in 1944. "Song of the Dark Ages" describes soldiers digging trenches, uncovering relics of the Stone Age. Young imagines that in time the earth will cover the trenches with green sod, but sufficient traces will remain for people to find them: "You see the toil they made: / The age of iron, pick, and spade, / Here jostles with the Age of Stone." The final stanza equates the trench soldier with the troglodyte savage:

> Yet either from that happier race
>   Will merit but a passing glance;
> And they will leave us both alone:
> Poor savages who wrought in stone—
>   Poor savages who fought in France.

Of those war poets who asserted nature's ultimate triumph over the destructive activity of man, most were civilians. Distance from the actual fighting allowed more room for optimism. Sir William Watson (1858–1935) drew extensive criticism during his long career. His opposition to the Boer War made him unpopular for some time, and the holy wrath he expressed against the Kaiser in several poems during the Great War went too far even for many prowar enthusiasts, although Watson received a knighthood in 1917 for his propagandistic war poetry. As a poet, Watson had a limited gift. In the *Bookman,* critic W. L. Phelps commented that "the William Watson of the last twenty-five years [1893–1918], a fiery, eager, sensitive man, with a burning passion to express himself on moral and political ideas, learned the mastery of his art before he had anything to say."[1] Watson, who began writing poetry in 1880, certainly practiced his art long before the 1914–18 War. Watson published one verse, however, which stands apart from his other war poems. "The Yellow Pansy," which appeared in the first issue of *To-Day* in March 1917, tried to place the war in a much larger perspective than that of rivalry between England and Germany. A yellow pansy in a garden in the early spring suggests significance (with the help of Shakespeare's line "There's pansies—that's for thoughts") in a commonplace occurrence:

> 'Twas Nature saying by trope and metaphor:
>   "Behold, when empire against empire strives,
> Though all else perish, ground 'neath iron war,
>   The golden thought survives."

The poem suffers from such poetic usages as *'Twas, Behold,* and *'neath,* which remove the verse from contemporary speech.

Another civilian poet, Harold Monro (1879–1932), is best known for the support he gave other poets and for his Poetry Bookshop, which published Edward Marsh's *Georgian Poetry* anthologies. Monro was educated at Cambridge and, during the war, received a commission in an antiaircraft battery of the Royal Artillery before being posted to the War Office. His best-known war poem, "Youth in Arms," includes a section entitled "Carrion," which describes nature's final victory over the soldier. The poem addresses a dead soldier who, if not found, will become part of the earth on which he lies: "In a little while your limbs will fall apart; / The birds will take some, but the earth will take most your heart." The ultimate fate of the soldier is to become part of the natural order: "You are fuel for a coming spring if they leave you here; / The crop that will rise from your bones is healthy bread." After calling the soldier's demise his "second birth," the poem reiterates the eventual melding of the body with the earth: "No coffin-cover now will cram / Your body in a shell of lead; / Earth will not fall on you from the spade with a slam, / But will fold and enclose you slowly, you living dead." Despite its attempt to describe a harmony with nature, the poem suffers from its gruesome detail as well as from discordant diction (e.g., earth "slamming" from a spade).

Humbert Wolfe (1885–1940) argues the inevitable victory of nature over war, but in a much more comprehensive sense. Wolfe, a Liberal Jewish civil servant, was an officer in the Ministry of Munitions during the war. Later, following his frequent literary skirmishes with G. K. Chesterton, he became known for his light, satirical verse. He celebrates the final conquest of nature over military machinery in "France":

> The corn outlasts the bayonet,
> Whose blades no blood nor rest can fret,
> Or only the immortal rust
> Of poppies failing in their thrust.

For Wolfe, the returning vegetation can "Reverse the errors of Versailles" by establishing peace over the battlefield:

> For all the living these will cloak
> The things they spoiled, the hearts they broke;
> And where these heal the earth will be
> For all the dead indemnity.

Despite nature's triumph over the devastation of the war, the haunting memory of destruction lingers. Vance Palmer (1885–1959), an Australian poet who worked as clerk, journalist, freelance writer, and bookkeeper before traveling in Europe, America, and Asia, served in France during the war. In his poem "The Farmer Remembers the Somme," Palmer indicates that, even after the soldier returns to his home, the effects of the war will remain. The poem opens with the returned farmer's question,

> Will they never fade or pass—
> The mud, and the misty figures endlessly coming
> In file through the foul morass,

And the grey flood-water lipping the reeds and grass,
And the steel wings drumming?

Although the farmer has returned to his familiar countryside, wartime experiences continue to disturb him:

I have returned to these;
The farm, and kindly Bush, and the young calves lowing;
But all that my mind sees
Is a quaking bog in a mist—stark, snapped trees,
And the dark Somme flowing.

As the memory of the Somme destroys the peace of the rural setting for at least one generation, so the war has left its mark on the poetry written about it. The clash of modern war with chivalry resulted in changes in chivalric verse, and the contrasts between harmonious peace and destructive war have also altered the content of the pastoral. Surprisingly few poets applied the pastoral strategy to protest the war, but the understated contrasts between war and the natural order were occasionally effective, and a new understanding of war's realities emerged from descriptions of war scenes. Even poets working deliberately within traditional conventions and expectations found their work altered by the encroachments of modern war. Thus, Palmer's poem shifts emphasis from the effect of the war on the land to the psychological consequences that war's destruction holds for those who fought and survived.

The Great War brought changes to the elegiac mode as well. War had become inglorious slaughter at the hands of an artillery gunner five miles away who had no personal involvement with, or even knowledge of, injury he might have inflicted. The machine gun rendered frontal attacks suicidal, and poison gas reduced combatants to mere victims. At the outset, elegies offered consolation in glory won and duty met. Eventually the pity of war that Wilfred Owen later came to epitomize, and the beginnings of protest against the apparently unending carnage, would both grow from the extent to which the unprecedented brutality of the Great War offered occasion for elegies.

Laurence Binyon (1869–1943) seems an unlikely poet to have written what Fussell has called "The most popular poem for quotation."[2] Binyon spent the greater part of his life working at the British Museum (1893–1933), supervising the Orientalia holdings after 1913. He had won the Newdigate Prize at Oxford in 1890 and had written nine volumes of poetry before the war, but the one work destined to keep his name alive was his "For the Fallen (September 1914)," which first appeared in the London *Times* on 21 September 1914. He had no direct knowledge of war when he wrote his poem, but later he worked with the Red Cross and visited the western front in

1916. His elegy bases its consolation on the fame and undying youth of the fallen. Throughout the poem Binyon describes the slain in imagery appropriate for classical elegy:

> They went with songs to the battle, they were young,
> Straight of limb, true of eye, steady and aglow.
> They were staunch to the end against odds uncounted:
> They fell with their faces to the foe.

One stanza is inscribed in gold above the entrance of the British Museum:

> They shall not grow old, as we that are left grow old:
> Age shall not weary them, nor the years condemn.
> At the going down of the sun and in the morning
> We will remember them.

Binyon's elegy inspired many imitations, such as Humbert Wolfe's "V. D. F. (Ave atque Vale)," but it remains the most satisfying classical treatment of contemporary loss.

Other poets focused on the soldier's sacrifice of life for the sake of duty. A. E. Housman (1859–1936) wrote several poems depicting submissive heroism. "Here Dead Lie We," from *More Poems* (1936), represents an attitude toward duty's call that many soldiers could appreciate:

> Here dead lie we because we did not choose
>   To live and shame the land from which we sprung.
> Life, to be sure, is nothing much to lose;
>   But young men think it is, and we were young.

The consolation is implicit: these have avoided dishonor by sacrificing their wellbeing for their country, an idea which may seem as outdated as the inversion of "lie we." In another poem, "Epitaph on an Army of Mercenaries," Housman honored those who fell at the First Battle of Ypres (that Kaiser Wilhelm called them "mercenaries" was an inflammatory fabrication of the British propaganda machine). The poem appeared in the London *Times* on 31 October 1917. After describing the deaths of the "mercenaries," Housman praised their achievement: "What God abandoned, these defended, / And saved the sum of things for pay."

Perhaps the most tragic of the war poets was Ivor Gurney (1890–1937), since for him the war never ended. By the time he was seventeen he had begun to write verse and set others' poetry to music, and in 1911 he entered the Royal College of Music in London, where he published two volumes of verse and wrote songs that were performed publicly. At the outbreak of the war he enlisted in the Gloucestershire Regiment in the ranks. He fought and was wounded in the Battle of Arras on 7 April 1917, but he recuperated

quickly enough to fight in the Battle of Passchendaele, where he was gassed
on 22 August 1917. Gurney, who had suffered a nervous breakdown before
the war, was discharged one month before the Armistice for shell shock. By
1922 he had become so unstable that he was confined to a private mental
home outside Gloucester and then to City of London Mental Hospital,
where he died in 1937. He continued to write war poetry in the belief that
the war was still going on. He had published two collections of poetry,
Severn and Somme (1917) and *War's Embers* (1919), before his confinement.

Gurney's "The Target," from *War's Embers*, describes the feelings of a
soldier who has killed an enemy only because duty and necessity compelled,
recalling Hardy's "The Man He Killed" (1909). Gurney's poem, despite its
broken meter, conveys in colloquial speech the moral confusion of a survivor
who knows his duty but is not very comfortable with it:

> I shot him, and it had to be
> One of us! 'Twas him or me.
> "Couldn't be helped," and none can blame
> Me, for you would do the same.

The speaker resolves to ask his victim's pardon should he also die, and the
poem becomes a lament for the living as well as for the dead:

> All's a tangle. Here's my job.
> A man might rave, or shout, or sob;
> And God He takes no sort of heed.
> This is a bloody mess indeed.

The reader's sympathy is with the speaker, who can barely justify his
actions, or his survival, because his conscience troubles him.

Gurney's "To His Love," a pastoral elegy, shifts to pity for the fallen. Two
stanzas establish that a dead youth's body is "not as you / Knew it" at home.
The third stanza reveals the growing discrepancy between conventional
descriptions of noble deaths and horrid mutilations common at the front:
"You would not know him now . . . / But still he died / Nobly. . . ." By the
end of the poem, the nature of the youth's death has rendered tributes to
courage and glory inadequate:

> Cover him, cover him soon!
>   And with thick-set
> Masses of memoried flowers—
>   Hide that red wet
>   Thing I must somehow forget.

Although this is far from the brutal imagery of a wagon wheel crushing a
corpse in Isaac Rosenberg's "Dead Man's Dump," it starts in that direction.

The shift from traditional exaltation of the fallen to pained shock at a corpse's mutilation has made conventional elegy more difficult.

E. A. Mackintosh's "In Memoriam," like his "Recruiting," frustrates the expectations aroused by the title. Instead of focusing on a man's death, "In Memoriam" examines the effect of death on two survivors, a soldier's father and his officer. In the first two stanzas, the poem addresses the father's grief. At the end of the second stanza, the speaker identifies himself: "And I was his officer." Mackintosh pointedly compares the two mourners: "You were only David's father, / But I had fifty sons." The father can recall a son's childhood, but the officer must watch him die:

> Happy and young and gallant,
> They saw their first-born go,
> But not the strong limbs broken
> And the beautiful men brought low,
> The piteous writhing bodies,
> They screamed "Don't leave me, sir",
> For they were only your fathers,
> But I was your officer.

Pity for the living who still must endure the hardships of ignominious trench warfare has supplanted concern for the dead.

Roland Leighton (1895–1915) tried to arouse pity by focusing on the life that the fallen must leave. The son of two writers (his father of boys' adventure stories, his mother of romantic novels), Leighton was educated at Uppingham, where he took prizes in the classics and became quartermaster-sergeant in the Officers' Training Corps. He volunteered for service shortly after the war began and was placed in a front-line unit on 31 March 1915. On the night of 22 December 1915, while leading his platoon on a wire-mending expedition, Leighton was wounded by machine-gun fire and died the following morning. He wrote only a dozen war poems, and these usually upheld the traditional virtues. "Ploegsteert" recalls Brooke:

> I have seen blood and death, but all has ending,
> And even Horror is but made to cease;
> I am sickened with Love that lives only for lending,
> And all the loathsome pettiness of peace.

After these lines, Leighton shifts to a more overtly chivalric appeal: "Give me, God of Battles, a field of death, / A Hill of Fire, a strong man's agony. . . ." Here is confusion similar to that of Gurney's "The Target," for Leighton has combined his sense of war's horror with his knowledge that it is temporary, a contempt for prewar peace (reminiscent of Brooke's "And all the little emptiness of love") with a direct request for a soldier's death.

In "Hédauville," dated November 1915 and intended for Vera Brittain, Leighton's fiancée and herself a war poet, Leighton merges pastoral imagery with a soldier's perception of life (without him) after the war. Leighton's verse reveals his admiration for Brooke as well as his ability to express his feelings in simple and direct language. He tells his beloved that, should he not return, she may meet someone else:

> And if he is not quite so old
> As the boy you used to know,
> And less proud, too, and worthier,
> You may not let him go—
> (And daisies are truer than passion-flowers)

> It will be better so.

One basis for later protests against the war was the feeling that the swollen casualty lists resulted from military and political ineptitude, coupled with indifference to the soldier's plight. That the first rumblings of protest would grow from the elegiac mode was almost inevitable. The first indications were poems and reports revealing the appalling extent of the deaths. J. Griffyth Fairfax (b. 1886), an Australian-born captain in the Royal Army Service Corps who served in Mesopotamia and was four times mentioned in dispatches, found the numbers of the dead overwhelming in one sense but not in another. In "The Forest of the Dead" he describes the rows of crosses over fallen soldiers in terms of a forest: "Cross after cross, mound after mound, / And no flowers blossom but are bound, / The dying and the dead, in the wreaths." Fairfax describes the vastness of the forest, but not to abandon hope:

> These, having life, gave life away:
> Is God less generous than they?
> The spirit passes and is free:
> Dust to the dust; Death takes the clay.

Although Fairfax has indicated the great numbers of the slain without hesitation, he offers consolation in the promise of an afterlife. However, Fairfax's unfortunate use of short, singsong lines diminishes the effect of his poem.

Major Maurice Baring (1874–1945), son of Lord Revelstoke and educated at Cambridge, served in the Intelligence Corps before becoming a major in the RAF. Of Baring, Marshal Foch commented that "there never was a staff officer in any country, in any nation, in any century, like Major Maurice Baring."[3] The effect of the prolonged war on Baring's outlook appears in a contrast between an elegy written in 1916 and one written two years later. The first, "In Memoriam: A. H.", in memory of Auberon Herbert, Lord

Lucas, who was killed on 3 November 1916, is a traditional funeral ode. Edmund Gosse has called it "one of the few durable contributions to the literature of the present war,"[4] but Gosse was wrong. A few lines give some feeling of the whole:

> God, Who had made you valiant, strong and swift
> And maimed you with a bullet long ago,
> . . . .
> Gave back your youth to you,
> And packed in moments rare and few
> Achievements manifold
> And happiness untold,
> And bade you spring to Death as to a bride,
> In manhood's ripeness, power and pride,
> And on your sandals the strong wings of youth.

The later poem, "August, 1918 (In a French Village)," differs in several respects, including reference to the enormous number of the fallen. The last six lines contrast sharply to the earlier ode:

> Sleep, child, the Angel of Death his wings has spread;
> His engines scour the land, the sea, the sky;
> And all the weapons of Hell's armoury
>
> Are ready for the blood that is their bread;
> And many a thousand men to-night must die,
> So many that they will not count the Dead.

Here is no hint of a just cause, or glorious battle, or noble purpose, or eternal fame, but only the casualty list in the offing.

Ernest Rhys (1859–1946), co-founder of the Rhymer's Club in 1895 with W. B. Yeats, took a less personal tack. In "Lost in France," subtitled "Jo's Requiem," Rhys presents an elegy that ignores the war entirely. He devotes the first eleven lines of his twelve-line poem to the victim's former physical prowess ("He could see a crow / Three miles away"), passing over the circumstances of death to conclude with a simple but forceful statement: "And he is dead." Instead of attempting to attribute significance to the death, Rhys places it as a contrasting detail that emphasizes the highly personal response of the mourner. Only the title enables one to recognize this as a war poem. The force of Rhys's understatement is itself a protest.

Sergeant Leslie Coulson (1889–1916), like W. N. Hodgson, frequently voiced an optimism and idealism that would not survive, but in his elegies he went farther than Hodgson in his growing resentment. Coulson, who joined the 12th London Battalion of the 2nd Royal Fusiliers in September 1914, fell on 7 October 1916 while leading a charge. His *From an Outpost and Other*

Poems (1917) was so popular that ten thousand copies sold in less than twelve months. In "Who Made the Law?", written only a few days before his death, Coulson struck an early note of protest. His indictment of the senseless slaughter derives its force from the contrast of traditional pastoral images and brutal deaths:

> Who made the Law that men should die in meadows?
> Who spake the word that blood should splash in lanes?
> Who gave it forth that gardens should be boneyards?
> Who spread the hills with flesh, and blood, and brains?
>   Who made the Law?

Other images of blood splashed on bark of trees and bones crackling underfoot arouse outrage rather than pity for the victims of the pointless slaughter. His "—But a Short Time to Live," published posthumously in the *Poetry Review* early in 1917, reveals soldiers' awareness of the fleeting moments before death. Instead of citing remembered pleasures to console those who must leave them, Coulson emphasizes how those pleasures make it more difficult to die:

> Our little hour—how short it is
>   When Love with dew-eyed loveliness
> Raises her lips for ours to kiss
>   And dies within our first caress.
> Youth flickers out like wind-blown flame,
>   Sweets of to-day to-morrow sour,
> For Time and Death relentless, claim
>   Our little hour.

Despite its romantic imagery, Coulson's poem offers no assurance that the dead have gained from their sacrifice.

Many of these poems retain defects of artificiality in their archaic diction, inappropriate imagery, and discordant meter. However, one can also find changes in poetic tradition, notably when poets attempt to place rhythms and phrases of colloquial speech in their verses and when they exploit the incongruity of older poetic conventions that fail to describe a new kind of war. The war poets' use of nature imagery to contrast the destruction of warfare with nostalgic longings for peaceful English settings, and their use of the elegy to question the growing casualties of the war, mark the initial step in the movement toward public protest. Even poets working deliberately within traditional conventions and expectations found their work altered by the disturbing realities of modern warfare.

PART II

Shifts in Technique and Attitude

5

The Imagists

THE PREWAR IMAGIST MOVEMENT BEGAN PARTLY AS A REACTION AGAINST Georgianism, but its shift of emphasis also made Imagist poetry peculiarly apt for describing the war. The contrast between Georgianism and Imagism, described by Vivian de Sola Pinto, was striking:

> The Georgians had assumed that there was still an upper middle class with a living poetic culture, and that it was possible by means of a few minor reforms to achieve a renewal of the classic English poetic tradition. . . . The Imagists, although they were only minor poets, had the merit of perceiving and declaring that this was no longer possible. They were the first true "modernist" group in the sense that they no longer attempted to communicate with a general public of poetry lovers which had ceased to exist, but concentrated on searching for a means of expressing the modern consciousness for their own satisfaction and that of their friends. The pretence that humanity was steadily progressing towards the millennium was to be abandoned and the poets had to recognize that they were living in a new dark age of barbarism and vulgarity where the arts could only survive in small islands of culture, which was no longer the possession of a securely established social class but which had to be fashioned anew by a self-chosen *élite* that managed to escape the spiritual degradation of a commercialized world. . . . The Imagists . . . wanted to create a very precise and concentrated expression of a new sort of consciousness for which the traditional techniques were inadequate.[1]

Dora Marsden and Harriet Shaw Weaver's the *New Freewoman* changed into the *Egoist* in 1913 to serve as an Imagist vehicle, Ezra Pound published the *Des Imagistes* anthology in 1914, and *Some Imagist Poets* anthologies appeared in 1915, 1916, and 1917.

Despite the brevity of the group's activity, there was a considerable long-term influence. Richard Aldington's autobiography, *Life for Life's Sake* (1941), addresses the question "What did the Imagists achieve between 1912 and 1917?":

> Well, they did some useful pioneering work. They dealt a blow at the post-Victorian magazine poets, whose unappeased shades still clamour

for Imagist blood. They livened things up a lot. They made free verse popular—it had already been used by Blake, Whitman, and Henley and by many of the French Symbolistes. And they tried to attain an exacting if narrow standard of style in poetry. And to a considerable extent T. S. Eliot and his followers have carried on their operations from positions won by the Imagists.[2]

The principles of Imagism, enumerated by Aldington in his preface to *Some Imagist Poets* in 1915, now seem simply rules for good writing. These are (1) "To use the language of common speech, but to employ always the exact word . . .", (2) "To create new rhythms," chiefly through free verse, (3) "To allow absolute freedom in the choice of subject," (4) to present concrete images in lieu of abstract generalities, (5) "To produce poetry that is hard and clear, never blurred nor indefinite," and (6) to apply "concentration" as "the very essence of poetry." These principles enhanced the development of modernist verse as well as more realistic and controlled responses to the war.

T. E. Hulme (1883–1917) provided both the initial impulse and the theoretical basis for the Imagist movement, but he wrote little of the poetry. In 1908 he founded the Poets' Club (which included no other Imagists until the following year), read and discussed experimental Imagist poems, and wrote short verses to illustrate Imagist principles. The posthumous *Speculations* (1924), edited by Herbert Read, includes only half a dozen poems (the entire Hulme canon consists of thirty verses). Hulme met F. S. Flint shortly after founding the Poets' Club, and, since Flint was already an advocate of *vers libre*, free verse soon became an Imagist principle. Interest in Japanese drama verse forms encouraged economy, or "concentration," and, when Ezra Pound coined the term *Imagisme* by adding a French suffix to *image*, the movement had evolved sufficiently to arouse interest.

Hulme approved of the war. He has been described as an "intellectual militarist" whose opposition to such antimilitaristic works as Bernard Shaw's *Arms and the Man* was fierce. Hulme enlisted in the Royal Artillery, was wounded in France, returned to the front after convalescence in England, and died under shell fire near Nieuport, France, in 1917. The efforts of Ezra Pound, T. S. Eliot, and Herbert Read prevented Hulme's lapsing into obscurity. As the "begetter" of Imagism he brought together poets of new talent, both English and American. The eleven contributors to *Des Imagistes* in 1914 included Richard Aldington, H. D. (Hilda Doolittle), F. S. Flint, Ford Madox Hueffer (Ford), James Joyce, Amy Lowell, Ezra Pound, and William Carlos Williams. Amy Lowell edited the three *Some Imagist Poets* anthologies, much to Pound's disgust since he disapproved of the "Amygist" movement. D. H. Lawrence became a nominal member of the group, but the Imagists remained essentially those whom Hulme and Pound had brought together in the first anthology.

In his poem "Trenches: St Eloi," Hulme describes men in the trenches, artillery positions behind the lines, and then the observer's state of mind. The first section, in ten lines, describes the trenches at night:

In the silence desultory men
Pottering over small fires, cleaning their mess-tins:
To and fro, from the lines,
Men walk as on Piccadilly,
Making paths in the dark,
Through scattered dead horses,
Over a dead Belgian's belly.

From this beginning, Hulme moves to statements: only the Germans have rockets, and cannon lie hidden behind the lines. At the end of the poem, Hulme stops short of protest's "curative realism" (graphic description designed to shock readers out of complacency). For Hulme's speaker, "Nothing suggests itself. There is nothing to do but keep on." By insisting that any subject is appropriate for poetry and by using stark images, Hulme and his following helped later poets describe the brutalities of the war, but Hulme's viewpoint required an "intrusion" at the end lest some readers regard his poem as critical of the war effort.

Ezra Pound (1885–1972) has also been associated with the development of Imagism, although his main contribution was to popularize the movement. He also browbeat editors into printing works by unknown poets. Shortly after the publication of *Des Imagistes*, Pound abandoned the movement to pursue Vorticism with Wyndham Lewis. Within three years the American Pound went far beyond the protests of several British poets, Sassoon included, by rejecting nationalistic patriotism entirely. His satire of England's response to the war, best expressed in *Hugh Selwyn Mauberley* (1920), was Juvenalian in its intensity, reaching its climax in Poem 5:

There died a myriad,
And of the best, among them,
For an old bitch gone in the teeth,
For a botched civilization. . . .

Pound's retrospective view of the war combines the pity (and allusion to Horace) of Wilfred Owen with the bluntness of Sassoon:

Died some, pro patria,
    non "dulce" non "et decor" . . .
walked eye-deep in hell
believing in old men's lies, then unbelieving
came home, home to a lie,
home to many deceits,
home to old lies and new infamy;

usury age-old and age-thick
and liars in public places.

Some traces of Imagism remain, including free verse, the rhythms of common speech, economy of expression, and concrete imagery. In Canto 16,
Pound included brief descriptions of writers and artists he knew who had
fought in the war, including Aldington, Wyndham Lewis, Hemingway, and
Henri Gaudier. His description of T. E. Hulme's role is brief but illuminating:

> And ole T. E. H. he went to it,
> With a lot of books from the library,
> London Library, and a shell buried 'em in a dug-out,
> And the Library expressed its annoyance.
>   And a bullet hit him on the elbow
> . . . gone through the fellow in front of him,
> And he read Kant in the Hospital, in Wimbledon,
> in the original,
> And the hospital staff didn't like it.

Ford Madox Ford (1873–1939) made his greatest contribution to the
Imagists and other unknown writers in his *English Review,* which he
founded in 1908 with Arthur Marwood and edited until 1910. The *English
Review* fostered both Imagism and Vorticism by supplying a forum for
obscure writers of merit. In addition to publishing controversial works by
Ezra Pound and Thomas Hardy (whose poem "A Sunday Morning Tragedy"
was the ostensible, if apocryphal, reason for founding the *English Review*),
Ford introduced D. H. Lawrence, Wyndham Lewis, and Norman Douglas
to the reading public. According to Ford's biographer Frank MacShane,
Ford entertained "a circle of poets that included Ezra Pound, W. B. Yeats,
Hilda Doolittle and her husband Richard Aldington, D. H. Lawrence, F. S.
Flint and, later on, T. S. Eliot."[3] Ford was not officially an Imagist, but "he
was attached to the movement in much the same way Ford Madox Brown
had been connected with the Pre-Raphaelite Brotherhood. Many of the
points made in the Imagist manifesto had been voiced by Ford years before,
some as early as 1902."[4]

At the outbreak of the war, Ford's German origins and surname (which he
adamantly refused to change from "Hueffer" until 1919) aroused suspicion,
and his involvement in a divorce scandal complicated matters by publicizing
his German connections. Ford had become involved with Violet Hunt,
whose Pre-Raphaelite background resembled Ford's, but his wife reneged on
her promise to allow a divorce and sued Ford for "Restitution of Conjugal
Rights." The judgment, which she won, required Ford to pay £3 per week
for the support of wife and children. Since he had been paying three times

that amount voluntarily, he defied this "aspersion of his honour" and went to Brixton Gaol for ten days in protest. In 1910, Ford and Violet Hunt visited his relatives in Germany, where he attempted to establish residency to obtain a divorce. He left without a divorce decree, but he introduced Hunt as "Mrs. Ford Madox Hueffer" when he was interviewed by the press. The legal Mrs. Hueffer sued two periodicals for misusing "her" name. Angered by the resulting scandal, Ford's wealthy and conservative aunt dropped him from her will, and legal expenses ultimately forced Ford into bankruptcy. The publicity linked Ford with Germany, later making his loyalty to England a subject of speculation.

Ford overcompensated by becoming positively fervid in his support of an English victory. Including *The Good Soldier* (1915), a prewar novel which was not a war book despite its title, Ford had written twenty novels, eight volumes of poetry, and other work before August 1914. Shortly after the German invasion of Belgium, Ford wrote "Antwerp," a chauvinistic poem. One section describing a Belgian refugee in London reveals Imagist influence in its austere diction:

> She has a dead face;
> She is dressed all in black;
> She wanders to the bookstall and back,
> At the back of the crowd;
> And back again and again back,
> She sways and wanders.

"Antwerp," however, includes such rhetorical intrusions, as "There is so much pain" and "Oh poor dears!" In Silkin's view, the poem "shows that, unlike those war poets for whom the brutality of war proved the desirability of stopping it, Ford treats the experience as proof of the depth and propriety of patriotic feeling."[5] Ford wrote two propaganda pamphlets embarrassingly vehement in their attacks on Germany. Commissioned by C. F. G. Masterman, chief of the world's first propaganda machine (known only as "Wellington House" until after the war), Ford's *When Blood is Their Argument* (1915) attacks the Prussian influence on German education, scholarship, literature, language, music, and tradition. *Between St. Dennis and St. George* (1915) combines further attack on Germany with defense of the "traditional" unity of France and Great Britain.

A more dramatic instance of Ford's patriotism, however, was his enlistment in the Army in 1915, although he was over military age. Commissioned as a subaltern in the Welsh Regiment, he went to France in July 1916. In the last month of the Battle of the Somme, poison gas changed Ford's voice permanently to a stertorous rasp. He advanced to captain in January 1918, and in two months he was an acting brevet major, a rank he held until he resigned his commission in January 1919. Ford chronicled his war experiences in his tetralogy *Parade's End* (1924–28), including the physical hardships which led, eventually, to shell shock. In a letter to Frank Stewart dated 23 June 1920, he described losing his memory in July 1916, not knowing even his name for thirty-six hours (Tietjens in the tetralogy suffers a similar affliction). Ford's letter to his daughter dated 10 December 1916 mentions that, of the fourteen officers who had arrived with him at the front, five months earlier, only he had survived.

These experiences did not dim Ford's patriotic ardor, but they changed the direction of his poetry. "Footsloggers" reaffirms the need to fight:

> But today it's mud to the knees
> And khaki and khaki and khaki . . .
> And love of one's land
> Very quiet and hidden and still. . . .
>
> What is love of one's land?
> Ah, we know very well
> It is something that sleeps for a year, for a day,
> For a month, something that keeps
> Very hidden and quiet and still,
> And then takes
> The quiet heart like a wave. . . .

Written at the end of 1917, the poem reflects both Ford's greater awareness of the realities of soldiers' lives ("Of digging at the double and strafes and fatigues") and his conviction that there was no alternative to defeating Germany, but his frequent interpolations of propagandistic and patriotic rhetoric undermine the force of his trench images.

Ford's best war poem, "That Exploit of Yours," anticipates Owen's "Strange Meeting" and conforms to principles of Aldington's manifesto. Although it resembles later poems of "curative realism," it stops short of questioning the purpose of the struggle. The poem begins with the line "I meet two soldiers sometimes here in Hell." They are not traditional heroes. One, caught stealing apples, "Was stuck by a pitchfork." The other died when his horse fell "on some tram-lines / In Dortmund." When these two meet, both exclaim, "I at least have done my duty to Society and the Fatherland!" Ford's poem moves to its sardonic conclusion:

> It is strange how the cliché prevails. . .
> For I will bet my hat that you who sent me here to Hell
> Are saying the selfsame words at this very moment
> Concerning that exploit of yours.

The target of Ford's poem is not the traditional hero, but unworthy pretenders basking in the reflected glory of heroism.

D. H. Lawrence (1885–1930), like Ford, aroused the suspicions of English chauvinists. During the war, in Bergonzi's phrase, Lawrence was "an 'internal *émigré.*' "[6] Despite frequent applications, the Lawrences could not obtain permission to leave England. On one occasion, they had to move from their rented cottage at Cornwall (an economic hardship since their rent was only £5 per year), ostensibly to prevent their signaling German submarines. The authorities kept a political file on Frieda and knew Lawrence as a minor figure of the antiwar movement. His health prevented his conscription, but boards frequently called him for physical examinations. His outspoken pacifist convictions frequently aligned him with the Bloomsbury group. Lawrence considered a German victory preferable to continuation of the war, but he was uncharacteristically tolerant of those who differed with him. In a letter to Sir Edward Marsh dated 5 January 1917, Lawrence rejected the label "pacifist" on the grounds that the war may be right for some men, that his objections pertained only to "this war," and that all men have the right to pursue their individual destinies regardless of Lawrence's position. Lawrence believed, however, that the war demonstrated the triumph of mechanical industry over humanity, and, although he wrote many poems which captured the spirit of the English home front, he avoided the subject of the war's validity by confining his verse to description based on direct observation.

Despite the independence of his talent, Lawrence had contributed to Georgian and Imagist anthologies. David Daiches has called Lawrence's association with both movements "pure accident, and he was really an enemy within both camps, . . . He wrote as he had always written, and the Imagists accepted him as a brother."[7] His volume of poetry *Bay* (1919) includes two elegies that express his pity for the slain without questioning their allegiance to the cause—"Bread Upon the Waters" and "Obsequial Ode." His "Tommies in the Train" describes soldiers without political comment:

> What are we
> Clay-coloured, who roll in fatigue
> As the train falls league after league
> From our destiny?

"Bombardment" reveals no antiwar bias except in the implicit horror of exploding shells:

> The Town has opened to the sun.
> Like a flat red lily with a million petals
> She unfolds, she comes undone.
>
> A sharp sky brushes upon
> The myriad glittering chimney-tips
> As she gently exhales to the sun.

Hurrying creatures run
Down the labyrinth of the sinister flower.
What is it they shun?

A dark bird falls from the sun.
It curves in a rush to the heart of the vast
Flower: the day has begun.

The poem employs the precise, exact imagery which Aldington's manifesto demanded. Lawrence has captured the moment of panic as bombardment begins. Compared with overwritten poems vilifying "Huns," "Bombardment" is most striking for its simplicity.

The early career of Richard Aldington (1892–1962) paralleled the development of the Imagist movement. Indeed, one might even argue that the Imagists became Aldingtons and H. D.s rather than the other way around, for the Imagist manifesto and principles popularized by Pound partly derived from verse which Aldington and H. D. had already written. The son of a Portsmouth barrister, Aldington took a serious interest in poetry in 1907 and enrolled in University College, London, in 1910. The next year he left school to begin a career as a writer and supported himself by his pen for the next half-century as poet, critic, novelist, and biographer. When Ezra Pound saw Aldington's poetry early in 1912, he declared that it was Imagist verse, although Aldington maintained that his early connection with Imagism rested on pure coincidence. When he published three poems in the November 1912 issue of Harriet Monroe's *Poetry*, he became the first (and youngest) poet associated publicly with the movement. Although H. D., who married Aldington in 1913, ultimately won regard as the most representative Imagist, Aldington was more helpful to the cause. He wrote the Imagist manifesto, and he edited the *Egoist* from 1914 until his enlistment in 1916. He edited the *Imagist Anthology, 1930* to show that Imagism was still alive. By 1930, however, most of the Imagists, including Aldington, had moved to other pursuits.

Aldington's early collections of poetry—*Images Old and New* (1915), *Images of War* (1919), *Images of Desire* (1919), and *Exile and Other Poems* (1923)—adhere to the principles of the manifesto. The poetry reflects classical and Mediterranean influence and employs *vers libre*, unorthodox rhythms, and language freed from literary artificiality. Aldington, the first soldier to publish Imagist trench poetry, reconciled his poetry with his observations. Although he tried to enlist in August 1914 at the instigation of T. E. Hulme, only to be declared "unfit," and did enlist in 1916 after the passage of the Conscription Act, Aldington had no illusions about the war. In *Life for Life's Sake,* Aldington described his method of writing in the trenches: "I had jotted down poems in a small pocket-book during the war, for no other reason than the consolation of writing something; and unexpectedly I found I could sell them for five or six times as much as I got before the war."[8] In *Death of a Hero* (1929), the best description in fiction of the postwar disillusionment of the British soldier, Aldington referred to "the alleged vogue for 'war poets,' which resulted in the parents of the slain being asked to put up fifty pounds for the publication (which probably cost fifteen) of poor little verses which should never have passed the home circle."[9] For Aldington, ease of publication led to no compromise of poetic principle in his verse, which anticipated the pity of Owen, the protest of Sassoon, and the "curative realism" of others.

Images of War includes several poems which present the pity of war's destruction, including "Three Little Girls," which, unlike much of Aldington's war verse, follows a regular metrical pattern. Marianne, Madeline, and Alys are "Three little girls with fathers killed / And mothers lost, / Three little girls with broken shoes / And hard sharp coughs" who "sold us sweets / Too near the shells." The poem's descriptive imagery conveys pity for the children without lapsing into sentimentality or pathos. "To Those Who Played for Safety in Life," like Sassoon's "Base Details," contrasts the trench soldier to those at home:

> I also might have worn starched cuffs,
> Have gulped my morning meal in haste,
> Have clothed myself in dismal stuffs
> Which prove a sober City taste;
> . . . .
> I might have earned ten pounds a week!

"The Blood of the Young Men" contrasts the useless sacrifice of soldiers at the front to the lots of those at home:

> Old men, you will grow stronger and healthier
> With broad red cheeks and clear hard eyes—
> Are not your meat and drink the choicest?
> Blood of the young, dear flesh of the young men.

Aldington's "curative realism" includes "Eumenides," which brutally evokes morbidity:

> That boot I kicked
> (It had a mouldy foot in it)
> The night K's head was smashed
> Like a rotten pear by a mortar.

The earlier "Soliloquy—1" undermines belief in the unflinching heroism of the chivalric tradition:

No, I'm not afraid of death
(Not very much afraid, that is)
Either for others or myself;
Can watch them coming from the line

On the wheeled silent stretchers
And not shrink,
But munch my sandwich stoically
And make a joke, when "it" has passed.

But—the way they wobble!—
God! that makes one sick.
Dead men should be so still, austere,
And beautiful,
Not wobbling carrion roped upon a cart . . .

Well, thank God for rum.

In the narrative "Trench Idyll," two men sit in the trenches, one "on a lump of frozen earth" and the speaker "on an unexploded shell." After they talk of the pleasures of London, their conversation turns to experiences at the front. The other soldier recalls morbid details of decay:

"Well, as to that, the nastiest job I've had
Was last year on this very front
Taking the discs at night from men
Who'd hung for six months on the wire
Just over there.
The worst of all was
They fell to pieces at a touch.
Thank God we couldn't see their faces;
They had gas helmets on . . ."

This description applies Imagist principles of the rhythms of common speech, the "exact" image, and free verse.

Aldington's best war poetry offers objective treatment of the front's realities. "Picket" describes a moment of half-light, when there are

Three soldiers huddled on a bench
Over a red-hot brazier,
And a fourth who stands apart
Watching the cold rainy dawn.

Amid the "familiar sounds of birds," "Wearily the sentry moves / Muttering the one word: 'Peace.'" In "Machine Guns" Aldington captures the visual effects of rapid fire:

Gold flashes in the dark,
And on the road
Each side, behind, in front of us,
Gold sparks
Where the fierce bullets strike the stones.

In "Bombardment," Aldington presents an economical picture of trench warfare, moving from a general view to the more confined view from the trench. His poem ends with a pointed contrast between the nerve-racking cringing beneath an artillery barrage and the sudden hush:

Four days the earth was rent and torn
By bursting steel,
The houses fell about us;
Three nights we dared not sleep,
Sweating, and listening for the imminent crash
Which meant our death.

The fourth night every man,
Nerve-tortured, racked to exhaustion,
Slept, muttering and twitching,
While the shells crashed overhead.

The fifth day there came a hush;
We left our holes
And looked above the wreckage of the earth
To where the white clouds moved in silent lines
Across the untroubled blue.

Aldington's war poetry offers a much wider range of immediate sensation and a more realistic perception of the war than do the verses of most of the trench poets.

Herbert Read (1893–1968) applied principles of Imagism long after the Armistice. Aldington tried to keep Imagism alive by publishing an Imagist anthology in 1930, but his poetry had departed from the war and from Imagism after *Exile and Other Poems* in 1923. Read, however, who wrote his first poems in 1915, found Imagism effective. In 1939, he recalled, "The War came, but that did not make any essential difference to our poetry. I myself wrote imagist poems in the trenches, and did not see or feel any inconsistency in the act. War was one thing, and poetry was another; and if war was to be expressed in poetry, the imagist technique was as adequate as any other."[10] In *The Contrary Experience* (1963), he indicated the problem that war imposed on poetry: "But as the war went on, year after year, and there seemed no escape from its indignity except death, some compromise between dream and reality became necessary. The only worthy compromise, I even then dimly realized, was a synthesis—some higher reality in which the freedom of the mind and the necessity of experience became reconciled."[11] Such emphasis was necessary not only for the poetry, but also for the poet: "We were trying to maintain an abstract aesthetic ideal in the midst of terrorful and inhuman events. In my own case I am certain that this devotion to abstract notions and intellectual reveries saved me from a raw reaction to these events."[12] What saved the man hurt the poetry, however, for often Read's verse embraces the "higher reality" at the expense of the intensity of feeling it attempts to convey.

Of his early life, Read remarked, "In spite of my intellectual pretensions, I am by birth and tradition a peasant." The son of a Yorkshire farmer, Read graduated from the University of Leeds and fought as an infantry officer for three years of the war, enlisting in 1915. He rose to the rank of captain in 1917, receiving the MC in 1917 and the DSO in 1918. After demobilization, he entered the Civil Service, first with the Treasury and then with the Victoria and Albert Museum, before embarking on an exclusively literary career. Of Read's *Naked Warriors* (1919), T. S. Eliot remarked, "It is the best war poetry that I can remember having seen. It is better than the rest because it is more honest. . . ."[13]

Read's early war poetry does not have the immediacy of Aldington's, for Read wrote most of his poetry after the Armistice, in retrospect. His poetic purpose derived from the Imagist philosophy: "It is one of my aims to restore poetry to its true role of a *spoken* art. The music of words—the linking of sounds—the cadence of phrase—unity of action. Each poem should be *exact*, expressing in the *only* appropriate words the emotion experienced."[14] This purpose, which he recorded while still in the trenches, remains evident in his later poetry.

Three comparatively early poems offer "curative realism." "The Happy Warrior," which, in Fussell's words, "brutally inverts Wordsworth's celebration of the honorable, well-conducted soldier,"[15] has drawn faint praise from Johnston, who felt that "the realistic and satiric impulse is not much different from Sassoon's; it has merely been compressed to conform to the Imagist principle of verbal economy."[16] The poem demonstrates the compatibility of modern experience and Imagist techniques, including *vers libre*, rhythms of common speech, and painfully precise imagery:

> His wild heart beats with painful sobs
> his strain'd hands clench an ice-cold rifle
> his aching jaws grip a hot parch'd tongue
> his wide eyes search unconsciously.
>
> He cannot shriek.
>
> Bloody saliva
> dribbles down his shapeless jacket.

I saw him stab
and stab again
a well-killed Boche.

This is the happy warrior,
this is he. . . .

Although some of the diction ("parch'd tongue," "painful sobs") seems characteristic of Victorian verse, the tormented "happy warrior" deflates traditional notions of innate heroism.

The movement of "Truth for a Change" is from the traditional concept of the willing hero ("Such a lad as Harry was / Isn't met with every day. / He walked the land like a god . . .") to the sudden impact of his quick death:

I saw him stretch his arms
Languid as a dozing panther,
His face full to the clean sky—
When a blasted sniper laid him low:
He fell limp on the muddy boards
And left us all blaspheming.

"Fear" is more overtly rhetorical than most Imagist efforts. In the first stanza, Read provides a definition:

Fear is a wave
beating through the air
and on taut nerves impinging
till there it wins
vibrating chords.

Read compares a man's nerves with the strings of an instrument to reveal the sudden change fear brings:

All goes well
so long as you tune the instrument
to simulate composure.

(So you will become
a gallant gentleman.)

But when the strings are broken
then you will grovel on the earth
and your rabbit eyes
will fill with the fragments of your shatter'd soul.

The shift from composure to panic is pointedly abrupt and is much more comprehensible in this poem than the panic which led to execution in Frankau's "The Deserter."

Read demonstrates exemplary economy in "Winter at Ypres," although the image "rat-locks of Maenades" is a far cry from the Imagist's "unadorned image":

> Thy ruins etched
>   in silver silhouettes
>   against a turquoise sky.
>
> Lank poles leap to the infinite,
>   their broken wires
>   tossed like the rat-locks of Maenades.

"The Refugees" presents a situation in a few bold strokes:

> We shall hold the enemy towards nightfall,
> and they will move
> mutely into the dark behind us,
> only the creaking cart
> disturbing their sorrowful serenity.

In the narrative of "Liedholz," inspired by a German prisoner Read captured during a raid in August 1917, Read reduces a complex situation to stark facts: "Liedholz shot at me / And I at him." The similarities of captive and captor also require few words: "In broken French we discussed / Beethoven, Nietzsche, and the International." Read's "The Execution of Cornelius Vane" is a masterpiece of brevity. Two days after Vane had fled from battle, "He entered a village and was arrested. / He was hungry, and the peace of the fields / Dissipated the terror that had been the strength of his will." Instead of holding Vane up as a warning, as Frankau did in "The Deserter," Read makes him sympathetic.

"My Company," written in 1931, according to critic Andrew Rutherford, "is the only one [of Read's poems] which seems to do full justice to the complexity of his responses."[17] Read catches the soldier's sense of comradeship with his fellows, starting with a definition of his men: "You became / in many acts and quiet observances / a body and a soul, entire." Then he refers to songs of homesickness, communal drinking, and combat that lead to an awareness of "unity." The poem's speaker realizes that, in future days, "I know that I'll wander with a cry: / 'O beautiful men, O men I loved / O whither are you gone, my company?'" After the speaker establishes his emotional bond with his men, his observations draw their significance from that bond: "My men, my modern Christs, / your bloody agony confronts the world." In the third section, the speaker describes a man beyond recovery:

> A man of mine
>   lies on the wire;

And he will rot
and first his lips
the worms shall eat.
It is not thus I would have him kiss'd,
but with the warm passionate lips
of his comrade here.

In the last section, the speaker accepts his fate: "Then again I assume / my human docility, / bow my head / and share their doom." Read's use of romantic love imagery here resembles that of Rosenberg and Owen, who also juxtaposed sensual images with war's horrors. Had Read written only this poem about the war, his place among the trench poets would remain assured.

Read applied some principles of Imagism to poetry of war as late as World War II, but T. E. Hulme did not survive the war, and other British Imagists shifted from poetry to fiction. Ford Madox Ford rendered his wartime experiences in *Parade's End* (1924–28), while Richard Aldington wrote of his in *Death of a Hero* (1929). D. H. Lawrence found his novel *Kangaroo* (1923) the appropriate vehicle for his response to the war years. The Imagists also became exiles and expatriates for the most part, Ford settling in Paris, Aldington following suit somewhat later, Pound moving through Paris to Italy, and Lawrence eventually settling in New Mexico. As they moved to other countries and other forms, they also encouraged a new literary generation that has displaced Imagism. Ford devoted both time and money to supporting younger writers. Ezra Pound's sponsorship of Aldington and Eliot was typical of his willingness to promote new talent, and Aldington championed, among others, T. S. Eliot and Herbert Read. After establishing techniques now accepted as principles of good writing, the Imagists waned as their influence on modernists changed the direction of England's poetic tradition and as they individually moved on to other interests. Their prewar approach to poetry, however, enabled them to respond much more realistically and directly to the changes imposed by the war.

6

Searchers for Perspective

WHEN JOHNSTON WROTE HIS COMPREHENSIVE STUDY OF THE POETRY OF World War I, he criticized the "limited" perspective of lyrical and narrative war poetry in order to advance his preference for more "objective" and "detached" views of the war. In many ways his bias is unreasonable, for it ignores the need poets felt to describe the reality of the trenches so that civilians would have to confront it. This demanded a more subjective approach. Johnston's bias also places greater emphasis on what a poet says than on how the poet says it. Although the commonplace nature of most war poetry makes that shift of emphasis appealing, the poet's view alone will not elevate the poetry. Sometimes what may appear to be evidence of a poet's objectivity only reveals the poet's indifference, or, at the least, lack of feeling. If verses jotted hastily in the trenches rarely went beyond the poet's personal involvement in the struggle, trench poets nevertheless captured an immediacy that more carefully wrought retrospective verses lacked. Several poets tried to embrace a larger perspective of the war, and perhaps for that very reason their poetry is hardly so memorable as the verse of Sassoon, Owen, Rosenberg, and others who tried to communicate their sense of what trench warfare actually involved.

Although he died before the Battle of the Somme, Charles Hamilton Sorley (1895–1915) came closer than any of the other trench poets to Johnston's standard of objectivity. Sorley was a surprisingly perceptive critic at an early age. In a paper which he read on 3 November 1912, praising John Drinkwater, Sorley criticized the artificiality of post-Victorian poetry: "The voice of our poets and men of letters is finely trained and sweet to hear; it teems with sharp saws and rich sentiment: it is a marvel of delicate technique: it pleases, it flatters, it charms, it soothes: it is a living lie."[1] Sorley's poetry proves embarrassing for those who wish to define the 1916 Battle of the Somme as a turning point in war poets' awareness, for he took a startlingly modern view of the conflict long before the Somme. Robert Graves identified (in 1929) Sorley, Rosenberg, and Owen as "the three poets of importance killed during the war."[2]

Sorley spent his early years at Cambridge, where his father became a professor in 1900. In 1908 Sorley won a scholarship to Marlborough College, where his enthusiasm for football, debate, and Officers' Training Corps rivaled Brooke's. When Sorley won a scholarship to University College, Oxford, in 1913, his family felt he should acquire some education abroad as a preliminary. Accordingly Sorley spent some months at Schwerin and then at the University of Jena. While on a walking tour of Germany he was arrested on 2 August 1914, but he was released and returned to England before Germany and England were officially at war. Sorley found much to admire in Germany despite his disapproval of the students' corps of German universities. As early as July 1914 he complained of the unduly harsh "fagging" system, compulsory drunkenness, offensive behavior to outsiders, and flagrant anti-Semitism that he found at Jena. However, his objectivity compelled him to add that, since most of his friends at Jena were Jews, he heard "the worst side."[3] Sorley applied for a commission on 7 August 1914 and became a subaltern in the Suffolk Regiment. When his training ended he received orders for France, where he became a captain in August 1915. He died in the action at Loos on 13 October 1915.

Although his quick response to the call was typical of his generation, his attitude toward the war was not. The common cry did not alter his grasp of reality: ". . . why the term 'slackers' should be applied to those who have not enlisted, God knows. Plenty of slackers here, thank you. I never was so idle in my life."[4] Sorley's independence of mind appears most striking in his view of the relationship between a just cause and victory:

> For the joke of seeing an obviously just cause defeated, I hope Germany will win. It would do the world good and show that real faith is not that which says "we *must* win for our cause is just," but that which says "our cause is just: therefore we can disregard defeat." All outlooks are at present material, and the unseen value of justice as justice, independent entirely of results, is forgotten. It is looked upon merely as an agent for winning battles.[5]

Sorley called Hardy's line "Victory crowns the just" the "worst line he ever wrote,"[6] and earlier he rejected Brooke's idealization of death in battle. Sorley's perception of the nature of the war prevented his accepting either Hardy's or Brooke's facile views. He reached Sassoon's ultimate position after only two months at the front: "I hate the growing tendency to think that every man drops overboard his individuality between Folkestone and Boulogne, and becomes on landing either 'Tommy' with a character like a nice big fighting pet bear and an incurable yearning and whining for mouthorgans and cheap cigarettes: or the Young Officer with a face like a hero and a silly habit of giggling in the face of death."[7]

Although Sorley's war poetry consists of only nine poems, these reveal an impressive complexity of attitude and range of experience. By September 1914, Sorley had written three remarkable poems. "All the Hills and Vales

Along" is far removed from the spirit of Hardy's "Men Who March Away"
or the celebration of Grenfell's "Into Battle." Sorley forms a deliberately
ironical contrast between the men's spirit and impending death. Like Grenfell's poem, Sorley's depends on reminders of the natural order, but whereas
Grenfell's Nature affirmed the fighting man, Sorley's remains indifferent to
human activity and offers nothing to sustain the soldier. The speaker addressing the men remains marvelously detached:

> All the hills and vales along
> Earth is bursting into song,
> And the singers are the chaps
> Who are going to die perhaps.

The speaker reminds the soldiers that the indifferent earth which

> bore with joyful ease
> Hemlock for Socrates,
>
> . . . .
>
> Shall rejoice and blossom too
> When the bullet reaches you.

The poem wishes the men on "To the gates of death with song" in a cheerful
meter more appropriate to a comic song than to a treatment of men about to
die in battle, adding significantly to the poem's irony.

Sorley's sonnet "To Germany," written during the first weeks of the war,
combines his acute sense of war's tragedy with his historical perspective:

> You are blind like us. Your hurt no man designed,
> And no man claimed the conquest of your land.
> But gropers both through fields of thought confined
> We stumble and we do not understand.
> You only saw your future bigly planned,
> And we, the tapering paths of our own mind,
> And in each other's dearest ways we stand,
> And hiss and hate. And the blind fight the blind.
>
> When it is peace, then we may view again
> With new-won eyes each other's truer form
> And wonder. Grown more loving-kind and warm
> We'll grasp firm hands and laugh at the old pain,
> When it is peace. But until peace, the storm
> The darkness and the thunder and the rain.

The poem reflects Sorley's feeling, as he expressed it in October 1914, that
"If this war proves (as I think it will) that you can kill a person and yet
remain his greatest friend—or, less preferably, be killed and yet stay

friends—it'll have done a splendid thing."[8] Owen was to develop this concept in "Strange Meeting."

"A Hundred Thousand Million Mites We Go" presents the conflict in a much vaster scope than do poems confined to a few feet of trench:

> A hundred thousand million mites we go
> Wheeling and tacking o'er the eternal plain,
> Some black with death—and some are white with woe.
> Who sent us forth? Who takes us home again?

Ironically, Sorley's perspective owes much to his inexperience of combat. The perception of battles in historical terms occurs more readily to those not directly involved. Sorley's view of the battle as between armies rather than between individuals suggests a report from the staff tent rather than from the line:

> And there is murmuring of the multitude
> And blindness and great blindness, until some
> Step forth and challenge blind Vicissitude
> Who tramples on them: so that fewer come.

After Sorley acquired experience of combat, he turned to matters closer to the individual. Instead of merely describing trench life, however, Sorley examined questions of significance. In his final poem, the sonnet "When You See Millions of the Mouthless Dead," responding to the publication of Brooke's *1914 and Other Poems,* Sorley presents the "obverse" of the sentimental attitude he had disparaged in Brooke's sonnets. He begins with a warning to those tempted to follow Brooke's lead and then defends his view of what poets should say in response to the war dead:

> When you see millions of the mouthless dead
> Across your dreams in pale battalions go,
> Say not soft things as other men have said,
> That you'll remember. For you need not so.
> Give them not praise. For, deaf, how should they know
> It is not curses heaped on each gashed head?
> Nor tears. Their blind eyes see not your tears flow.
> Nor honour. It is easy to be dead.
> Say only this, "They are dead." Then add thereto,
> "Yet many a better one has died before."
> Then, scanning all the o'ercrowded mass, should you
> Perceive one face that you loved heretofore,
> It is a spook. None wears the face you knew.
> Great death has made all his for evermore.

The poem arouses pity for the slain without sensory description of carnage or battle. The sonnet's impact rests on its understatement.

No other poet entirely matched the objectivity, maturity, and profundity of Sorley's verse during the war, but a few approached aspects of Sorley's achievement. Arthur Graeme West (1891–1917), like Sorley, received a scholarship to Oxford, where he was studying when the war began. Like Sorley he applied for a commission, but his poor eyesight made him ineligible, so he enlisted as a private in the Public Schools Battalion. He fought in France from November 1915 to March 1916 and then, when the need to replace fallen officers became acute, he spent some months in Scotland at Officers' Training Camp. In September 1916 he returned to France as an officer, where he remained until sniper fire killed him in April 1917.

West's experiences during the Battle of the Somme inspired a crisis and rebellion similar to Sassoon's. Earlier, at Officers' Training Camp, growing disillusionment with the war inspired West to write a letter to his adjutant, informing him that he would "not rejoin the Army nor accept any form of alternative service" and that he "would rather be shot than do so."[9] However, he did not mail the letter. According to critic Dennis Welland, West "returned to France, not in the spirit of altruistic responsibility to his comrades that took Owen and Sassoon back, but because of an understandable reluctance to give pain and distress to his family."[10] This prevented West from anticipating Sassoon's protest by almost exactly a year, while the intensity of his personal conflict with his role as a soldier prevented his developing Sorley's independent cast of mind.

Two of West's poems compare favorably with most verse of the war. "The Night Patrol," written in March 1916, appeared in the posthumous *The Diary of a Dead Officer* (1918). The poem depicts the trenches with stark realism and reveals an antiheroic bias. It offers this description of the trenches:

> Only the dead were always present—present
> As a vile sickly smell of rottenness;
> The rustling stubble and the early grass,
> The slimy pools—the dead men stank through all,
> Pungent and sharp; as bodies loomed before,
> And as we passed, they stank; then dulled away
> To that vague factor, all encompassing,
> Infecting earth and air.

Much more consistent with Sorley's position is West's recognition of the common plight of Englishmen and Germans: "I have contracted hatred and enmity for nobody over here, save soldiers generally and a few N.C.O.'s in particular. For the Hun I feel nothing but a spirit of amiable fraternity that the poor man has to sit just like us and do all the horrible and useless things that we do, when he might be at home with his wife or his books, as he preferred."[11]

Like Sorley, West wrote a poem directed at Brooke and his imitators. Instead of using restrained language, West lashes them. "God! How I Hate You" cites failures of post-Victorian romanticism in terms which Sorley might have approved. The poem frequently echoes phrases from *Quest of Truth: Poems on Doubt, War, Sorrow, Despair, Hope, Death, Somewhere in France,* by H. Rex Feston, an Exeter undergraduate whose book appeared posthumously.

> God! How I hate you, you young cheerful men,
> Whose pious poetry blossoms on your graves
> As soon as you are in them . . .
> > Hark how one chants—
> "Oh happy to have lived these epic days"—
> "These epic days"! And *he'd* been to France,
> And seen the trenches, glimpsed the huddled dead
> In the periscope, hung in the rusty wire: . . .

He sneers at the notion of camaraderie in a common cause:

> On earth, the love and fellowship of men,
> Men sternly banded: banded for what end?
> Banded to maim and kill their fellow men—
> For even Huns are men.

At the end of the poem, he takes umbrage with Brooke's "Now, God be thanked Who has matched us with His hour" and with McCrae's "In Flanders Fields":

> Ah, how good God is
> To suffer us to be born just now, when youth
> That else would rust, can slake his blade in gore,
> Whose very God Himself does seem to walk
> The bloody fields of Flanders He so loves!

West shares Sorley's distaste for the "sentimental attitude," but he betrays the subjective intensity of his feelings. Where Sorley responds in reasoned tones, West tries to crush the detested opposition. However, West does share Sorley's rejection of sentimental responses and his recognition of the German soldier's suffering.

Max Plowman (1883–1941) revealed his appreciation of a "cosmic perception" of the war approaching Sorley's. Plowman served as an officer in the 10th West Yorks Regiment and fought at the Somme. His experiences of war moved him to become an outspoken pacifist between the wars, and he served as Secretary of the Peace Pledge Union from 1937 until 1938, when he became editor of the *Adelphi*. Plowman published *A Lapful of Seed* (poems) in 1917 and later published a memoir, *A Subaltern on the Somme in 1916* (1927) under the pseudonym "Mark VII." Plowman's best poem, "Going Into the Line," combines individual soldiers' uncertainty with the perception of their comparative insignificance. When an order arrives for a platoon to move from Pommiers Redoubt, the men's reaction reveals their sense of misgiving:

> So soon!
> At 3.15. And would return here . . . when?
> It didn't say. Who would return? P'raps all,
> P'raps none.

After devoting thirty lines to an officer's reflections, Plowman shifts to Sorley's larger perspective: "Poor craven little crowd of human mites! / Now they were crawling over the scarred cheese, / . . . . / Each thinking his own thought. . . ."

Plowman balances momentary reflections with the larger view until the fifth stanza returns to the officer:

> Peace now, and dear delight in serving these,
> These poor sheep, driven innocent to death:
> . . . .
> Peace, peace with all, even the enemy,
> Compassion for them deep as for his own:
> Quietness now amid the thunderous noise,
> And sweet elation in the grave of doom.

In addition to the larger perspective that eluded most trench poets, Plowman, writing this poem in August 1916 during the Somme Offensive, was able to describe the immediate terrors of battle, introduce a note of protest against useless slaughter, include the enemy among those for whom he desired peace, and balance a sense of objectivity with realistic description. However, Plowman's perspective is not enough to compensate for the triteness of his diction. As the war continued, Plowman's poetry moved closer to pacifism—"The Dead Soldiers" (1917) includes the judgment that "killing men is always killing God"—but he managed to avoid the strident urgency of those who recoiled from the destruction of war.

Two other poets approached Sorley's broad conception of war to a lesser extent. Maurice Hewlett (1861–1923), who wrote historical novels and spent some time as a civil servant, was in his fifties when the war began and was one of the established writers invited by C. F. G. Masterman to Wellington House to assist the British propaganda machine. Although Hewlett saw little of the war, his "In the Trenches" was better than most civilian poems trying to convey a sense of trench warfare. Hewlett focuses on a soldier's mind as it wanders from the scene of war. References to the actual fighting are few and brief. Except for mentioning "shells fly screaming / And men and horses die," Hewlett wisely refrains from "realism." His soldier recalls the pastoral setting of his native Wiltshire in four short stanzas and then interrupts his reflection to consider that

> 'T was more than I could compass,
> For how was I to think
> With such infernal rumpus
> In such a blasted stink?

Then another thought sets Hewlett's poem apart from the common run, for the soldier's imagination turns to his counterpart in the German lines "Whose gills are turning yellow / As sure as mine are. . . ." Hewlett's soldier realizes that his enemy, watching the same moonlit landscape and no doubt thinking of his own home, "longs as dearly, / With heart as full as mine." This identification of a common yearning, rare enough among soldiers, was virtually unheard of among civilian poets.

W. J. Turner (1884–1946), an Australian-born novelist, essayist, and poet, transcended partisan views in another fashion. Like Sorley, Turner had an intellectual's grasp of the conflict, but unlike Sorley he had little poetic talent. While his responses were less complex than Sorley's, he avoided any undue allegiance to a national or political cause. Turner emigrated to London in 1907 and worked as a clerk in an import/export firm until 1913, when he became a fulltime writer. Although he met Rupert Brooke and the Georgians before the war and contributed to the Georgian anthologies of 1916–17 and 1918–19, he eluded identification with the movement. Turner was a lieutenant in the Royal Garrison Artillery (antiaircraft section) from 1916 to 1918. This did not prevent his dedicating his first collection of poetry, *The Hunter and Other Poems* (1916), to Francis Meynell, then in prison as a conscientious objector. Turner had little affinity for the partisan view: "I have no political convictions, except that I think it is impossible to have a really civilised society unless every member of it is assured, without work, of his livelihood."

Turner, as a garrison officer, had no more experience of the front than did most civilians, but he saw through the conventional views of martial heroics. His "The Hero" offers a definition which repudiates the general view:

> To be brave is not enough,
> It is not enough to be rough;
> To be smooth is not enough,
> Cunning is not enough;
> It is not enough to know the truth.

After similarly rejecting vengeance, pity, ruthlessness, and righteousness, Turner describes the elusiveness of the hero's quest for his answer:

It is not disclosed to him who does what he is bidden;
Even constant persistence
Along the line of most resistance
Is not enough, is not enough.

Turner also provides a metaphysical conceit:

He knows that to be a hero
Is like the mathematical zero.
In itself it is nothing but it multiplies by ten
The virtues of *other* men.

He anticipates Yossarian of Joseph Heller's *Catch-22* by half a century: "He must be so sane that he may appear mad." In Turner's view, the hero is "only the man that everybody would be / If he followed the secret passion in his heart," a man of compassion. This is far from earlier paeans to martial heroics, but it is also far from being effective verse, for, except for its rhymes and a few attempts at simile, it reads as an abstract essay of definition and as an argument couched in phrases too vague to be either convincing or moving.

The search for perspective was less rewarding for Wilfrid Gibson (1878–1962), a Georgian poet who was an innovator in his realistic treatment of the problems of the lower classes. Gibson, called "the poet of the industrial poor," recorded the point of view of the other ranks, addressing the war's impact on the class which provided most of the soldiers. Gibson, whose sole profession was writing, took a clear-headed view of the conflict. When Rupert Brooke decided to enlist in 1914, Gibson tried to talk him out of it. Later, however, Gibson applied for a commission and was rejected no fewer than four times before enlisting as a private in the Army Service Corps. He was briefly at the front before he embarked in December 1916 on a lecture tour of the United States. Although his collection of poetry, *Battle* (1915), had earned considerable praise, his popular appeal on the lecture circuit resulted from his being advertised (accurately) as a close friend of Brooke and (inaccurately) as Brooke's "disciple." Gibson's efforts do not measure up to Sorley's, but he provides a refreshing contrast to prevailing patriotic encomia. As John Wilson notes, "Instead of schoolboy heroics and epic violence we have the musings and dreams of the private soldier, typically a lad of Gloucestershire or Northumberland, who had been torn out of his familiar surroundings and flung into an absurd context which he cannot understand."[12] In the process of searching for a meaningful context, however, Gibson occasionally fell into excesses of sentimentality.

Gibson's efforts included flawed attempts at realism which fail to convey an accurate picture of trench warfare. His poem "The Bayonet" attempts, in the words of critic Arthur Waugh, "to whittle poetry down to its barest core, in the effort to present a keen and undecorated outline of fact."[13] However, as the first stanza of "The Bayonet" reveals, simplicity of diction does not automatically render a "fact" convincing:

> This bloody steel
>   Has killed a man.
> I heard him squeal
>   As on I ran.

"Between the Lines" is more convincing. A soldier caught in No Man's Land reflects on his situation in 152 lines. He recalls another soldier who managed to bring butter back to the trench,

> Butter enough for all, and held it high,
> Yellow and fresh and clean as you would wish—
> When plump upon the plate from out the sky
> A shell fell bursting . . . Where the butter went,
> God only knew! . . .

The soldier's recollections include several descriptions of such trench phenomena as constant shellfire and abrupt death, close calls, and a hope that pilots would return to their lines in safety "Even if they were Germans."

The narrative ends with the soldier's resolve to return to his trench:

> He, too, must try
> To win back to the lines, though, likely as not,
> He'd take the wrong turn: but he could n't lie
> Forever in that hungry hole and rot,
> He'd got to take his luck, to take his chance
> Of being sniped by foes or friends. He'd be
> With any luck in Germany or France
> Or Kingdom-come, next morning . . .

Had Gibson restricted his narrative to the soldier's reactions and observations instead of providing excessive explanation for each of the soldier's turns of thought, the poem might have rivaled West's "The Night Patrol" for balance and objectivity.

Gibson devoted several short poems to narratives of soldiers' deaths, most of them heavy-handedly ironical. "The Joke" (which strongly resembles Kipling's "A Son") describes in eight lines a soldier who, raising his head to whisper a joke, falls under sniper fire. "Breakfast" follows the same pattern. A soldier raises his head to make a bet on a football game, "And cursed, and took the bet; and dropt back dead." In "The Father," another soldier dies as he tells for

The fiftieth time
Without a change
How three-year-old
Prattled a rhyme,
They got the range
And cut him short.

In other brief narratives, Gibson focuses on the unbidden recollections of home that tormented men in the trenches. "Dick Milburn" determines to pick some almonds when they ripen, "But, now the almond-shells are brown and ripe, / Somewhere in No-man's-land he's lying dead, / And other lads are pinching them instead." In "Mark Anderson," a soldier dies near a "glass / Of water that he could not drink." Some contrasts appear disappointingly contrived. "Tombstones," for example, presents the irony of a tombstone polisher who now lies in an unmarked grave. In "The Ring," a man at his induction physical, naked except for his wedding band, ultimately dies, and the ring is "tumbled somewhere in the Flanders mud." These formulaic poems approach dripping pathos.

Gibson was more successful when he tried to present the war in terms of its psychological impact on soldiers, but his reliance on formula weakens the effect of his attempts. He frequently depicted shell-shocked soldiers clinging to remnants of their civilian pasts. "In the Ambulance" records the ravings of a soldier who has lost his legs and who repeats a description of his garden: "Two rows of cabbages, / Two of curly-greens, / Two rows of early peas, / Two of kidney-beans." "The Messages" alternates the words of a shell-shocked soldier with the information that he has been deafened, dazed, and maimed in battle. The soldier cannot remember the messages or names of five dying soldiers who have entrusted him to convey their last words. "Retreat" tells of a retreating soldier, "Half-stunned, half-blinded, by the trudge of feet" who repeats (four times in a twelve-line poem) "All-heal and willow-herb and meadow-sweet." "Mad" tells of a soldier who, "Neck-deep in mud," returned to his schooldays and yelled *April Fool!* before laughing "like mad." These attempts to depict mental imbalance are variations of one simple plot. Any one of these poems loses its effectiveness when the reader encounters a second.

However, Gibson wrote five poems which achieve some measure of control and transcend the limited personal view of many war poets. "Philip Dagg," in six lines, describes a soldier who felt the raking of machine-gun fire, realized that he was dying, "And stumbled blindly, muttering *Cheerio! / Into eternity, and left no trace.*" Gibson's tribute to Rupert Brooke, published as the prefatory poem to *Friends* (1915–16), employs simple language and short, unallusive lines to convey Gibson's sense of loss:

He's gone.
I do not understand.

I only know
That as he turned to go
And waved his hand
In his young eyes a sudden glory shone,
And I was dazzled by a sunset glow,
And he was gone.

"The Conscript" emphasizes the fate of cannon fodder. The examining physicians, "Indifferent, flippant, earnest, but all bored" watch "an endless stream of naked white / Bodies of men" as they decree "mangled limbs, blind eyes, or a darkened brain" for those deemed "fit." The chairman announces each verdict "with easy indifferent breath." Gibson contrasts the victims of war to indifferent civilians without losing control of the poem.

In two dramatic monologues, "The Question" and "His Father," Gibson appears relatively objective as soldiers muse ironically on domestic situations that the war has interrupted. "The Question" for one soldier is whether "the old cow died or not." He cannot prevent the question's recurrence "Over and over like a silly song," and he realizes that "if I'm hit, I'll never know / Till Doomsday if the old cow died or not." Another soldier in "His Father" recalls that he left for the front without shutting off the spigot of a cask of beer, and his reflections on his father's reaction are comic: "he'll not care if we lose or win / And yet be jumping-mad about that beer." The soldier is amusedly aware of his father's ire: "I'd give my stripes to hear / What he will say if I'm reported dead / Before he gets me told about that beer!" The contrast between the soldier's past and present occurs without the descent into pathos that has marred a few of Gibson's narratives. No less a poet than Isaac Rosenberg read Gibson's work in the trenches and pronounced himself delighted by the "naturalness" of some of the poems.

W. B. Yeats (1865–1939) is difficult to place in the context of war poetry, for he recognized the subjective nature of trench poetry and dismissed the war as irrelevant to the Irish struggle for independence. When he edited the *Oxford Book of Modern Verse* in 1936, he excluded virtually all war poets except Herbert Read. When Yeats found that his exclusion of Wilfred Owen's work had drawn considerable hostility, he complained in a letter to Dorothy Wellesley that Owen was "all blood, dirt & sucked sugar stick. . . . There is every excuse for him but none for those who like him."[14] When Edith Wharton asked Yeats for a war poem in 1915 he drafted his "A Reason for Keeping Silent," which began "I think it better that at times like these / We poets keep our mouths shut; for in truth / We have no gift to set a statesman right. . . ." For later publication as "On Being Asked for a War Poem," Yeats refined the diction of this draft.

Yeats maintained this stance until, in 1918, Major Robert Gregory, son of Yeats's friend and patron Lady Gregory, died in Italy. Yeats wrote three poems concerning Gregory: "An Irish Airman Foresees His Death," "In

Memory of Major Robert Gregory" (which lists Gregory's decorations for bravery), and "Elegy" (unearthed by critic T. R. Henn).[15] "An Irish Airman Foresees His Death" focuses not on the conflict, but on Gregory's reasons for volunteering. The monologue states that Gregory foresaw his death, that he had no hatred for Germany or love for England, that he had no illusions that the war would benefit Ireland, that he remained unmoved by war frenzy, and that he felt compelled by no sense of duty or by any fear of authority:

> I balanced all, brought all to mind,
> The years to come seemed waste of breath,
> A waste of breath the years behind
> In balance with this life, this death.

"In Memory of Major Robert Gregory" expresses Yeats's sense of loss. Of twelve stanzas, Yeats devotes the first five to describing "friends that cannot sup with us," including Lionel Johnson, John Synge, and George Pollexfen, before introducing Gregory as "my dear friend's dear son" in the sixth. In the next five stanzas Yeats follows the pattern of a traditional encomium, recalling Gregory's love of life and his accomplishments as "Soldier, scholar, horseman," as well as Yeats's dashed hopes for Gregory's future as an artist. In the last stanza Yeats comments that he had intended to introduce a longer series of friendships that had influenced him, "but a thought / Of [Gregory's] late death took all my heart for speech."

In "Elegy," Yeats reflects on something far more important to him than the war—the Irish situation. Yeats establishes his priorities in the opening lines:

> Some nineteen German planes, they say,
> You had brought down before you died.
> We called it a good death. Today
> Can ghost or man be satisfied?

Yeats then refers to "the cause you served, that we / Imagined such a fine affair." The cause is that of Irish independence, and the results have been disappointing. British soldiers murder Irish tenants, shoot Irish patriots, and leave no place of safety for the weak. Yeats concludes that all has been for nothing: "Then close your ear with dust and lie / Among the other cheated dead." Yeats's ability to see the Great War in its larger context owes much to his indifference to English war aims, compared with his concern for the Irish plight. His "cheated dead" indicates some affinity with the views of Sorley, West, and Gibson, however, while his refusal to glorify Gregory for heroic acts accords with Turner's rejection of prewar conceptions of heroism. Like the other searchers for perspective, Yeats refused to limit his elegies to conventional views.

7

Comedy and Reality

IN HIS EARLY ESSAY ON THE WORK OF ROBERT GRAVES (1895–1985), T. STURGE Moore commented, "The more comprehensive the mind the more kinds of relief it seeks in laughter."[1] Edmund Gosse observed, "There could hardly be a more vivid contrast than exists between the melancholy passion of Lieut. [Robert] Nichols and the fantastic high spirits of Captain Robert Graves."[2] Much of that contrast stems from Graves's complex responses to the war. Since Graves has written more than one hundred books, including the well-known historical novel *I, Claudius* (1934) and the acclaimed critical study *The White Goddess* (1948), his war poetry is a small fraction of his literary achievement. However, the early poems are sufficiently striking to have earned him a place in literary history even had he not survived the war.

Graves's early years resembled, in one respect, those of Ford Madox Ford, for he was overshadowed by eminent relatives. On his mother's side, Graves was the descendant of a German family that included the historian Von Ranke. His father, Alfred Percival Graves, was a poet, editor, song writer, and expert on Irish folk songs. Graves went to school at Charterhouse, where he was active as a boxer and soccer player. Like many veterans, he completed his education after the war, at St. John's College, Oxford, where he encountered several reminders of the gulf separating soldier from civilian. In his autobiography, *Goodbye to All That* (1929), he recalled meeting one Thomas Earp, whose wartime contribution to Oxford's tradition had been to be sole member and recording secretary of no fewer than nineteen social and literary societies, which could thus continue "unbroken" after the war.

Graves, at nineteen, joined the Royal Welch Fusiliers when the war began. (As an honor, the unit retained the archaic spelling of *Welch*). He met Sassoon in France, where he saw more action at the front than did most of his contemporaries and at one point was so severely wounded that he was listed among the dead. The severity of his wound precluded further line duty. Graves convalesced, wrote poetry, and met Owen at Craiglockhart. Like Owen and Sassoon, Graves was the victim of shell shock, then called neurasthenia. He shared Sassoon's belief that the war was unnecessarily prolonged, and his response may have predated Sassoon's. Graves claimed that when he showed Sassoon some early war poems, Sassoon

frowned and said that war should not be written about in such a realistic
way. In return, he showed me some of his own poems. One of them
began:
    Return to greet me, colours that were my joy,
    Not in the woeful crimson of men slain. . .
Siegfried had not yet been in the trenches. I told him, in my old-soldier
manner, that he would soon change his style.[3]

By 1916, Graves's war experiences included front line duty in two of the
war's bloodiest battles (the actions at Loos and the Somme), severe injury,
convalescence, and a nervous reaction which lasted long after the Armistice.
In his poetry, Graves expressed his sense of the soldier's endurance, the
failure of British institutions, outrage at the brutality of war, and the soldier's
agony. Although he was unable to resolve all the contradictions of his
responses, his war poetry expressed his struggle with his belief that "To fight
and kill is wrong— / To stay at home wronger."

Graves began writing poetry early. Like Nichols and Sassoon, he published poems in *Georgian Poetry, 1916–1917*. Harold Monro's Poetry Bookshop published Graves's *Over the Brazier* (1916), which included both
prewar and early war verse. "In many respects," as Bergonzi points out,
"Graves, in his early work, was a quintessential Georgian, with a taste for
ballad-like forms, unpretentious, small-scale subjects with a rural flavour,
and a particular inclination to folk-lore and fairy-tale."[4] Graves's second
volume of verse, *Fairies and Fusiliers* (1917), written during his convalescence, contains much of his better war poetry. Graves's rebellious spirit
was evident in his earliest efforts. As critic Daniel Hoffman remarked of
Graves's preference for the poetry of John Skelton, "To resurrect Skelton in
1917, when criticism as yet had done little to mitigate Pope's scornful jape
that 'Beastly Skelton heads of houses quote,' took a bit of nerve. Already
Graves was determinedly going his own way, against the grain of the literary
establishment and equally against the counter-establishment of the avant-
garde."[5] Graves's rejection of the contemporary poetic establishment was
clear to Edmund Gosse, who remarked that Graves "likes rough metre, bad
rhymes and squalid images: we suspect him of an inclination to be rude to
his immediate predecessors,"[6] but Graves's rejection of the counter-establishment was also evident in his early poems.

Holding contradictory attitudes toward the war, Graves developed a
protective callousness and a comedic approach to enable him to control his
experience. Graves was proud of his battalion, publicly nonchalant in the
face of death, contemptuous of established English values, and outraged at
the carnage of the war. He recognized his retreat from contradictions, which
he persistently stated ironically: "We held two irreconcilable beliefs: that the
war would never end and that we would win it."[7] He also frequently
exploited incongruity: "But, having come through the war, I refused to die

of influenza."[8] Looking back on the war, Graves upheld, if not the heroic stance, the British tradition of "side": "Myself, I value the Kaiser's war as having given me not only an unsurpassable standard of danger, discomfort, and horror by which to judge more recent troubles, but a confidence in the golden-heartedness and iron endurance of my fellow countrymen (proved again during Hitler's war), which even the laxity of this new plastic age cannot disturb."[9]

This affirmation, perhaps offered in the spirit of "Assume a virtue if you have it not," appeared frequently in Graves's portraits of soldiers under stress. "It's a Queer Time," written before Graves saw action, alternates descriptions of the trenches with the mind's unbidden retreats into the prewar world. Each stanza, describing sudden visions from the civilian past which confront a soldier in the line, ends with the refrain, "It's a queer time." In the last stanza, as a shell falls into the trench, suddenly there is "Elsie . . . tripping gaily down the trench, / Hanky to nose," leading the soldier to reflect, "Funny! because she died ten years ago! / It's a queer time." Although Graves pictures (in advance) the psychological stress of combat, he accepts the war. In "The Shadow of Death," after a poet certain of his death regrets verse he left unwritten, he decides that "To fight and kill is wrong— / To stay at home wronger." In his eulogy "Not Dead," Graves argues, as did Binyon and Grenfell, that the soldier has not really died: "Over the whole wood in a little while / Breaks his slow smile."

Other poems imply an idealistic, even ennobling picture of soldiers' sufferings despite Graves's ironical twists. "Sergeant-Major Money (1917)" describes the "virtues" of an old soldier, whose "Old Army humour was so well-spiced and hearty / That one poor sod shot himself, and one lost his wits." After their fill of Money's command, two men from the other ranks bayonet him in a canteen. The "after-action" summary is a display of soldierly detachment:

> Well, we couldn't blame the officers, they relied on Money;
> 　We couldn't blame the pitboys, their courage was grand;
> Or, least of all, blame Money, an old stiff surviving
> 　In a New (bloody) Army he couldn't understand.

Graves frequently goes beyond Kipling's colloquialisms (*bloody, sod, the batty* major), while the "Colonel, who drank" and the battalion that "hadn't one Line-officer left, after Arras" would be out of place in Kipling's prewar celebrations. There remains the poem's potentially heroic understatement that such events do occur and that one must therefore accept them. Graves's "Strong Beer" is almost a call to action. After asking "Tell us, now, how and when / We may find the bravest men?" he prefers to "Leave the lads who tamely drink / With Gideon by the water brink" in favor of robust frequenters of rural pubs, "jolly rascals, lads who pray, / Pewter in hand, at close of day, / 'Teach me to live that I may fear / The grave as little as my beer.' " ("Teach me to live" almost certainly parodies the popular hymn, "O, Master, Let Me Walk with Thee.")

The idealism which dominated most early verse also appeared in Graves's poems. In "1915," expressing nostalgia for pastoral England, Graves yearns for escape into a remembered haven:

> Dear, you've been everything that I most lack
> In these soul-deadening trenches—pictures, books,
> Music, the quiet of an English wood,
> . . . .
> And Peace, and all that's good.

Later poems express Graves's sense of camaraderie with the soldiers of his unit. "Two Fusiliers" begins "And have we done with war at last? /Well, we've been lucky devils both." The poem lists miseries that have bound the two soldiers and concludes that, after facing death, "we found / Beauty in Death, / In dead men, breath." Like Graves's statement that it is "wronger" to remain at home, this poem supports the martial attitude without denying the discomforts of soldiering.

Despite early concessions to chivalric tradition, Graves rejected twentieth-century militarism and materialism in his poetry as early as *Over the Brazier.* In "Big Words," a young sentry tries to convince himself that he will "feel small sorrow" if he "must die to-morrow." His reasons include "faith in the wisdom of God's ways," true love after a series of false ones, and memories of peace. However, these fail to sustain the boy: "But on the firestep, waiting to attack, / He cursed, prayed, sweated, wished the proud words back." In "Over the Brazier," men discuss their plans for after the war. At first the narrator pictures "A cottage in the hills, / North Wales, a cottage full of books," where he could write, but his comrade rejects postwar England:

> "No, Home's played out:
> Old England's quite a hopeless place:
> I've lost all feeling for my race:
> The English stay-at-home's a tout,
> A cad; I've done with him for life."

The narrator realizes that "this silly / Mad War has now wrecked" the plans of his companions, and he wonders "what / Better hopes has my little cottage got?"

In "Goliath and David," published in 1917, Graves ironically undermines concepts of heroism and his own earlier idealism. The poem, a funeral ode for David Thomas, killed at Fricourt in March 1916, reshapes the biblical story to reflect the reality of modern war. David boasts "That he's killed lions, he's killed bears, / And those that scorn the God of Zion / Shall perish so like bear or lion." He has placed his faith in God, with a predictable result: "(God's eyes are dim, His ears are shut)" and David falls. In the last four lines, David is in an unmistakably modern context:

> "I'm hit! I'm killed!" young David cries,
> Throws blindly forward, chokes . . . and dies.
> And look, spike-helmeted, grey, grim,
> Goliath straddles over him.

Military tradition also fails in "The Leveller." The title, referring to John Shirley's "Death, the Leveller," contrasts two men killed by the same shell, one a stripling and the other a grizzled veteran. Shirley's poem stresses that kings die as surely as do peasants. Graves's poem ironically reverses the reader's expectations of how two soldiers met their deaths: the veteran sobs like a child, and the youth "Died cursing God with brutal oaths." Graves's more decisive irony, however, occurs in his presentation of the typical military response. The sergeant, whose responsibilities include writing letters "To cheer the womenfolk" of the fallen, copies out the same note for both men:

> "He died a hero's death: and we
> His comrades of 'A' Company
> Deeply regret his death: we shall
> All deeply miss so true a pal."

The note is equally inappropriate for both men and provides a sample of the military reluctance to be honest about warfare, as well as of the insincerity of the military style.

Graves's much more widely known spoof of military rhetoric, "The Persian Version," came later, parodying the language of the bureaucrat. According to the Persians, the Battle of Marathon was a clash between Greeks and "a mere reconnaissance in force / By three brigades of foot and one of horse / (Their left flank covered by some obsolete / Light craft . . .)." The report ends with the Persian apologist's assessment: "Despite a strong defence and adverse weather / All arms combined magnificently together." The staff rhetoric, in addition to minimizing defeat to mask the ineptitude of military bunglers, implies that accepting any other version would be unpatriotic. Although the tone is playful, the light touch hides a deadly seriousness.

Siegfried Sassoon once criticized Graves for seeming "to want the War to be even uglier than it really was." Early in their friendship, according to Graves, the two agreed to "scandalize the jolly old Gosses and Stracheys" by presenting an antiestablishment view of the conflict.[10] Graves referred to the continuation of the war as "merely a sacrifice of the idealistic younger generation to the stupidity and self-protective alarm of the elder." He felt that the real victims of the war were the "officers who had endured two years or more of continuous trench service" and who consequently "became dipsomaniacs," and he found it comparatively easy to sustain his rage against the perpetrators of the war. However, as his efforts on Sassoon's behalf revealed, there was a practical side to his nature. After Sassoon wrote a letter to his commanding officer, stating his belief that the war had been unnecessarily prolonged and refusing to contribute further to it, Graves used influential connections to suppress the newspaper accounts of the letter, arranged a medical board to ward off a court martial, and provided testimony to convince the board that Sassoon's protest had resulted from shell shock.

Graves's refusal to join Sassoon in a widely publicized airing of their common views and his efforts to extricate Sassoon from his predicament reveal the contradictory pull of opposing values. On the one hand, Graves recognized and recoiled from the horror of war. On the other, he would not commit himself to an action that presumed knowledge of a solution or suggested that participation in the war was "wronger." Graves depicted the morbid reality of the trenches in some of his verse, but he felt that realistic description was sufficient protest. The most striking expression of Graves's "curative realism" was "A Dead Boche," which was among the first poems to describe the physical realities of battle, focusing on the putrefaction of a corpse:

> To you who'd read my songs of War
>   And only hear of blood and fame,
> I'll say (you've heard it said before)
>   "War's Hell!" and if you doubt the same,
> To-day I found in Mametz Wood
> A certain cure for lust of blood:
>
> Where, propped against a shattered trunk,
>   In a great mass of things unclean,
> Sat a dead Boche: he scowled and stunk
>   With clothes and face a sodden green,
> Big-bellied, spectacled, crop-haired,
> Dribbling black blood from nose and beard.

The poem forces inexperienced readers to face the horror of the trenches and to place it into a moral context.

"The Trenches (*Heard in the Ranks*)" does this also and suggests a larger perspective of the war:

Scratches in the dirt?
No, that sounds much too nice.
Oh, far too nice.
Seams, rather, of a Greyback Shirt,
And we're the little lice
Wriggling about in them a week or two,
Till one day, suddenly, from the blue
Something bloody and big will come
Like—watch this fingernail and thumb!—
Squash! and he needs no twice.

A similar context appears in "The Next War," from *Fairies and Fusiliers*.
Watching boys play at war, an elder comments,

Another war soon gets begun,
A dirtier, a more glorious one;
Then, boys, you'll have to play, all in;
It's the cruellest team will win.
So hold your nose against the stink
And never stop too long to think.

Graves came no closer to effective protest because to do so would have required a much stronger personal conviction of certainty than he could muster.

As Graves's verses show, spiritual stress is largely responsible for his attempt to regain the sense of control that the war took from him. In *The Common Asphodel* (1949), Graves recalled that "until the pressure of war was removed by the Armistice, poetry of idealism stank in the nostrils of all who had done any serious fighting." His memories of the victimized soldiery were bitter. Graves wrote a letter to the editor of the *Times Literary Supplement* which asserted that "the average British soldier of 1914–18, unlike his predecessors, the scum of the gaols who sacked Badajoz, had to be duped into the toughness and immorality that made a successful civilized fighter, by lying propaganda and a campaign of organized blood lust. This was the peculiar dirtiness of the Great War."[11] Graves suffered considerably from hallucinations of war that did not leave him until well after 1918: "Shells used to come bursting on my bed at midnight, even though Nancy shared it with me; strangers in daytime would assume the faces of friends who had been killed. When strong enough to climb the hill behind Harlech and revisit my favourite country . . . I would find myself working out tactical problems, . . . where to place a Lewis-gun if I were trying to rush Dolwreiddiog Farm. . . ."[12]

In two poems, Graves reveals that part of his problem was his lack of anything certain on which to base his perspective. "Dead Cow Farm" describes the ancient myth of the First Cow who licked the earth and humanity into existence:

> Here now is chaos once again,
> Primaeval mud, cold stones and rain.
> Here flesh decays and blood drips red,
> And the Cow's dead, the old Cow's dead.

The poem uses myth to describe the unsettling effect of the war on confidence in a natural order. Similarly "Escape," occasioned by his having been reported "Died of Wounds," describes a dream that includes Graves's descent into hell, his refusal to remain among the dead, his search for weapons to fight his way out, and his ultimate ploy of drugging Cerberus with "morphia that I bought on leave." The beast lapses into unconsciousness and falls, blocking the exit, but "Too late! for I've sped through. / O Life! O Sun!" Despite the light touch, Graves's poem reveals how greatly his close brush with death has disturbed him. Detachment has been a psychological necessity, not a poetic artifice.

Edgell Rickword (b. 1898) also combined a humorous approach with description of the sordid physical realities of trench warfare, but with a difference. Graves's personal struggle resulted from contradictory impulses which he never fully resolved. Rickword seems to have been less directly engaged. Both Graves and Rickword found the basis for their poems in an internal reality rather than in external events, but whereas Graves focused more on emotional responses, Rickword's inward turning was self-consciously literary. Rickword admired Donne and other "metaphysical" poets, and his first book of verse, *Behind the Eyes* (1921), reveals his early appreciation of the French Symbolistes. Unlike Graves, who continued after the war to develop his poetry and to write scores of books on varied subjects, Rickword limited himself to verse, editing, and biography. A friend of W. J. Turner, Rickword is best known for the *Calendar of Modern Letters* (1925–28), which published work by D. H. Lawrence, Edwin Muir, John Crowe Ransom, A. E. Coppard, Robert Graves, and T. F. Powys. He also edited two volumes of *Scrutiny* (the title of which F. R. Leavis later appropriated). Rickword, a between-the-wars communist, stopped publishing poetry in 1930 except for one public satire called "Ode to the Wife of a Non-interventionist Statesman" (1938), which attacked a politician's refusal to support the Republican government during the Spanish Civil War. He edited *Contemporary Poets* in 1980.

"Winter Warfare" is more comprehensive than most war verse in that it treats the suffering of both sides as equal. In the poem, winter becomes two officers, Hauptmann Kälte and Colonel Cold, who "stiffen all":

> Those who watched with hoary eyes
>   saw two figures gleaming there;
> Hauptmann Kälte, Colonel Cold,
>   gaunt in the grey air.

> Stiffly, tinkling spurs they moved
>   glassy-eyed, with glinting heel
> stabbing those who lingered there
>   torn by screaming steel.

Rickword has created symbols for the biting cold of the trenches, has included the German as well as the English victims, and has maintained a light touch in his description of their torment. However, the poem's lightness does not convey the emotional intensity of Graves's poetry.

Like Graves, Rickword could record physical horrors of the trenches with disturbing immediacy. Graves's "A Dead Boche" represented the body of a slain enemy as a repulsive object. In "Trench Poets," Rickword represents the corpse of a comrade in terms which recall the soldier's humanity:

> I knew a man, he was my chum,
> but he grew blacker every day,
> and would not brush the flies away,
> nor blanch however fierce the hum
> of passing shells.

Rickword mixes description with literary allusions. The soldier attempts to revive the corpse with readings from Donne, fails, and tries Tennyson:

>   I racked my head
> for healthy things and quoted *"Maud."*
> His grin got worse and I could see
> he sneered at passion's purity.

(The speaker had probably read these lines, which describe a young man's resolve to fight in the Crimea:

> And as months ran on and rumour of battle grew,
> "It is time, it is time, O passionate heart," said I
> (For I cleaved to a cause that I felt to be pure and true)
> "It is time, O passionate heart and morbid eye,
> That old hysterical mock-disease should die.")

After the stench drives away the soldier, rats devour the corpse. Graves's poem placed physical decay into a moral context, but Rickword's merely plays reality and literary fancy against each other.

In a parody of Andrew Marvell's "A Dialogue Between the Soul and Body," Rickword wrote "The Soldier Addresses his Body." The soldier tells his body, "I shall be mad if you get smashed about, / we've had good times together, you and I." He then mentions "a world of things we haven't done," including lands unseen, wines untasted, and joys unsampled. The last stanza repudiates the soldier's desire for new experience, however, and rejects the value of verse:

> Yes, there's a world of things we've never done,
> but it's a sweat to knock them into rhyme,
> let's have a drink, and give the cards a run
> and leave dull verse to the dull peaceful time.

Rickword's use of colloquialism is much less convincing than Graves's. Rickword's comic verses suffer in comparison with Graves's poetry partly because they convey no sense of Rickword's personal engagement with the sufferings he addresses and because they seem to make their points too facilely. There is little sense of agony or anguish in Rickword's verse, or of the poet's struggle in his literary treatments of the war.

Satire and Protest

SIEGFRIED SASSOON (1886–1967) WAS THE FIRST SOLDIER POET TO ACHIEVE public notoriety as an opponent not only of the war, but also of those whose complicity allowed it to continue. His satiric targets included virtually everyone except fighting soldiers of both sides—civilians content to accept the casualties of the war as inevitable, staff officers whose incompetence contributed to the carnage, churchmen who abetted efforts to prolong the war, and profiteers who combined insensibility and greed to become "hard-faced men who did well out of the war." During the war, Sassoon's *The Old Huntsman and Other Poems* (1917), "A Soldier's Declaration" (July 1917), and *Counter-Attack and Other Poems* (1918) drew attention to the war's effects.

Nothing in Sassoon's prewar life suggested he would become a public spokesman. Born in Kent, Sassoon was the second of three sons of Alfred Sassoon, who separated from his wife when Sassoon was five, and Theresa Thornycroft, whose family included several distinguished Victorian sculptors. Sassoon's connections were various. Cousins on his father's side intermarried with Rothschilds, and his father's sister Rachel at one point edited two rival London newspapers, the *Observer* and the *Sunday Times* (she owned one, her husband the other). Sassoon attended Clare College, Cambridge, first in law and then in history, but he left without taking a degree. On an income of approximately £500 per year, he devoted his energies to cricket, fox-hunting, book-collecting (chiefly for the bindings), and poetry. By 1912 Sassoon had published nine volumes of verse, but he did not achieve recognition until 1913, when he published *The Daffodil Murderer*, a parody of Masefield. Both Edmund Gosse and Edward Marsh took an interest in Sassoon's verse, and Marsh convinced Sassoon to move in May 1914 to London, where he met Rupert Brooke and other Georgians.

Sassoon possessed an incredible physical and moral courage that prewar circumstances had not allowed to surface beyond his determination to master fox-hunting. When the war began, however, his response was immediate. By 5 August 1914 the twenty-eight-year-old Sassoon was in uniform as a cavalry trooper. As he recorded in *Memoirs of a Fox-Hunting Man* (1928), he "did not need Hardy's 'Song of the Soldiers' ["Men Who March Away"] to warn me that the Remounts was no place for me,"[1] and he transferred to the Royal Welch Fusiliers as an infantry subaltern. Recalling the first weeks of the war, Sassoon commented, "Many of us believed that the Russians would occupy Berlin (and, perhaps, capture the Kaiser) before Christmas. The newspapers informed us that German soldiers crucified Belgian babies. Stories of that kind were taken for granted; to have disbelieved them would have been unpatriotic."[2] He also recalled, "Courage remained a virtue. And that exploitation of courage, if I may be allowed to say a thing so obvious, was the essential tragedy of the War, which, as everyone now agrees, was a crime against humanity."[3]

Sassoon survived the war chiefly through luck. While he was training with the Sussex Yeomanry in January 1915, his horse stumbled over a hidden strand of barbed wire, and Sassoon broke his arm. He did not arrive at the front until November 1915, with his early idealism intact. Little in Sassoon's early poetry distinguished it from Brooke's except for Brooke's superior talent as a poet. Sassoon's "Absolution" reveals the extent to which abstractions dominated his verse before Sassoon saw action: "War is our scourge; yet war has made us wise, / And, fighting for our freedom, we are free." "France" describes soldiers as "serene" when death is near and argues that "they are fortunate, who fight / For gleaming landscapes swept and shafted / And crowned by cloud pavilions white." When his younger brother Hamo died at Gallipoli in August 1915, Sassoon wrote "To My Brother," an elegy which concludes "But in the gloom I see your laurell'd head / And through your victory I shall win the light."

One early poem, "The Kiss," as Sassoon recalled with chagrin, attempts to satirize "the barbarities of the famous bayonet-fighting lecture. . . . The difficulty is that it doesn't show any sign of satire."[4] The poem, addressing "Brother Lead and Sister Steel," can read as a fire-eating poem because it offers no clue to resolve the ambiguity of the last stanza:

> Sweet Sister, grant your soldier this:
> That in good fury he may feel
> The body where he sets his heel
> Quail from your downward darting kiss.

Still, the poem does reveal Sassoon's early tendency to respond to an outrageous occurrence in verse.

Sassoon's conduct during the war exemplified the highest ideals of courage. He won the Military Cross for bringing back wounded men after a raid, and during the Somme Offensive he singlehandedly occupied a section of German trench. As an officer, his consideration and concern for his men recall the spirit of Read's "My Company." As C. E. Maguire reports, "Ordered to rehearse his men—already much over-rehearsed—for an attack, he led them into a wood and read the *London Mail* to them."[5] Nicknamed

"Mad Jack" by his men, Sassoon, like Julian Grenfell, made independent forays into No Man's Land to stalk German snipers. During the Battle of Arras in April 1917, Sassoon received a neck wound and returned to England for convalescence. He had met Ottoline Morrell in 1916, in whose home he spoke with pacifists and conscientious objectors for the first time. With the encouragement of Bertrand Russell, Lady Ottoline, and Middleton Murry, Sassoon wrote "A Soldier's Declaration" and mailed it to his commanding officer. Russell had the letter mentioned in the House of Commons. Robert Graves was quick to minimize the consequences of the protest by arranging for a medical board, but Sassoon, whose statement during wartime could have resulted in court martial and even execution for treason, had no reason to expect that he would avoid trial or punishment.

Sassoon's protest differs from today's notions of pacifism. Instead of protesting killing on humanitarian grounds, he opposed the victimization of the fighting soldier:

> I believe that the purposes for which I and my fellow soldiers entered upon this War should have been so clearly stated as to have made it impossible to change them, and that, had this been done, the objects which actuated us would now be attainable by negotiation. I have seen and endured the sufferings of the troops, and I can no longer be a party to prolong these sufferings for ends which I believe to be evil and unjust. I am not protesting against the conduct of the War, but against the political errors and insincerities for which the fighting men are being sacrificed.

Sassoon did not object to a war that sought and attained specified goals. His major grievance was that only part of the population bore the burden. He ends his declaration by condemning "the callous complacency with which the majority of those at home regard the continuance of agonies which they do not share, and which they have not sufficient imagination to realize."[6] After his medical board, Sassoon became a patient of W. H. R. Rivers at Craiglockhart, where he spent some months convalescing. At Craiglockhart Sassoon met Wilfred Owen, whom he influenced beyond his understanding. Only after the war, according to Sassoon, did he realize the importance of Owen's work. Sassoon could have safely spent the rest of the war at Craiglockhart, but he chose to return to the front.

In *Sherston's Progress* (1936), Sassoon gave as reasons for his return to the front his personal wellbeing, his feeling for his men, and his desire to continue his protest. The effects of the war continued to plague him (he once told Graves of hallucinations of corpses lying on London streets), and he felt that "Army life away from the actual Front is demoralizing."[7] For Sassoon, "The only way to forget about the War was to be on the other side of the Channel,"[8] and he felt it was "Better to be in the trenches with those whose experience I had shared and understood than with this medley of civilians who, when one generalized about them intolerantly, seemed either being broken by the War or enriched and made important by it."[9] He justified his return to the front, ironically, in terms of

> exasperation against the people who pitied my "wrongheadedness" and regarded me as "not quite normal." In their opinion it was quite right that I should be safely out of it and "being looked after." How else could I get my own back on them but by returning to the trenches? Killed in action in order to confute the Under-Secretary for War, who had officially stated that I wasn't responsible for my actions. What a truly glorious death for a promising young Pacifist! . . .[10]

Sassoon's return to the front was not immediate. He was stationed in Egypt in February 1918, where he felt almost as uncomfortable among noncombatant officers as he had among civilians. However, his unit transferred to France in May 1918, where he served as a company commander (his second-in-command, a bespectacled subaltern, was Vivian de Sola Pinto). Sassoon resumed his stalking as "Mad Jack." When he returned from a foray into No Man's Land on 13 July 1918, after harassing a German machine-gun nest, his sergeant mistook him for a German and shot him in the head. Sassoon spent the rest of the war convalescing in England.

He had written the poems for *Counter-Attack and Other Poems* during his stay at Craiglockhart and must have viewed at least one effect of the volume with disgust. According to L. Hugh Moore, "Winston Churchill so admired ["Counter-Attack"] that he memorized it, seeing it, not as a protest against war, but as a means of increasing the war effort because it showed what the English soldiers endured."[11] Despite later appreciation of Sassoon's pioneering protests, several of his contemporaries dismissed them. Middleton Murry found that the verses of *Counter-Attack* "express nothing, save in so far as a cry expresses pain," and another of Murry's comments anticipates one of Johnston's conclusions by fifty years: "Without the perspective that comes from intellectual remoteness there can be no comprehension, no order and no art."[12] Arnold Bennett had tried to dissuade Sassoon from issuing his declaration of protest. Gosse, respecting Sassoon's sincerity, objected to the verse on similar grounds: "His temper is not altogether to be applauded, for such sentiments must tend to relax the effort of the struggle, yet they can hardly be reproved when conducted with so much honesty and courage."[13] Sassoon's development as a satirist transcended techniques peculiarly Georgian. His rigidly bipolar view of ethical extremes made his poetry effective, although his perception of absolute truths sometimes limited his realism. Sassoon's poems were occasional. When the occasion passed, so did his prominence as a poet.

Before Sassoon's poetry, few civilians could know what the trenches were really like. The soldiers themselves, in their letters and infrequent leaves, kept silent, due partly to a feeling of decency and partly to civilians' incomprehension. In retrospect, Sassoon's satire seems heavy-handed when he dwells on the horrors of the trenches and on the villainy of those responsible, but civilians' prevailing ignorance of modern warfare demanded blunt depiction. The unprecedented carnage and unforeseen suffering were more shocking to Sassoon's audience than any pacifist argument could be. His aim was to force the noncombatant to contemplate the realities of the front. The task required some poetic innovation—Sassoon once commented that he had been the first to use the word *syphilitic* in a poem—but his impact derived chiefly from his new subject matter.

The antichivalric "A Working Party" presents a modern "hero" who is commonplace, dull, weary, and unimaginative:

> He was a young man with a meagre wife
> And two small children in a Midland town;
> He showed their photographs to all his mates,
> And they considered him a decent chap
> Who did his work and hadn't much to say,
> And always laughed at other people's jokes
> Because he hadn't any of his own.

Unlike the nondescript of Asquith's "The Volunteer," Sassoon's soldier does not experience an ennobling death: as he fortified his trench with sandbags, "the instant split / His startled life with lead, and all went out." Sassoon's most gruesome depiction occurs in the first stanza of "Counter-Attack":

> The place was rotten with dead; green clumsy legs
> High-booted, sprawled and grovelled along the saps;
> And trunks, face downward, in the sucking mud,
> Wallowed like trodden sand-bags, loosely filled;
> And naked sodden buttocks, mats of hair,
> Bulged, clotted heads slept in the plastering slime.
> And then the rain began,—the jolly old rain!

A war correspondent's bloodlessly abstract report—"The effect of our bombardment was terrific"—inspired "The Effect," which introduces the palpable realities behind the journalist's empty phrase: "When Dick was killed last week he looked like that, / Flapping along the fire-step like a fish, / After the blazing crump had knocked him flat. . . ."

In "The Rear Guard (Hindenburg Line, April 1917)," Sassoon describes a lost soldier who angrily kicks a reclining figure for not responding to his request for directions. His flashlight reveals "the livid face / Terribly glaring up, whose eyes yet wore / Agony dying hard ten days before; / And fists of fingers clutched a blackening wound." Sassoon duplicates the surprise and shock of the soldier, who, "with sweat of horror in his hair," emerged from the trench, "Unloading hell behind him step by step." Sassoon also described soldiers' departures from traditional attitudes. In "Stand-To: Good Friday Morning," a sentry ill with fatigue, sick of the rain, offers a prayer that belies civilian expectations of a Happy Warrior: "O Jesus, send me a wound to-day, / And I'll believe in Your bread and wine, / And get my bloody old sins washed white."

Sassoon was at his best when attacking those who mismanaged the war. "The General," which nearly resulted in the censor's refusal to allow the publication of *Counter-Attack and Other Poems*, satirizes the ineffectiveness of military leadership with masterful economy:

> "Good-morning; good-morning!" the General said
> When we met him last week on our way to the line.
> Now the soldiers he smiled at are most of 'em dead,
> And we're cursing his staff for incompetent swine.
> "He's a cheery old card," grunted Harry to Jack
> As they slogged up to Arras with rifle and pack.
>
> *   *   *   *
>
> But he did for them both by his plan of attack.

The poem demonstrates Sassoon's most frequent satiric device, reserving a bitterly ironical twist for the last line. The poem is not pacifistic: Sassoon does not object to the general because he is a military man, but because he does not wage war well enough.

"Base Details" emphasizes the opposition Sassoon frequently exploited between the men doing the fighting and the others (garrison officers wore scarlet tabs to distinguish them from line officers, causing combatants to refer often to the "Red Badge of Funk"):

> If I were fierce, and bald, and short of breath,
>   I'd live with scarlet Majors at the Base,
> And speed glum heroes up the line to death.
>   You'd see me with my puffy petulant face,
> Guzzling and gulping in the best hotel,
>   Reading the Roll of Honour. "Poor young chap,"
> I'd say—"I used to know his father well;
>   Yes, we've lost heavily in this last scrap."
> And when the war is done and youth stone dead,
> I'd toddle safely home and die—in bed.

Whereas "The General" is a narrative, "Base Details" moves closer to dramatic irony in a monologue, although Sassoon stops short of having an officer condemn himself in his own words.

The opening lines of "Banishment" reveal Sassoon's regard for the men of the trenches:

> I am banished from the patient men who fight.
> They smote my heart to pity, built my pride.
> . . . .
> Their wrongs were mine; and ever in my sight
> They went arrayed in honour.

At the end of the poem, Sassoon justifies his soldier's declaration and his ultimate return to the trenches in terms of his feeling for his men: "Love drove me to rebel. / Love drives me back to grope with them through hell; / And in their tortured eyes I stand forgiven." Sassoon's satire derives force from his conviction that only malice or incompetence could explain others' willingness to allow the fighting to continue.

Had one only the record of Sassoon's verse, one might conclude that the war was fought between soldiers and civilians. As critic Joseph Cohen has observed, Sassoon's "approach was direct and his technique simple: he emphasized and re-emphasized the contrast between the relative comfort and safety of the homefront and the misery and insecurity of the trenches. While the poetic worth of his formula was questionable, its communicative potential was unlimited."[14] Sassoon referred to his "acute antagonism toward anyone whose attitude to the War was what I called 'complacent'— people who just accepted it as inevitable and then proceeded to do well out of it, or who smugly performed the patriotic jobs which enabled them to congratulate themselves on being part of the National Effort."[15]

His contempt for civilians who desired to win the war at all costs appears frequently. In "Ancient History," he has "Adam, a brown old vulture in the rain" recall Cain affectionately and Abel contemptuously: " 'Afraid to fight; was murder more disgrace? . . . / *God always hated Cain*' . . . He bowed his head— / The gaunt wild man whose lovely sons were dead." In "How to Die" he ridicules civilian misapprehensions of reality. In the first half of the poem, he presents an idealized version of a soldier's death, complete with "skies / Where holy brightness breaks in flame." Then comes a realistic picture of soldiers who die "with sobs and curses, / And sullen faces white as chalk." Sassoon's ironical conclusion, reserved for the end, is that soldiers die "not with haste / And shuddering groans; but passing through it / With due regard for decent taste." Unlike the early "The Kiss," this poem's consistency enables one to recognize the irony.

"The Hero" makes it almost impossible for a reader to miss the point. Sassoon called the plot of the narrative "Brother officer giving white-haired mother fictitious account of her cold-footed son's death at the front." In the second stanza, the officer reveals that he has lied, and in the third he expresses his contempt for Jack, "cold-footed, useless swine" who panicked in the trenches, tried to effect his transfer home, and died ingloriously, "Blown to small bits" by a shell. The poem inspires conflicting sympathies. One can pity the officer who puts the coward's death in a good light for the mother, one can pity "that lonely woman with white hair," and one can even pity Jack, for the last lines reveal him as a victim for whom no one cares except his mother. The poem almost meets the objection that Sassoon's poetry does not communicate the truth of his conflicting loyalties. Although Sassoon was aware of civilians' ignorance, he invites sympathy with an officer who deliberately ennobles the slain.

"Suicide in the Trenches" is Sassoon's most blatant lapse into overt propaganda. In the first stanza, a soldier maintains an "empty joy" that does not interfere with his peace of mind. In the second, "cowed and glum," after experiencing winter in the trenches, "He put a bullet through his brain." Had Sassoon left the stark biography to speak for itself, the poem might have been more effective, but, after a typographical separation that suggests the impossibility of transition, Sassoon shifts from simple narrative to pointed accusation:

> You smug-faced crowds with kindling eye
> Who cheer when soldier lads march by,
> Sneak home and pray you'll never know
> The hell where youth and laughter go.

Sassoon could not resist the opportunity of an easy target.

Sassoon is more sophisticated in "To Any Dead Officer," which presents one side of a telephone conversation between a living officer and his dead comrade. The monologue moves quickly through a description of the officer who had "hated tours of trenches" and desired to live, but who fell, machine-gunned, "in a hopeless dud-attack" and appeared in "the bloody Roll of Honour." After a typographical separation, Sassoon indicates his specific target:

> Good-bye, old lad! Remember me to God,
>   And tell Him that our politicians swear
> They won't give in till Prussian Rule's been trod
>   Under the Heel of England . . . Are you there? . . .
> Yes . . . and the War won't end for at least two years;
> But we've got stacks of men . . . I'm blind with tears,
>   Staring into the dark. Cheerio!
> I wish they'd killed you in a decent show.

Sassoon's expression of his hatred for excessive patriotism approaches the rabid. In "Blighters," Sassoon attacks the frenzied jingoism of the music hall, using an experience from a convalescent leave that recalls E. A. Mackintosh's

"Recruiting." Civilians heartily approve "prancing ranks / Of harlots" as they sing "We're sure the Kaiser loves our dear old Tanks!" Sassoon imagines a tank coming down the aisle to clear the stage of the performers, to end jokes that "mock the riddled corpses round Bapaume." Similarly, "Fight to a Finish" presents soldiers taking revenge on civilians after the war. At a celebration designed to "cheer the soldiers who'd refrained from dying," the "Grim Fusiliers" fix bayonets, charge the civilians, deal "Yellow-Pressmen" their just deserts, and go "To clear those Junkers out of Parliament." The poem neither introduces nor attempts to change any idea but is merely a moment of wishful thinking. "They" is also weak, primarily because the target presents no real challenge. The role of the clergy in encouraging the war made a bishop too obvious a target even for civilians, while at the front many churchmen were beneath contempt for the hypocrisy of exhorting others to fight while remaining outside the fighting areas themselves. In "They," a bishop says that returning soldiers "will not be the same; for they'll have fought / In a just cause," will have opposed Anti-Christ, and will have "challenged Death and dared him face to face." To this the soldiers respond "We're none of us the same!", since one has lost his legs and another his sight, a third has received a bullet through the lungs, and a fourth has contracted syphilis. Like the poems of soldiers' revenge on civilians, "They" communicates little except the poet's resentment.

Sassoon's poems of brutal reality and vindictive satire, particularly when compared with Owen's verse, have obscured his attempts to convey a sense of pity for the soldier/victim, most of which did, to be sure, appear in combination with satiric thrusts aimed at the insensitive civilian. Sassoon's disgust for the acquiescent obscured his other feelings. He had personal experience of civilians' indifference. According to Robert Wohl, Lady Brassey told Sassoon that "he had nothing to lose in going back to France as he was not the bearer of a great name."[16] Sassoon frequently attacked such attitudes. One of his more successful satires is "Lamentations," which uses a *persona* instead of an authorial intrusion to make its point. The poem reveals the insensitivity of one soldier who sees a second soldier shaken by inconsolable grief at the death of his brother:

> I found him in the guard-room at the Base.
> From the blind darkness I had heard his crying
> And blundered in. With puzzled, patient face
> A sergeant watched him; it was no good trying
> To stop it; for he howled and beat his chest.
> And, all because his brother had gone west,
> Raved at the bleeding war; his rampant grief
> Moaned, shouted, sobbed, and choked, while he was kneeling
> Half-naked on the floor. In my belief
> Such men have lost all patriotic feeling.

Two locutions, "it was no good trying / To stop it" and "all because his brother" has died, establish the narrator's lack of feeling and prepare the reader for the final irony of the poem.

Sassoon uses a similar technique in "Survivors," employing a speaker who discusses shell shock victims with little understanding of their plight. The speaker feels that the soldiers will soon recover, that "they'll be proud / Of glorious war that shatter'd all their pride," but Sassoon assures the reader's sympathy for the patients: they are "boys with old, scared faces, learning to walk," they suffer from "dreams that drip with murder," and they are "Children, with eyes that hate you, broken and mad." The memorable phrases of the poem focus on the suffering of the patients.

Sassoon's response to insensitive civilians was either to lash the target directly or to dramatize an unsympathetic situation. In "Glory of Women" Sassoon attacks women who allow their patriotic chauvinism to prevail over pity:

> You love us when we're heroes, home on leave,
> Or wounded in a mentionable place.
> You worship decorations; you believe
> That chivalry redeems the war's disgrace.
> You make us shells. You listen with delight,
> By tales of dirt and danger fondly thrilled.
> You crown our distant ardours while we fight,
> And mourn our laurelled memories when we're killed.
> You can't believe that British troops "retire"
> When hell's last horror breaks them, and they run,
> Trampling the terrible corpses—blind with blood.
>   O German mother dreaming by the fire,
>   While you are knitting socks to send your son
>   His face is trodden deeper in the mud.

Sassoon's anger seems hardly fair since he is condemning attitudes he himself had held before he went to the trenches. However, he explicitly decries support of the war effort by the ignorant who "delight" in "tales of dirt and danger."

More effective as a criticism of insensitivity is "Does It Matter?", which dramatizes the plight of a soldier crippled by the war. The second stanza is particularly fine:

> Does it matter?—losing your sight? . . .
> There's such splendid work for the blind;
> And people will always be kind,
> As you sit on the terrace remembering
> And turning your face to the light.

The effect of combining the clichés of consolation with vivid description is to make the victim pathetic, partly because he is subjected to the "sympathy" of the indifferent. In "The One-Legged Man," whose "Thank God they had to amputate!" deflates civilian expectations of a soldier's unflagging fighting spirit, the poem's effect results from the reader's recognition that, if one prefers amputation to the front, war must indeed be horrible. In "Does It Matter?" the reader cannot help feeling that the victim would be better dead than an object of insincere pity.

In "Dreamers" and "Attack," Sassoon communicates his pity for soldier/victims. In the sonnet "Dreamers," the octave discusses soldiers in abstract generalizations and, standing alone, would not have been out of place in a Victorian anthology of romantic war poetry. The sestet, however, offers an officer's concrete observations, conveying his pity for his men:

> I see them in foul dug-outs, gnawed by rats,
>   And in the ruined trenches, lashed with rain,
> Dreaming of things they did with balls and bats,
>   And mocked by hopeless longing to regain
> Bank-holidays, and picture shows, and spats,
>   And going to the office in the train.

By limiting himself to straightforward "reporting," Sassoon conveys more feeling than when his focus shifts to his audience. "Attack" describes dawn as the men attack:

> Lines of grey, muttering faces, masked with fear,
> They leave their trenches, going over the top,
> While time ticks blank and busy on their wrists,
> And hope, with furtive eyes and grappling fists,
> Flounders in mud. O Jesus, make it stop!

The technique of expressing pity through the eyes of an officer/narrator worked well in other poems. In "The Dug-Out," written in July 1918, the speaker addresses a soldier sleeping in the trench. Usually poets described the dead as sleeping, but Sassoon inverts this: "You are too young to fall asleep for ever; / And when you sleep you remind me of the dead." "In the Pink" describes the thoughts of an officer whose duties include censoring the letters written by his men. He reads between the lines of a soldier's letter to his sweetheart which ends "This leaves me in the pink." In contrast to the soldier's assurances, the officer understands what the soldier is actually thinking: "to-morrow night we trudge / Up to the trenches, and my boots are rotten." The officer summarizes the soldier's situation: "To-night he's in the pink; but soon he'll die. / And still the war goes on—*he* don't know why."

Sassoon's remarkable "Repression of War Experience" (which takes its title from a paper read by W. H. R. Rivers to the Royal Society of Medicine on 4 December 1917) delineates the thought processes of a shell shock victim who cannot keep his mind from the war. The soldier's thoughts return to war when other subjects cannot hold his attention:

> Now light the candles; one; two; there's a moth;
> What silly beggars they are to blunder in
> And scorch their wings with glory, liquid flame—
> No, no, not that,—it's bad to think of war. . . .

When the soldier lights his pipe, he notes that his hand is steady. When he examines a shelf of books, he sees them "dressed" in the colors of uniforms, a "jolly company" waiting in formation, "quiet and patient." After a typographical separation, Sassoon has the soldier consider his situation:

> You're quiet and peaceful, summering safe at home;
> You'd never think there was a bloody war on! . . .
> O yes, you would . . . why, you can hear the guns.
> Hark! Thud, thud, thud,—quite soft . . . they never cease—
> Those whispering guns—O Christ, I want to go out
> And screech at them to stop—I'm going crazy;
> I'm going stark, staring mad because of the guns.

This dramatic presentation of the shell shock victim's suffering is among Sassoon's more successful efforts.

Sassoon's achievement as a war poet does not depend on his poetic techniques, which are essentially Georgian, but on the insights that he forced upon the modern consciousness. Chiefly through his poetic protests the public became aware of the brutal reality of trench warfare, the disproportionate burden of suffering borne by the fighting soldier, and the growing disparity between soldiers and civilians. His satires of indifferent civilians, jingoistic patriots, and military incompetents communicated a sense of reality not accessible through the newspapers. His success has obscured his attempt to convey his sense of the pity of war. Sassoon was able to respond to the new world that the war introduced, but, when the Armistice ended the war, it also ended Sassoon's effectiveness as a poet.

During the war Sassoon was not alone in his poetical expressions of dissatisfaction. Several other poets directed satire against civilian and political targets, and some went beyond Sassoon's protest against the conduct of the war. Sassoon was the first, at great risk, to accuse openly those whose complicity was responsible for the prolongation of the war and to reach a large audience with his protests. However, others later attacked the same targets in their verse, and some writers articulated protests comparable to those of the late 1960s and early 1970s.

After Sassoon, the most effective of the war satirists was Osbert Sitwell (1892–1969), son of Sir George Sitwell, 4th Baronet. He was in the Grenadier Guards from 1912 to 1919, and he served with E. W. Tennant at the front. After the war, with his siblings Edith and Sacheverell, Sitwell edited the six "cycles" of *Wheels* (1916–21), largely in reaction to the Georgian poetry anthologies. According to Frank Swinnerton, "Being excluded, either by their own act or by the repulsion of the editorial canon, from 'Georgian Poetry,' they established a counterblast to which they gave the name 'Wheels'; and to this all three contributed greatly, adding jovial and insulting annotations with which they lambasted uncomplimentary reviewers."[17]

Sitwell frequently singled out the older generation for abuse. "Arm-Chair," a monologue of dramatic irony, opens with lines recalling Sassoon's "Base Details": "If I were now of handsome middle-age, / I should not govern yet, but still should hope / To help the prosecution of this war." The poem summarizes activities of civilians who plant victory gardens, write letters to the *Times*, send their sons to France, and encourage others to do the same. "If I were old or only seventy," the poem's speaker would become either a military leader or a politician, send grandsons to France, and make the "Bishops go nigh mad with joy" by not making peace until all the younger generation had been crippled in battle. In the last stanza, the speaker regrets that, younger than ninety, he is not old enough to govern, and he ends with a wish: "O let me govern, Lord, at ninety-nine!" Sitwell also attacks the older generation in "The Eternal Club," in which old men commiserate with Joseph concerning the conduct of Jesus:

> Warming their withered hands the dotards say:
> "In our youth men were happy till they died.
> What is it ails the young men of to-day—
> To make them bitter and dissatisfied?"

Joseph's cronies do not understand his son's reaction to the money-changers in the temple, denial of family, Sermon on the Mount, or protest against the *status quo*.

Sitwell is effectively ironical in his use of *personae*. His targets frequently condemn themselves from their own mouths. In "Hymn to Moloch," the older generation prays to Moloch, from the safety of home, to refrain from saving youth at the front:

> Lord, it is the better way
> Swift to send them to the grave.
> Those of us too old to go
> Send our sons to face the foe,
> But, O lord! *we* must remain
> Here, to pray and sort the slain.

Sitwell's attacks on civilians at home introduced a new bitterness to antiwar writing. He entitled his Armistice Day poem "Corpse Day."

Other poets, including Rudyard Kipling, attacked elders for their abuse of the young. Kipling's "Common Form" suggests an epitaph for the fallen, including his own son, who died early in the war: "If any question why we died, / Tell them, because our fathers lied." Thomas Burke (1886–1945), best known for his Limehouse stories, did not serve in World War I but worked in the American Division of the Ministry of Information during World War II, when he was in his fifties. "Of the Great White War," from *The Song Book of Quong Lee of Limehouse* (1920), recorded the perverse gratification that the deaths of the young provided for the old. After the speaker observes "how the aged cried aloud in public places / Of honour and chivalry and the duty of the young," the young "suddenly became old, / And marched away to defend the aged." The old became young,

> And mouthed fair phrases, one to the other, about the Supreme
>   Sacrifice,
> And turned to their account-books, murmuring gravely:
> Business as Usual.
> And brought out bottles of wine and drank the health
> Of the young men they had sent out to die for them.

Burke suggests that the psychological source of the generation gap is the invidious hatred that age directs at youth.

Other poets lashed out at civilian insensibility. Francis Brett Young's "The Pavement" focuses on the lack of concern "In bitter London's heart of stone" for "a soldier's body thrown / Unto the drabs that traffic there." For Young, "Out of the jaws of Passchendaele / They had sent him to this nether hell." The concluding stanza, recalling Sassoon's "Blighters" and "Fight to a Finish," is separate from the rest of the poem:

> I would that war were what men dream:
>   A crackling fire, a cleansing flame,
> That it might leap the space between
>   And lap up London and its shame.

Alfred Noyes, Victorian in his support for the Allies, was also disgusted by civilian conduct during the war. Shortly after the Armistice he attacked the mindless hedonism that became epidemic after the shooting stopped:

> The cymbals crash,
>   And the dancers walk;
> With long silk stockings,
>   And arms of chalk,
> Butterfly skirts

> And white breasts bare;
> And shadows of dead men
> Watching 'em there—

The most incisive indictment of civilian insensitivity to the sufferings of the soldiers was "High Wood" by "Philip Johnston," which appeared in the *Nation* on 16 February 1918. A guide conducts a tour of High Wood, a bloody battleground during the Somme Offensive, and points out barbed wire, trees damaged by shell fire, a mound under which slain soldiers lie, and other curiosities. He interrupts himself in midsentence to caution a tourist:

> Madame, please,
> You are requested kindly not to touch
> Or take away the Comp'ny's property
> As souvenirs: you'll find we have on sale
> A large variety, all guaranteed.
> As I was saying, all is as it was,
> This is an unknown British officer;
> The tunic having lately rotted off.
> Please follow me—this way . . . the *path* sir. *please* . . .

Months before the Armistice, "Johnston" predicted the civilian postwar indifference that others would satirize only in retrospect.

Several poets objected to inept political and military leadership during the war. Among the most blunt critics was Rudyard Kipling, whose "A Dead Statesman" is brutally direct:

> I could not dig: I dared not rob:
> Therefore I lied to please the mob.
> Now all my lies are proved untrue
> And I must face the men I slew.
> What tale shall serve me here among
> Mine angry and defrauded young?

Similar is Kipling's "Mesopotamia (1917)," which in six stanzas contrasts the plight of the young who fell and the rise of political leaders, "idle-minded overlings who quibbled while they died" and contributed "The slothfulness that wasted and the arrogance that slew." Each stanza ends by asking whether the inept and corrupt leaders will "come with years and honour to the grave?" or "confirm and re-establish each career?" (virtually every wartime leader went on to further honors despite the criminal ineptitude that characterized their war "service"). "Mesopotamia (1917)" rivals Sassoon's verse in its unmitigated bitterness, its bipolar contrast between sympathetic victim and malicious victimizer, and its certainty of conviction.

G. K. Chesterton (1874–1936) took a similar stance in his "Elegy in a Country Churchyard." Chesterton, whose younger brother Cecil died in the war, was as bitter as Kipling, but his expression was more felicitous and much more concise. The first of three short stanzas establishes that "men that worked for England / They have their graves at home." The second refers to the war dead, who "have their graves afar." The last, which echoes *Paradise Lost*'s "secret conclave" of Satan and his followers, drives Chesterton's point home:

> And they that rule in England,
> In stately conclave met,
> Alas, alas for England
> They have no graves as yet.

Colin Ellis (1895–1969) takes a more general approach toward failures of leadership. In "International Conference," his definitions of nations' political aims leave no room for argument:

> To kill its enemies and cheat its friends,
> Each nation its prerogative defends;
> Yet some their efforts for goodwill maintain,
> In hope, in faith, in patience, and in vain.

When Ellis selects a more specific target, his choice of the church recalls Sassoon's "They." During the war Ellis, a lieutenant and forward observation officer at the capture of Vimy Ridge, won the MC, and he had sufficient experience to recognize the disparity between the church's espousal of a "just" cause and the war's actual conditions. "Spaniel's Sermons," after identifying the chaplain as fearful for his place, addresses the chaplain's role in the war:

> But when the shells begin to fly
> He calls our quarrel just
> And bids us keep our powder dry
> And place our God in trust.

The betrayal of the fighting soldier for political ends was a frequent theme of wartime protest. William Norman Ewer (b. 1885) focused on the political exploitation of soldiers in "Five Souls." The poem presents five fallen soldiers, each of whom claims "I gave my life for freedom—This I know / For those who bade me fight had told me so." These soldiers include men of both sides: a Pole fighting for Russia, an Austrian fighting against Russia, a Frenchman fighting in Belgium, a German fighting in Lorraine, and a Scot fighting in Belgium. That all five claim to be fighting for freedom, as defined by their leaders, attempts to satirize political duplicity, but the simplistic structure of the poem makes it so predictable, even on a first reading, that it is ineffective.

Alan Patrick Herbert (1890–1971) attacked the political and military use of soldiers' sacrifices. A lieutenant in the Royal Naval Division who fought at Gallipoli and the Somme, wounded and invalided out, Herbert knew whereof he spoke. In "After the Battle," he addresses leaders to caution them against exploiting the troops. After the battle, "we shall have the usual Thanks Parade, / The beaming General, and the soapy praise." Herbert, however, realizes that the leaders desire only the gains that will accrue to them. The men "have bled to boost you up a rung— / A K. C. B. [Knight Commander of the Order of the Bath] perhaps, perhaps a Corps—." After informing the leaders that the men want only to forget the battle, Herbert warns them to keep their plans for future actions to themselves as long as possible.

John Collings Squire (1884–1958), literary editor of the *New Statesman* from 1913 to 1917 and an early encourager of Edmund Blunden, wielded considerable literary influence during the war and after. His faulty eyesight exempted him from service, and, according to Frank Swinnerton, "by the end of the First World War he had unrivalled power in London critical journalism."[18] In "The Trinity," soldiers in France cry "God for Harmsworth! England and Lloyd George!", parodying "God for Harry! England and Saint George!" (*Henry V*) with references to Harmsworth, a newspaper magnate, and Lloyd George, whose political opportunism during the formation of the Coalition Government secured his political future. In Squire's poem, the connection between soldiers' casualties in France and Lloyd George's political rise is explicit.

Satires of wartime profiteering and the advantages gained by wartime civilians were frequent. Sitwell's "Judas and the Profiteer" pointedly equates the profiteers' betrayal of the soldier with Judas's betrayal of the Nazarene. Judas, descending to hell, meets "his only friend—the profiteer" who informs Judas that he was foolish "to sell / For silver pence the body of God's Son, / Whereas for maiming men with sword and shell / I gain at least a golden million." Judas, however, has a ready retort: "You deserve your gold; / It's not His body but His soul you've sold!" Poet and critic T. Sturge Moore (1870–1944), in "War and Peace, 1915," focuses on man's inherent greed as a reason for his preferring war to peace. After arguing that the God of War "Honours the worthless and neglects the worthy," Moore asks, "Should Peace return from Paradise / Would men not reabuse her reign?" He cites extortioners who will not "Renounce the lordship of hard cash." For Moore, "deep within War's cavernous smoke and noise, / Brave faces kiss

Peace, ruined men rejoice!" Moore, whose poem appeared in *To-Day* (January 1919) after the Armistice, can ironically prefer the late war to the continuing economic corruption and exploitation of peace.

One economic target frequently criticized was labor. Many felt that workers demanding higher wages and improved working conditions during wartime were taking unpatriotic advantage, forgetting that the miserable conditions of the English working class had brought the country to the verge of a general strike that only the outbreak of the war averted. Kipling's "Batteries Out of Ammunition" explicitly links workers' gains with soldiers' deaths: "If any mourn us in the workshop, say / We died because the shift kept holiday." Another noncombatant who attacked workers' economic gains was Dugald Sutherland MacColl (1859–1948), who spent the war years as Keeper of the Wallace Collection. His "The Miners' Response" has an epigraph from a speech by the Minister of Munitions: "We must keep on striking, striking, striking . . ." MacColl feels that the workers have taken the Minister's advice too literally:

> We do: the present desperate stage
> Of fighting brings us luck;
> And in the higher war we wage
> (For higher wage) *We struck.*

G. K. Chesterton's "France" attacks the economic opportunism of French civilians rather than of English ones. After introducing his subject by alluding to France's occupation by the Germans, he attacks the venality of French politicians and profiteers:

> The rulers smote, the feeble crying "War!"
>   The usurers robbed, the naked crying "Peace!"
>
> And her own feet were caught in nets of gold,
>   And her own soul profaned by sects that squirm,
> And little men climbed her high seats and sold
>   Her honour to the vulture and the worm.

The poem concludes with the hope that France "Clear the slow mists from her half-darkened eyes." The focus of anger is not on those who require war, but on those who interfere with the Allies' ability to prosecute it.

Some protests went beyond Sassoon's brutal reality to address the ethics of war. Chesterton's "For a War Memorial" argues that the truly unfortunate participants in the war are not the hucksters, senates, schools, or usurers who have in their various ways allowed the war to continue, but soldiers who "died / To prove they were not dead." Their tragedy is that their deaths were without meaning, even to themselves. F. W. Harvey's "To the Devil on

His Appalling Decadence" takes a similar attitude toward the futility of soldiers' deaths: "Oh, 'Krieg ist Krieg,' we know, and 'C'est la guerre!' / But Satan, don't you feel a trifle sick?"

Many emphasized the ubiquity of death. Herbert Asquith's "Nightfall" asks, "Is this a Kingdom? Then give Death the crown, / For here no emperor hath won, save He." A. A. Milne (1882–1956), best known as the creator of Winnie the Pooh, emphasizes futility with a much lighter touch. Milne, who had fought at the Somme as a lieutenant in the Royal Warwickshire Regiment, received his commission after Robert Graves's father, A. P. Graves, introduced Milne to the colonel of the regiment. That his war poetry is satirical owes much to his experience as assistant editor of *Punch* from 1906 to 1914. In "Gold Braid," from *The Sunny Side* (1922), Milne makes his point indirectly:

> Same old trenches, same old view,
>   Same old rats as blooming tame,
> Same old dug-outs, nothing new,
>   Same old smell, the very same,
> Same old bodies out in front,
>   Same old *strafe* from two till four,
> Same old scratching, same old 'unt,
>   Same old bloody war.

The purpose of the war becomes lost in the constant presence of filth, decay, and death. A similar approach to war protest came from H. Smalley Sarson, who served in the ranks. He often published poems in the *Poetry Review,* and his volume of poetry, *From Field and Hospital,* appeared in 1916. As early as September 1916 his protests against war's destruction were in print. His "The Shell," after describing the flight of an artillery round, ends in protest:

> The brains of science, the money of fools
> Had fashioned an iron slave
> Destined to kill, yet the futile end
> Was a child's uprooted grave.

A few poets anticipated in their verse the approach to war protest of the 1960s and 1970s. Robert Palmer (1888–1916), who served as a captain in the 6th Battalion, Royal Hampshire Regiment, was wounded in Mesopotamia in January 1916 and died of wounds incurred at the Battle of Umm-Al-Hannal. Arthur Balfour had stood as Palmer's godfather, and Palmer knew both A. P. Herbert and Julian Grenfell. His poem "How Long, O Lord" appeared in the London *Times* on 15 October 1915. Palmer's sonnet begins "How long, O Lord, how long, before the flood / Of crimson-welling carnage shall abate?" He presents the carnage as offensive to the heavens and castigates the "nations great" which "sink to the state / Of brute barbarians, whose ferocious mind / Gloats o'er the bloody havoc of their kind, / Not knowing love or mercy." His question, "Lord, how long / Shall Satan in high places lead the blind / To battle for the passions of the strong?", leads to a plea for men to regard hatred and pride as "their deadliest foe." By attributing desire for war to all nations involved and by identifying the slaughter as offensive to the Deity, Palmer transcends the more narrow protests against the conduct and prolongation of the war that did not question the war's necessity.

Paul Bewsher's attitude toward his role in a mechanized war, expressed in "Nox Mortis," establishes an ethically based protest against the fact of war, rather than merely criticizing inept prosecution of the struggle. He defines his role as having to "bear my poison o'er the gloomy land, / And let it loose with hard unsparing hand." The contrast between the peaceful solitude of the air and the devastation that bombs bring to those below afflicts Bewsher's conscience: "for I have blindly killed, / And nameless hearts with nameless sorrow filled." His concluding stanza protests the war for requiring him to inflict suffering as well as for forcing others to bear it:

> Thrice cursèd War
>   Which bids that I
> Such death should pour
>   Down from the sky.
> O, Star of Peace, rise swiftly in the East
> That from such slaying men may be released.

Bewsher's focus is on his ethical and moral dilemma. Like Owen, he seems a "conscientious objector with a very seared conscience." Instead of reviling civilians, politicians, profiteers, and others for interfering with the Allies' attempts to win the war, Bewsher faces the implications of his own actions and the responsibility that all participants in war must bear to varying degrees. This approach was extremely rare during the Great War.

9

Women and the War

DURING THE WAR, VIRTUALLY ANY SOLDIER'S POEMS, IRRESPECTIVE OF MERIT, were in great demand, verses by a "fallen" trench poet even more so. Frank Swinnerton indicated his opinion of the sudden interest in war poetry by entitling one chapter of *The Georgian Literary Scene* "The War-Time Afflatus, 1914–1918," but he did observe that the "disenchantment" of the soldier poets at least "was something true and original, the protest of some men who, coming from peace and hope into a shambles, had had their beautiful dreams of life broken"[1]

When Swinnerton turned his attention to the women poets, he revealed considerable contempt:

> You will find in the poems of the women of War-time no comparable disenchantment; and yet their number can hardly have been less than that of the poems by young men of the same period. Little exercises in verse were as common to women as they were to men; the records of heightened mood, intuitions of pain, comments upon the exceptional scene, slight dramatic lyrics in which—it was the temper of war-time— they pretended to speak in the persons of harlots, dead men, and children puzzled by sorrow and brutality. Poetry seemed so easy, such a tender, delicate means of expressing a sense of darkened homes, darkened minds, darkened streets; and free verse was such a simple medium for light pens to use. One had but to take paper and break a slightly sentimental prose into unequal lengths; and lo! one was part of the poetic impulse of the age. No wonder that there was a multitude of little books; the wonder, rather, was that there should be so few per head of the population.[2]

Examples of the pretense to speak from the front abound. One C. A. Renshaw ended the poem "My Mate" with a description of a soldier leaning over a dead comrade to exclaim, "God! let me touch his lips / And go, lest I forget I am a man!" The danger of the forgetting becomes understandable when one learns that "C. A." stands for "Constance Ada." She published *England's Boys: A Woman's War Poems* (1916), *Battle and Beyond* (1917), and *Lest We Forget: Poems* (1937). Similarly Margaret Louise Woods (1856–1945) published "The Gunner's Horses" in the *Graphic* on 19 June 1915.

This poem falls considerably short in its attempt to describe a gunner's reflections: "All I know / Is I looked for them in vain when the early sun shone low / Along the dusty plain." Gunners at the front were more likely to see mud than dust. Similarly unrealistic depictions appear in other collections, such as *Fighting Men* (1916) by Cicely Fox Smith (d. 1954). The reading of such volumes can arouse sympathy for Swinnerton's point of view. Swinnerton's bias has a firmer basis than mere sexism in one startling fact. Almost all the women war poets were hawks to varying degrees, and their appeals to chivalric tradition and to chauvinism frequently went beyond those of the men. Most women war poets encouraged the men to enlist, exhorted soldiers to continue fighting despite heavy losses, and praised women and other noncombatants for their share in the sacrifice.

However, although many of the women war poets adopted false voices as facilely and heedlessly as Swinnerton claimed, many women sought an active role in the struggle. Some, including Vera Brittain, eagerly accepted the hardships of auxiliary service as V.A.D. (Voluntary Aide Detachment) nurses, thereby occasionally coming as close to the front as many "scarlet Majors" and Anglican chaplains. Brittain has commented that "relatively few women played an active part in the First World War. They were, on the whole, merely aides operating behind the various fronts. Such roles as they did fulfill were modest, subsidiary, and insignificant. War was a man's business."[3] The majority of women poets, like the men, persisted in a view of war that had become outmoded with the arrival of the machine age. Partly because women did not experience trench life or actual combat, their verses lacked immediacy and realism when depicting war scenes, but the women felt the effects of the war as directly as many noncombatant male poets. The loss of relatives and friends, the experience of treating or visiting casualties in military hospitals, and the changes in civilian life wrought by the unexpected duration of the fighting inspired women to address the war in their verse.

Swinnerton, writing almost two decades after the Armistice, condemned the women poets' lack of "disenchantment" with some justice, but he ridiculed the women's poetical failings without adding that most of the male poets' verses shared these defects, and without acknowledging that the women poets provided the same range of responses as the men who addressed the war, soldiers and civilians alike. Women wrote calls to action in the spirit of Robert Bridges's "Wake Up, England," encouragement to continue the fight despite tragic losses in the vein of John McCrae's "In Flanders Fields," and appeals for heroism in the mode of Herbert Asquith's "The Volunteer." Some addressed the importance of women and other noncombatants who helped to prosecute the war. Others exploited the tradition of nature poetry to make implicit protests against the destruction of battle, as did Alec Waugh in "From Albert to Bapaume." Still others protested more explicitly, as did Wilfred Owen and Siegfried Sassoon. In Vera Brittain's work one can find the groping for meaning that critics have praised in the war poetry of Max Plowman, Isaac Rosenberg, Charles Hamilton Sorley, Edward Thomas, and Arthur Graeme West.

Some of the more popular and compelling calls to action came from the women poets. Although barely known today, Jessie Pope reached a wide audience with her verse. *Jessie Pope's War Poems* (1915), *More War Poems* (1915), and frequent contributions to periodicals consisted largely of blatant appeals to patriotism. Unwittingly she helped to inspire Owen's "Dulce et Decorum Est," one early draft of which Owen subscribed "To Jessie Pope etc." Her "The Call" alternates encouragement to enlist with attribution of ignoble motives to those who do not enlist:

> Who's for the trench—
>   Are you, my laddie?
> Who'll follow the French—
>   Will you, my laddie?
> Who's fretting to begin,
> Who's going out to win?
> And who wants to save his skin—
>   Do you, my laddie?

The juxtaposition of noble heroism and base cowardice will continue after victory:

> Who'll earn the Empire's thanks—
>   Will you, my laddie?
> Who'll swell the victor's ranks—
>   Will you, my laddie?
> When that procession comes,
> Banners and rolling drums—
> Who'll stand and bite his thumbs—
>   Will you, my laddie?

Critic Arthur E. Lane comments of Pope, "If the subject were not so serious, one could afford to laugh off Miss Pope as the faintly ridiculous lady she was. But it was she, not Owen, who had the public ear, and her jingling verse was a lie no less terrible for the inanity it displayed."[4] Other poets, such as Mary Symon, whose *Deveron Days* appeared in 1933, appealed without adding an explicit threat against laggards. In "A Call to Arms" (*Graphic*, 26 December 1914), she states the situation baldly:

> Your country needs you. Leave the plough
>   To rust in homeland sod,
> Give weakling hands your work to do,
>   Leave child and wife to God.

Her feeling for the warrior tradition becomes explicit in the diction of the first stanza: "The cry that thrilled our sires of old / Wakes Britain once again."

Others continued to support the war effort even after the discouragingly heavy losses. The Irish poet Katharine Tynan (1861–1931) published collections of her war poetry throughout the war, including *Flower of Youth* (1915), *The Holy War* (1916), *Late Songs* (1917), and *Herb o' Grace* (1918). She spent the war helping its victims by working as a nurse and by supporting soldiers' families while one of her sons fought in Palestine and the other in France. She was less eager to issue direct appeals than Pope, but she regarded the war as both necessary and just. Her picture of the war as an exercise in chivalry becomes apparent in "New Heaven," where she describes modern soldiers: "Paradise now has many a Knight, / Many a lordkin, many lords, / Glimmer of armour, dinted and bright, / The young Knights have put on new swords." The last stanza takes this view to its extreme:

> Paradise now is the soldiers' land,
>   Their own country its shining sod,
> Comrades all in a merry band;
>   And the young Knights' laughter pleaseth God.

She supports continuing the war despite casualities. In "To the Others," she tells a mother "Your son and my son, . . . / Should they be broken in the Lord's wars—Peace! / He Who has given them—are they not His?" The poem ends with the unmistakable conclusion that casualty lists should not deflect the nation from its "Holy War": "Your son and my son for the Great Crusade, / With the banner of Christ over them—our knights new-made." She does not always retreat into chivalric imagery, however. In "High Summer," she combines pastoral description with the refrain "They die in Flanders to keep these for me." Her preferred mode, nevertheless, is romantic, as she reveals in "The Old Soldier":

> Lest the young soldiers be strange in heaven,
>   God bids the old soldier they all adored
> Come to Him and wait for them, clean, new-shriven,
>   A happy doorkeeper in the House of the Lord.

Tynan's verse occasionally comments on her fear that a soldier might not return, but most of her poems are optimistic. She expressed her feeling that the war was necessary, that the Deity approved it, and that English chivalry would prevail.

Another Irish poet, Winifred M. Letts (b. 1882), provided similar encouragement and support by emphasizing the justice of England's cause, the gratitude that those at home felt for the soldiers, and the romantic nature of the struggle. In addition to children's books and plays, she published two volumes of verse, *Hallow-e'en, and Poems of the War* (1916) and *The Spires of Oxford and Other Poems* (1918). Her best known poem, "The Spires of Oxford," is an appreciation of students who "left the peaceful river . . . / to seek a bloody sod." (The response of trench soldiers to the second line is best left to the imagination.) For Letts, "They gave their merry youth away / For country and for God," and she ends the poem with the hope that "God bring you to a fairer place / Than even Oxford town." Despite her V.A.D. service at Manchester Base Hospital and elsewhere, she clung to a distinctly prewar vision of combat.

In "The Call to Arms in Our Street," she counsels a weeping mother to "Keep your tears until they go" and wonders who will find food for the children during the men's absence, but she also identifies the women's "proper" role: "We must smile and cheer them so." In "To a Soldier in Hospital," her comparison of war and a football match recalls Sir Henry Newbolt:

> An Empire's team, a rougher football field,
>   The end—perhaps your grave.
> What matter? On the winning of a goal
>   You staked your soul.

In this poem she shifts from recollection of schoolboy games to the soldier's affinity with the sufferings of Christ, a theme which she applies to the Army chaplain in "Chaplain to the Forces." Assuming the schoolboy code, she tells the chaplain,

> It is not small, your priesthood's price,
> To be a man and yet stand by,
> To hold your life while others die,
> To bless, not share the sacrifice,
> To watch the strife and take no part—
> You with the fire at your heart.

Service to "our great Captain Christ" requires the chaplain's patient endurance of his comparative safety. Such a view might excite mirth in the trenches, but many civilians for whom Letts wrote would not know any better.

Margaret Peterson (1883–1933), in the spirit of John McCrae's "In Flanders Fields," appeals to soldiers not to give up the struggle. In 1914 she wrote *A Woman's Message*, a broadside published by the Parliamentary Recruiting Committee, and in 1915 she published *A Woman's Message, 1915 (and Other Poems)*. Early in the war she worked in a British hospital lent to the French army and, following her success at winning the Andrew Melrose Prize (£250) for the best first novel of 1913, she abandoned poetry to write several novels. "A Mother's Dedication" appeals to a son to fight on:

> Dear son of mine, by all the lives behind you;
> By all our fathers fought for in the past;
> In this great war to which your birth has brought you,
> Acquit you well, hold you our honour fast!

No negotiated peace for her. In "The Great Sacrifice," which appeared in the *Graphic* on 3 April 1915, she prays, "Teach him, O Christ, how best to fight his fight, / Then teach him how to die." For her, Christ must "Grant that these soldiers, dying for their Cause, / Shall know it not in vain."

In similar spirit, Mildred Huxley encourages the next generation to continue, if necessary. In "To My Godson," she writes, "The lot is fallen, O child, to you / To finish all they had to leave, / And by their sacrifice achieve, / The manifold desires they knew." She offers the prospect of glorious death as consolation in "Subalterns: A Song of Oxford":

> They who had all, gave all. Their half-writ story
>   Lies in the empty halls they knew so well,
> But they, the knights of God, shall see His glory,
>   And find the Grail ev'n in the fire of hell.

The sincerity with which some women poets encouraged men to fight reaches its unwitting apex in "The War Shrine" by Emmeline Banbury (*Graphic*, 28 September 1918), with a parallel to the chief irony of Swift's projector in "A Modest Proposal": Banbury, reflecting on a war memorial, regrets that she, who has "no life to give," lacks sons to spare.

Several women poets focused on the fallen to provide further impetus for the war. In "A Cossack Charge," Jessie Pope reveals her immersion in the chivalric tradition. During the charge, "The narrow eyes are laughing, / The wine of war they're quaffing, / The glorious draught of swift, resistless death." Poetic exaltation of martyrs served to encourage others to follow their example. Among several tributes to Edith Cavell, the nurse executed by the Germans in Belgium after she helped prisoners to evade recapture, is "Nurse Edith Cavell" by Alice Meynell (1847–1922). Unlike those who emphasized German brutality without admitting that both French and British forces had done the same to civilians of both genders who had interfered with prisoners, Meynell focused on the thoughts of Cavell as she awaited her death. Cavell showed the same patience with which she had "outwatched the dying," found the vigil shorter than vigils over her patients, and "Ere the cock / Announced that day she met the Immortal Dead."

Appreciation of sacrifices by the lower classes came from a surprising source in the poems of Lady Judith Blunt, Baroness Wentworth (1873–1957). Her great-grandfather was Lord Byron; her grandfather, the first Lord Lovelace; and her father, Wilfred Scawen Blunt. Her approach was to praise the men of the ranks for their courage, which, before the war, had not emerged. In "Known to the Police," Wentworth describes a soldier "By training bad, by nature most perverse," whom a call to arms transformed: "To-day the wreck of him was laid to rest, / The cross of flame and honour on his breast." In "Rank and File," published in the *Graphic* less than two weeks before the Armistice, she claims,

> Not to the leaders, whose great names will live
> In Fate's proud chronicles of victory,
> Is due the greatest honour that we give
> To those who died, to those who still must die.
> Rather, to heroes' blood too cheaply shed,
> To unrecorded deeds, to those who lie
> In shambles of the unrecorded dead. . . .

Her focus on the power of war to redeem an unheroic life resembles that of Herbert Asquith in "The Volunteer." In "The Last Gun," published in the *Graphic* two weeks after the Armistice, a soldier remains

> Unbeaten to the last, though hope had fled,
> Breathless he fought with reckless hardihood;
> Dizzy and sick at heart and weak for food,
> Blinded with rage and pain, with aching head.
>   He would not fail . . . No power should make him yield,
>   Though all the world surrendered.

The poem is a thinly disguised chivalric appeal to continue to fight at all costs.

Several women used their verses to call attention to the extent of women's role in the war. Frequent among the themes of these verses was the burden of loss sustained by the women who remained at home. In "The Devonshire Mother," Marjorie Wilson focused on the fears of a mother for her son. Since Wilson worked in the War Relief Office and served as a V.A.D. nurse at Netley, she saw the reality of the apprehensions she expressed in her poems. In dialect, a mother relates her memories of her son's childhood, her constant hopes for his sudden return, her prayers that he be safe, and her confidence that the boy thinks of her. Like many of these poems, "The Devonshire Mother" visualizes the war as a call to which all classes have responded: "For there's Squire's son have gone for one, and Parson's son—and mine." The focus, however, is not on the soldier's role but on the mother's.

May O'Rourke, better known as Thomas Hardy's secretary and as the author of biographies of Hardy and of Margaret Sinclair, also emphasized the burden of those left to wait in ignorance. "In Memoriam, 1916," printed in the *Graphic* on 15 July 1916, is a Petrarchan sonnet that begins with the immediate effect of a soldier's death:

> Love and our dreams are over: Hope is dumb,
> Your coffin closed the darkness on my hours,
> Your grave has left its slime upon my flowers,
> I live your Death: . . .

The remainder of the sonnet addresses the problems of learning to live with the soldier's death and leads to a surprising ending:

> I curse the Thing that left you, damp and mute,
> In alien mould—then suddenly know you are
> Safer than I—and thank God on my knees!

The introduction does not prepare the reader for a conclusion derived from Rupert Brooke's sonnet "Safety" ("And if these poor limbs die, safest of all").

Agnes M. Mackenzie (1891–1955), later known as a Scottish historian and biographer, also focuses on bereft women in "Piob-Mhor" (*Graphic*, 26 June 1915). After introducing "Sorrow in the glens," which has resulted from "Brave men and strong" having gone to "a foreign resting," the poem emphasizes the women's loss:

> Sorrow at night, oh sorrow, sorrow:
> Sorrow of women among the Islands:
> Ay but the kites and the gleds are merry:
> Sorrow of women!

"To all Fathers and Mothers whose Sons have been Killed in the War" (*Graphic*, 12 January 1918) by Winifred Ellis goes farther in extolling the people at home for their sacrifice. The grieving parents become identical with God in their grief—He also gave an only Son:

> You, the Elect, can sympathise with God.
> You know the grief, the love, the awful pride,
> You only know what it means to give the Son.

Such poems, emphasizing the burden sustained on the home front, were common, although Ellis's attains new heights of presumption.

Others objected more explicitly to the prevailing view that this was only a man's war. May Wedderburn Cannan (b. 1893) served first as a V.A.D. nurse and then in the Intelligence Service. Her books include *In War Time: Poems* (1917) and *The Splendid Days: Poems* (1919). After the war she returned to

Oxford (she had been educated at Wychwood School) to work for the Oxford University Press, and later she was assistant librarian to the Athenaeum Club (London). She addressed women's roles specifically in "When the Vision Dies," urging women to realize that "this is your War; in this loneliest hour you ride / Down the roads he knew; / Though he comes no more at night he will kneel at your side / For comfort to dream with you." More explicit was Evelyn Underhill (Evelyn Stuart Moore, 1875–1941), widely known as a mystical writer and poet, whose study *Mysticism* appeared in 1911. Her "Non-Combatants" addressed the role of those not in uniform to argue that "We faltered not":

> Never of us be said
> We had no war to wage,
> Because our womanhood,
> Because the weight of age,
> Held us in servitude.
> None sees us fight,
> Yet we in the long night
> Battle to give release
> To all whom we must send to seek and die for peace.

Underhill specifies the agony of awaiting news from the front and emphasizes that "Theirs be the hard, but ours the lonely bed." She argues that noncombatants lack self-pity and do not complain as they accept their burden.

Most women active in the war were V.A.D. nurses. The contrast between subjective and objective views of V.A.D. service appears in two poems. Hellen Margaret Richmond's "The Crimson Cross" (*Graphic*, 17 August 1918) calls attention to the sacrifice demonstrated by the Red Cross, which, "Across the shell-torn plains of France, / Amid the havoc, blood and pain, / . . . brings good cheer and strength again / To those who faint beneath the night." In the poem, the Red Cross "calmly dares War's hideous woe / To aid in righting deadly wrong." Ultimately, the "men who march thro' Hell's wide doors, / In passing, murmur down the line, / 'We, about to die, salute thee!'" Her implication is that the soldiers of the trenches regard the sacrifices of the Red Cross nurses as greater than their own. In contrast, Letty Ison, whose "Song of a Night Nurse" appeared in the *Graphic* on 6 April 1918, is less interested in asserting the nurse's importance than in describing her growing hope that the war will soon end. In three short stanzas she contrasts midnight and dawn, winter and spring, and war and peace. The final stanza, in beautifully simple diction, conveys her hope:

> Sick faces sternly set
> Across the low lights stare.

'Tis war-time yet,
But peace is in the air.

The poem does not belabor the fatigue and depression of hospital duty to invite sympathy or gratitude for the V.A.D.

Like many of the trench poets, the women poets found pastoral contrast a means of criticizing the war. Alice Meynell wrote "Summer in England 1914" to describe the contrast between the apparent peacefulness of nature and the encroaching war. After two stanzas of idealized imagery, the contrast becomes explicit: "And when / This chaste young silver sun went up / Softly, a thousand shattered men, / One wet corruption, heaped the plain / After a league-long throb of pain." After returning briefly to traditional pastoral images of flocks, flowers, and serene skies, the poem ends with war's intrusion: "Yonder are men shot through the eyes. / Love, hide thy face / From man's unpardonable race!" Such contrasts form an explicit protest against the war.

Lady Gertrude Bone (1876–1962), a novelist whose husband was the artist Sir Muirhead Bone and whose son was critic and painter Stephen Bone, makes a similar protest in "From the Night," which contrasts the serenity of moonlight to the chaos of earth:

> If I saw crosses raised above faces,
>   Hid from the moon,
> I should say, "Shine thou, bright in sterility,
> Roll with thy seas of tranquillity, rainbows, and reverie.
> Smitten by a death, earth yet holdeth a gratitude—
>   Lo! the world hopeth!"

Two other poets better known for their prose made similar contrasts. Winifred Holtby (1898–1935), whose novel *South Riding* appeared in 1936, served in the WAAC in 1918 and became a close friend of Vera Brittain at Oxford after the war. Her poem "Trains in France," originally appearing in *Time and Tide*, describes how the sound of trains returns her thoughts to wartime France:

> And I,
> Who thought I had forgotten all the War
> Remember now a night in Camiers,
> When, through the darkness, as I wakeful lay,
>   I heard the trains,
>   The savage, shrieking trains,
> Call to each other their fierce hunting-cry,
> Ruthless, inevitable as the beasts
>   After their prey.

The novelist Dame Rose Macaulay (1881–1958), in "Picnic, July 1917," recalls the crashing of guns in France that contrasted sharply to normal expectations of a country picnic:

> Oh, we'll lie quite still, nor listen nor look,
> While the earth's bounds reel and shake,
> Lest, battered too long, our walls and we
> Should break . . . should break.

Although Macaulay referred to the war as a "capitalist's war" in *Potterism* (1920), she hastened to add that it was a "war that had to be won." Her belief in the war's necessity, however, did not blind her to the war's harrowing effects.

Fredegond Shove (1889–1949) presented her protest in "The Farmer," in which a farmer walks his fields in only apparent peace. "He seems to be the only man alive / And thinking through the twilight of this world," but the speaker knows that "there is war, / And has been now for three eternal years." The speaker imagines, behind the farmer, "Wide hosts of men who once could walk like him / In freedom, quite alone with night and day, / Uncounted shapes of living flesh and bone, /Worn dull, quenched dry, gone blind and sick, with war," and the poet awaits the day "when peace shall come / With stillness, and long shivers, after death." Gertrude Ford attempts a similar protesting contrast in "Nature in War-Time," in which she focuses on the damage to Nature caused by the war. She asks,

> Grieve not those meadows scarred and cleft,
>   Mined with deep holes and reft of grass,
> Gardens where not a flower is left,
>   Fouled streams, once clear as glass?

Her conclusion is that the earth affords "Such works as only God could limn / Wrecked by thy madness, Man!"

A few women poets explicitly cursed war and those who allowed it to continue. Emilia S. Lorimer took this tack astonishingly early. Her "Work and War" appeared in the *Poetry Review* on 5 November 1914. She contrasted the beautiful days of work, when "ploughing and building and weaving" men worked at constructive pursuits, with the war: "Another night cursed I, and will curse, the black warring race; / To-night, O for those days!" Another protesting poet, Jessie Annie Anderson, often wrote in a more traditional mode. Her "The Weeper in the Glen" (*Graphic*, 19 February 1918) mourns the death of a beloved and reflects how hard it will be "to think I'm shut in grief / That ithers should be free." In "The Wastage of War"

(*Graphic*, 14 December 1918), she describes women waiting for "men and lads who cannot come again" and then prays:

> Jesus of Pity, wake all women's souls
> To War's cruel, wasteful hideous misuse
> Of mortal Cups the Maker made to hold
> Souls and the Sacramental Wine of Love.

However, this poem did not appear until after the Armistice.

Elizabeth Shillito, whose poems frequently appeared in the *Graphic* during the war, emphasized the sacrifices of the war dead. Her sympathy was consistently with the victims of the war and more convincing than the facile and superficial feelings of most of her contemporaries. "The Failures," published in the *Graphic* on 5 October 1918, praised those whose sacrifices remained unrecognized:

> No honours from their King
> E'er shone upon their breast,
> Swift flights on glitt'ring wing,
>   And then—their rest.

This poem, inspired by the graveyard at a school for fliers, recognizes the sacrifices of those who did not live to finish their training. Another of her poems, "His Sacrifice," like Owen's "Mental Cases," focuses on the reality of shell shock:

> His life he gave not, but he gave
>   His peace of mind, his happy youth;
> Not his the calm within the grave,
>   But living pain that knows no ruth.

Although this poem is more abstract and more general in its language than Owen's, it reveals a remarkably early awareness of the sufferings of soldiers at the front. The poem appeared in the *Graphic* on 28 October 1916, much earlier than similar treatments by trench poets appeared in print.

Charlotte Mew (1869–1929), whose poetry Hardy admired, wrote the most sophisticated protest of the women poets. "The Cenotaph (September 1919)" places a war memorial into a context of protest that might have appealed to the dead soldiers:

> Only, when all is done and said,
> God is not mocked and neither are the dead.
> For this will stand in our Market-place—
>   Who'll sell, who'll buy
>   (Will you or I

Lie each to each with the better grace)?
While looking into every busy whore's and huckster's face
As they drive their bargains, is the Face
Of God: and some young, piteous, murdered face.

Such protests, as effective as those of actual combatants, could question the validity of sacrifice, but, since the women could not experience the trenches directly, the more realistic expressions that grew from experience of war remained outside their scope.

Although many women poets lacked talent for verse and suffered from misapprehensions of reality that even a first-rate talent could not have transcended, one woman poet, Vera Brittain (1896–1970), combined a genuine talent with a desire to grasp the significance of the war. The daughter of a small-town Midland manufacturer, she won an exhibition to Somerville College, Oxford, and was studying there when the war began. Despite objections from the faculty, she left Oxford to serve as a V.A.D. nurse in London, Malta, and France. Both her brother, Edward, and her fiancé, Roland Leighton, died in the war. Although her sorrow was great, she came to view the war from a perspective that transcended her personal losses. *Testament of Youth* (1933) is Brittain's memoir of her provincial upbringing, her early struggles for the feminist cause, her war experiences, and her disenchantment with the postwar indifference to her generation's sacrifices.

Robert Wohl has criticized her memoir for being "too self-indulgent, too self-pitying, and too lacking in self-irony to be good literature,"[5] but Brittain's perspective of the war's meaning was more objective than Wohl's criticism suggests. As early as 1917 she wrote to her brother, "I think that 'Before' and 'After' this war will make the same kind of division in human history as 'B.C.' and 'A.D.'" In retrospect, she realized, "At the time this seemed an extravagant and even absurd assessment, but after half a century it does not seem to me that I was so far wrong in my estimate of that tremendous perspective."[6] In her view, "The work of Sassoon and his near contemporaries was one long cry of protest precisely because they were the products of an exceptionally fortunate social era,"[7] and she foresaw that "If any of us is to have a future on this earth, it must depend on man's ability to reconquer his power over the machine, which he yielded in the First World War."[8] In verse which she wrote during and shortly after the war, collected in *Verses of a VAD* (1918) and *Poems of the War and After* (1934), she demonstrated a much more mature grasp of the struggle than any of the other women poets, and certainly than most of the men.

As early as 1914, Brittain's verses recognized the ironies of the war. In "August, 1914," she poses God reflecting that "Men have forgotten Me," and thus "since redemption comes through pain," God brought the war: "But where His desolation trod, / The people in their agony / Despairing cried:

'There is no God!' " Her view of heroics was hardly chivalric. In "To My Brother (In Memory of July 1st, 1916)," written 11 June 1918 (four days before Edward's death), Brittain referred to the Military Cross Edward had won during the Somme Offensive as less important than his "battle-wounds," which are "scars upon my heart," and she hoped that Edward would "endure to lead the Last Advance." Three months later, in "To a V.C.," she recalls Shillito's view of military medals:

> 'Tis not your valour's meed alone you bear
> Who stand the hero of a nation's pride;
> For on that humble Cross you live to wear
> Your friends were crucified.

She concludes that the medal "Is worn for them by you."

Brittain's poetry describing women's wartime suffering reveals a similar development. In February 1916, writing "Perhaps . . . To R. A. L." in memory of her fallen fiancé, she addresses her loss in extremely personalized terms:

> But, though kind Time may many joys renew,
> There is one greatest joy I shall not know
> Again, because my heart for loss of You
> Was broken, long ago.

A year later, in "The Troop Train;" she reveals greater control:

> And often I have wondered since,
>   Repicturing that train,
> How many of those laughing souls
>   Came down the line again.

In "The Last Post," the bugle asks,

> Whether the eyes which battle sealed in sleep
> Will open to *réveillé* once again,
> And forms, once mangled, into rapture leap,
> Forgetful of their pain.

However, she does not commit herself to a conclusion: ". . . stars above the camp shine on, / Giving no answer for our sorrow's ease."

Some of the soldier poets, notably Charles Hamilton Sorley, Max Plowman, Arthur Graeme West, and Edward Thomas, recognized their kinship with the German soldier instead of denying the humanity of the "Hun." In "The German Ward (*Inter Arma Caritas*)," written in September 1917, Brittain expresses her compassion for German casualties, drawing from her experiences as a V.A.D. with wounded German prisoners:

> . . . I learnt that human mercy turns alike to friend or foe
> When the darkest hour of all is creeping nigh,
> And those who slew our dearest, when their lamps were burning low,
> Found help and pity ere they came to die.

She visualizes a day when "much will be forgotten" of the war, but "I shall always see the vision of Love working amidst arms / In the ward wherein the wounded prisoners lay."

Like other women poets, Brittain comments on the forgotten or unheralded roles of women who served during the war. In "The Sisters Buried at Lemnos," written in October 1916, she offers her thoughts after passing the graves of three Canadian nurses:

> Seldom they enter into song or story;
>   Poets praise the soldier's might and deeds of War,
> But few exalt the Sisters, and the glory
>   Of women dead beneath a distant star.

She does not limit her social commentary to feminist concerns, however. "The Lament of the Demobilised," written in 1919 and published in *Oxford Poetry, 1920,* focuses on the plight of the returned soldiers as well as of the women who served: " 'Four years,' some say consolingly. 'Oh well, / What's that? You're young. . . .' " Brittain comments that "others stayed behind and just got on— / Got on the better since we were away" and adds that "no one talked heroics now," although the stay-at-homes had been willing to benefit from heroics during the war. The poem's conclusion is extremely direct:

> "You threw four years into the melting-pot—
> Did you indeed!" these others cry. "Oh well,
> The more fool you!"
> And we're beginning to agree with them.

Brittain managed to place the war into a perspective wider than that of most of her contemporaries, but she never compromised her feeling that the sacrifice of her generation was worthwhile (she ever remained an admirer of Rupert Brooke), and she frequently felt that those for whom the sacrifice had been made were hardly worthy of it.

One might criticize the chauvinistic excesses of some of the women war poets or ridicule their failure to provide the "curative realism" that might have awakened the British public to the horrors of the Great War. However, lacking direct experience of trench warfare, the women poets were remarkable in that their patriotic effusions were not very far beyond those of the soldiers who should have known better, and even more remarkable in that some of them—notably Mew, Shillito, and Brittain—were able to respond to the war in ways that a retrospective view can approve.

PART III
Innovative Responses

Edmund Blunden and Edward Thomas

EDMUND BLUNDEN (1896–1974) AND EDWARD THOMAS (1878–1917) HARDLY fit the usual definition of trench poets. Blunden's war poetry as such did not become available until after the war. Blunden did appear in the final volume of Marsh's *Georgian Poetry* series, but, as Bergonzi has observed, Blunden differed markedly from the Georgian norm: "Blunden's world of nature is not particularly wild or wayward in a Romantic fashion: it is ordered and in harmony with man, and it offers, above all, an image of civilization, the pattern of a pastoral, pre-industrial society. It goes a good deal deeper than the weekend-cottage view of nature of the typical Georgian."[1] Blunden's description of himself as "a harmless young shepherd in a soldier's coat" at the end of *Undertones of War* (1928) reflects his awareness of his place in a pastoral tradition. When his colonel, who had read a favorable review of Blunden's earlier "trifling collection of verses," quickly moved Blunden from line duty to battalion headquarters, he may well have saved Blunden's life, but Blunden still saw much of the worst fighting.

Thomas had only a few poems published in his lifetime, and those under the pseudonym "Edward Eastaway" (a family name). He tried to interest both Harold Monro and Edward Marsh in his verse, but to no avail. Monro, who had rejected T. S. Eliot's early work in 1914, returned several of Thomas's poems on the grounds that he had not had time to read them. When Thomas sent more poems early in 1915, hoping that Monro's Poetry Bookshop would publish them, Monro again rejected Thomas's verse. After Thomas's death, Marsh refused to consider his work on the grounds that he would not publish posthumous war poetry, justly fearing a plethora of submissions from the relatives of fallen poets. Thomas never did gain formal recognition from the Georgians as a poet, which makes his present association with Georgianism ironical.

Philip Hobsbaum has found a significant difference between Thomas and the Georgians: "The difference between Thomas and even the better Georgians is that his work is an advance on that of the poetry of a previous generation. His is a genuinely modern sensibility."[2] Thomas was particularly concerned that he not be identified as a war poet. Writing to his publisher Roger Ingpen, Thomas was explicit: "I beg you not to make use of my situation, as a publisher might be tempted to, now or in the event of any kind of accident to me, to advertise the book."[3] Thomas felt that most war poetry was occasional verse and, as such, was inferior. He deliberately refrained from creating overtly patriotic or curative poetry.

Thomas's quiet patriotism was an extension of his love for the English countryside. The tendency of most patriotic poets to be jingoistic in their appeals has made any patriotic appeal suspect. Perhaps Thomas's unquestionable acceptance of the need to defend England has unfairly associated him with what Swinnerton has called "The War-Time Afflatus." As Thomas's friend J. W. Haines has commented,

> The war tinges many [of Thomas's poems] and directly inspires not a few. Nor was his attitude to the War that of the War Poets in general; he was far older than most of them. He did not embrace it passionately like Rupert Brooke, nor revolt from it as passionately as did Wilfred Owen.[4]

In a letter to W. H. Hudson, Thomas wrote that "I thought Hardy's poem in *The Times* 'Ere the barn-cocks say / Night is growing gray,' the only good one concerned with the war."[5] His acceptance of the need to fight outweighs, in many critics' views, the merits of his verse.

Samuel Hynes links Thomas and Blunden in a poetic tradition separate from the Georgians on the one hand and the American-led modernists on the other:

> Thomas's proper poetic company is clear, then: it is that tradition of outsiders which descends in modern poetry from Hardy, through Frost to Thomas, and includes the early rhyming Lawrence, Edmund Blunden, Robert Graves, Andrew Young, and R. S. Thomas. Together these poets compose a major modern tradition, less noisy than the School of Pound, and without the convenience of a collective name (perhaps that is why this "quiet tradition" has never been anthologized as a group), but important nevertheless, poets of fine achievement.[6]

Blunden and Thomas, whose genuine affinity for the pastoral tradition should not be confused with Georgianism, shared an attitude of acceptance toward the war. Both Blunden and Thomas found that their observation of nature at the front helped to maintain their sense of balance, even to preserve sanity in the midst of unsettling events and reversals, as when Thomas was knocked down by a shell blast the day before his death, or when Blunden, after a shell had killed several men, found himself diverted by the sight of field mice playing in the trench.

Blunden, the son of a schoolmaster, had completed a public-school education at Christ's Hospital and had entered Queen's College, Oxford, on a classics scholarship when the war began. He enlisted in the Royal Sussex Regiment as a lieutenant in 1915, was in the trenches by May 1916, and survived two full years of the roughest fighting of the war, including action at La Bassee (1916), Hamel (September 1916), Thiepval during the Somme Offensive (October and November 1916), and Ypres during the Passchendaele Offensive (July 1917). He received the MC and suffered the effects of poison gas before he was invalided to a training camp in March 1918. Like other war poets he attempted to return to the front, but his requests for transfer were futile, and he was demobilized in 1919. At eighteen, he was among the youngest subalterns, and he was only twenty-two when he returned to Oxford. However, he left without taking a degree in 1920, joining the *Athenaeum* as assistant to Middleton Murry, whom he had known at Christ's Hospital. When the *Athenaeum* merged with H. W. Massingham's *Nation* in 1921, Blunden remained on the staff as a regular contributor. He sent copies of his verse to Siegfried Sassoon, who recognized Blunden's merit and helped to advance his poetic career, as did J. C. Squire, H. W. Massingham, Edward Marsh, and Robert Graves. In 1920 Blunden's *The Waggoner* was well received, and his collection *The Shepherd* (1922) won the Hawthornden Prize.

During the next fifty years Blunden enjoyed a varied academic career, which included teaching at the University of Tokyo (1924–27), becoming an Oxford Fellow at Merton College (1931–44), and teaching at the University of Hong Kong (1953–64). In 1966 he became Professor of Poetry at Oxford (selected over Robert Lowell), and his several honors included a C. B. E. (Commander of the Order of the British Empire) in 1951. His best-known work is the war memoir *Undertones of War,* which Fussell has called an "extended pastoral elegy in prose."[7] He wrote no fewer than 177 books and pamphlets, more than three thousand contributions to periodicals and newspapers, and several introductions to others' works. His prose spanned thirty volumes of occasional essays, scholarly editions, and literary biographies, including a biography of Shelley, as well as a monograph on the poets of World War I. His *Nature in English Literature* (1929) is a critical masterpiece. Blunden was extremely fortunate to survive two years of the war, find literary recognition early, and pursue a scholarly and literary career for more than half a century—a prospect which seemed highly unlikely for an asthmatic youngster whose encounter with poison gas almost finished him.

In several poems, Blunden indicated his belief that war, while horrible, was an inevitable burden for his generation and, as such, required dispassionate acceptance. In the poem "Some Talk of Peace," Blunden contrasts war and peace to reach an ironical conclusion. He calls war "in a way reserved, polite and dainty" despite its noisy destruction because the murder seemed outside man's power and "there was not much felt of cold designs." Peace, by contrast, although quieter, is more deadly: "She may not kill; she even keeps alive / Those whom their faces or their foes deprive / Of joy and equity," and Blunden's conclusion is that "we live in doubt / Whether her sins or War's more misery sow." In "Zero," Blunden combines a description of war's horrors with his belief that war is nevertheless his destiny:

> The swooning white of him, and that red!
>   These bombs in boxes, the craunch of shells,
> The second-hand flitting round; ahead!
>   It's plain we were born for this, naught else.

A note of nostalgia also appears in his verse. In "1916 Seen From 1921," he describes himself as "Tired with dull grief, grown old before my day" as he recalls "Long silent laughters, murmurings of dismay, / The lost intensities of hope and fear." Defining himself as "Dead as the men I loved," he recalls days when "my friend of friends and I" would "snatch long moments from the grudging wars, / Whose dark made light intense to see them by." Like many soldiers after the conflict, Blunden found himself drawn by a memory of camaraderie that would not recur in civilian life.

Blunden's acceptance of the war by no means reflected ignorance of war's horrors or unwillingness to express them, but he retained much more control over his narrative verse than did Sassoon. In "Escape" he describes a scene in the orderly room when a colonel receives a message that four dead officers, killed by an exploding shell, require identification. "A Mind"—later addressed as "Bunny" (Blunden's nickname)—immediately forms an inward prayer:

> Now God befriend me,
> The next word not send me
> To view those ravished trunks
> And hips and blackened hunks.

The colonel sends someone else, but the simplicity of diction in the fervent prayer communicates the sense of horror which has chilled the young officer.

When Blunden chooses to comment as a narrator on what he reports, he manages to avoid becoming intrusive. In "Third Ypres," Blunden's longest war verse, he maintains a dispassionate objectivity while describing scenes of horror. After beginning the poem with the soldiers' anticipation of victory (vain, since the offensive ultimately produced no gain), Blunden describes the soldiers' hope that the enemy's guns have been silenced:

> They move not back, they lie among the crews
> Twisted and choked, they'll never speak again.
> Only the copse where once might stand a shrine
> Still clacked and suddenly hissed its bullets by.
> The War would end, the Line was on the move,
> And at a bound the impassable was passed.
> We lay and waited with extravagant joy.

The rain begins, and "those distorted guns, that lay past use, / Why—miracles not over!—all a-firing!" The narrator addresses a "Poor signaller, you I passed by this emplacement" who is now a spectacle of horror with "lean green flies upon the red flesh madding." When a bullet kills a runner departing with a message, the narrator has time for only a brief comment: "Well I liked him, that young runner, / But there's no time for that."

Blunden, in a manner beyond Sassoon's power, continues to describe the horrors of the battle without belaboring them. His consistent understatement throughout conveys the soldiers' wavering expectations at each moment of battle until he reaches noon, when he shifts to his personal involvement. When he is one of four in a pillbox struck by a shell, the narrator temporarily panics and then brings himself out of his fear:

> Doctor, talk, talk! if dead
> Or stunned I know not; the stinking powdered concrete,
> The lyddite turns me sick—my hair's all full
> Of this smashed concrete. O I'll drag you, friends,
> Out of the sepulchre into the light of day,
> For this is day, the pure and sacred day.
> And while I squeak and gibber over you,
> Look, from the wreck a score of field-mice nimble,
> And tame and curious look about them; (these
> Calmed me, on these depended my salvation).

The narrator, describing an event which Blunden actually experienced, regains control.

Near the end of the poem Blunden establishes a perspective that transcends his unit's plight, for he recognizes "how for miles our anguish groans and bleeds, / A whole sweet countryside amuck with murder; / Each moment puffed into a year with death." As the rain continues, the narrator awaits his unit's relief, but he ends by wondering "But who with what command can now relieve / The dead men from that chaos, or my soul?" In "Third Ypres," Blunden has written a sustained narrative poem which communicates the actual uncertainties of battle from a consistently objective perspective that persists even when, in the actual experience, Blunden lost control for a while.

Blunden's strengths, despite his narrative achievement in "Third Ypres," were his pastoral descriptions and his understatements of irony. In "Thiepval Wood (September 1916)," he describes the effect of artillery on a peaceful sylvan scene:

> Then jabbering echoes stampede in the slatting wood,
> Ember-black the gibbet trees like bones or thorns protrude
>   From the poisonous smoke—past all impulses.

The carefully wrought phrasing reinforces the sense of panic amid destruction. In "Festubert: The Old German Line (May 1916)," Blunden describes the occupied section of trench with surprising economy:

> Still zipped across the gouts of lead
> Or cracked like whipcracks overhead;
> The grey rags fluttered on the dead.

In "Illusions," Blunden indicates that he finds beauty in the trenches and apologizes for this: "There are such moments; forgive me that I note them." He then adds that "there comes soon the nemesis of beauty" and describes that as well. He carefully limits many descriptions to accurate depiction of the palpable. In "A Farm Near Zillebeke," he writes,

> I stood in the yard of a house that must die,
> And still the black hame was stacked by the door,
> And harness still hung there, and the dray waited by.

The contrast between the peace of the deserted house and Blunden's ability to predict its demise is sufficient for his rhetorical purposes.

Blunden's war poems abound in ironical observation. In "The Zonnebeke Road," Blunden playfully addresses the soldiers:

> And yet the day is come; stand down! stand down!
> Your hands unclasp from rifles while you can,
> The frost has pierced them to the bended bone?
> Why, see old Stevens there, that iron man,
> Melting the ice to shave his grotesque chin:
> Go ask him, shall we win?

When Blunden recognizes the beauty of flowers in "Vlamertinghe: Passing the Chateau (July 1917)," he ends with a subtle comparison of flowers' colors and soldiers' blood:

> Such a gay carpet! poppies by the million;
> Such damask! such vermilion!
> But if you ask me, mate, the choice of colour
> Is scarcely right; this red should have been much duller.

"Zillebeke Brook (April 1917)" records Blunden's ironical observation that even the "conduit stream that's tangled here and there / With rusted iron and shards of earthenware" can, in its twisted muddiness, remind him of a clear stream in Kent: "And much too clear you bring it back to me, / You dreary brook deformed with cruelty, /Here where I halt to catch the day's best mood, / On my way up to Sanctuary Wood." In "Les Halles d'Ypres" he describes a ruin ("A tangle of iron rods and spluttered beams, / On brickwork past the skill of a mason to mend") and then finds odd contrast in pigeons who "come to the tower, and flaunt and preen, / And flicker in playful flight" as if nothing has happened. Blunden's careful eye caught several such contrasting details, which he presented in his verse without superfluous comment.

In "The Sentry's Mistake," Blunden describes the company's movement from the fighting to a peaceful rural scene which had not experienced "whining covey of shells." Blunden describes the men's delight with the stillness of the farm, the clearness of the brook, and the abundance of such natural bounty as cherries. In the last stanza, however, he introduces a sharp contrast to the respite of this scene:

> But now a flagged car came ill-omened there.
> The crimson-mottled monarch, shocked and shrill,
>   Sent our poor sentry scampering for his gun,
>   Made him once more "the terror of the Hun."

Blunden's use of the poetic tradition to underscore ironical contrast appears in "Trench Raid Near Hooge," which opens with an echo of Homer:

> At an hour before the rosy-fingered
>   Morning should come
> To wonder again what meant these sties,
> These wailing shots, these glaring eyes,
>   These moping mum. . . .

The poem moves through descriptions of "false dawns" from the "thunderous" guns and then reflects on the condition of the dead. Dawn's fingers played

>   with something of human pity
>   On six or seven
> Whose looks were hard to understand,
> But that they ceased to care what hand
>   Lit earth and heaven.

The poem serves to point out the inability of the epic posture to convey the sense of the mechanized war.

"Rural Economy (1917)" comments ironically on the war by adopting the metaphor of the careful husbandman:

> There was winter in those woods,
>   And still it was July:
> There were Thule solitudes
>   With thousands huddling nigh;

There the fox had left his den,
The scraped holes hid not stoats but men.

To these woods the rumour teemed
    Of peace five miles away;
In sight, hills hovered, houses gleamed
    Where last perhaps we lay
Till the cockerels bawled bright morning and
The hours of life slipped the slack hand.

In sight, life's farms sent forth their gear;
    Here rakes and ploughs lay still;
Yet, save some curious clods, all here
    Was raked and ploughed with a will.
The sower was the ploughman too,
And iron seeds broadcast he threw.

What husbandry could outdo this?
    With flesh and blood he fed
The planted iron that nought amiss
    Grew thick and swift and red,
And in a night though ne'er so cold
Those acres bristled a hundredfold.

Why, even the wood as well as field
    This ruseful farmer knew
Could be reduced to plough and tilled,
    And if he planned, he'd do;
The field and wood, all bone-fed loam
Shot up a roaring harvest-home.

A poem of more extended irony, "The Prophet," juxtaposes statements from a guidebook on the Netherlands and a soldier's comments on the prevailing conditions of the Belgian front, balancing Blunden's descriptions of military life with travel-book phrases out of their original context:

"The necessary cautions on the road" . . .
Gas helmets at the alert, no daylight movement?
"But lately much attention has been paid
To the coal mines." Amen, roars many a fosse
Down south, and slag-heap unto slag-heap calls.

The irony which most fascinated Blunden, however, was the contradiction between the reality of war and prewar expectations, as he revealed in "Report on Experience." In each of four stanzas, a statement of actual conditions leads to another purposeful, ironical statement that undermines the first. In the first stanza, one finds "the righteous forsaken," with

Blunden's observation that "This is not what we were formerly told." In the second stanza,

> I have seen a green country, useful to the race,
> Knocked silly with guns and mines, its villages vanished,
> Even the last rat and last kestrel banished—
>   God bless us all, this was peculiar grace.

Blunden's war verses reveal a range and variety rare among the war poets. Not only has he written verses that find beauty among ruins, play on the contrast between the works of nature and the work of man, present sustained narratives, and communicate some of the horrors of war, but also he has managed to maintain objective control of his verse. His poems are of pity, not self-pity, and he stays for the most part above his subjective responses to the experiences he describes, particularly in "Third Ypres." His fine eye for detail, his willingness to narrate without intrusion, and his appreciation of the ironies of war do not weaken his acceptance of his role in the war. Perhaps his cynical observation that his generation was "born for this, naught else" enabled him to maintain sufficient detachment to convey his sense of reality without lapsing into the distracting stridency of Sassoon or the self-consciousness of many of the other trench poets.

Edward Thomas was among the older officers of the war, enlisting at thirty-eight. Like Blunden, Thomas had a public-school education (St. Paul's), and he won a scholarship to Lincoln College, Oxford, where he married Helen Noble in 1899. In 1900 he left Oxford to begin a literary career that recalls the tribulations described in George Gissing's *New Grub Street*. According to Paul M. Cubeta, "His staggering output of about one million words in ten years included thirty books on literary history, commercial English travelogues on Windsor Castle, Wales, the Isle of Wight, and, more important, over 1,000 reviews, especially for books on nature and modern poetry, often used as dust-jacket copy. Books about books, scribbled for bread and babies' shoes."[8] With three children and a wife to support, Thomas forced himself to produce what he called "hack work." However, as a critic he was the first to review Ezra Pound's poetry favorably, and he also recognized the merit of Robert Frost's *A Boy's Will* (1913) and *North of Boston* (1914). His review of the former led to a meeting with Frost on 5 October 1913, and the two became fast friends. Frost suggested that Thomas rewrite some of his prose as nature poetry. Although Thomas did not write his first poem, "Up the Wind," until December 1914, he then followed Frost's advice.

The war squeezed Thomas out of the literary marketplace, and he sought help from the Royal Literary Fund, which provided £300. After considerable soul-searching and many heated arguments with his jingoistic father, Thomas decided to enlist in the Artists' Rifles in July 1915, and he spent two years in training in England. On January 1917 he arrived in France, and less than three months later he was killed at the beginning of the Battle of Arras. Although some have claimed that Thomas wrote only a few poems touching on the war (his last poem written two weeks before he arrived in France), his preoccupation with the war during his entire poetic career made, in at least that sense, almost all his verse war poetry. During most of the twenty-six months he spent writing the verse ultimately published in *Collected Poems*, Thomas was in uniform.

Apart from encouraging Thomas to turn to poetry, Frost had little to do with Thomas's poetical development. As Thomas's earlier prose and his letters to Frost reveal, the traits in common between these two poets evolved independently. The comparatively short span of Thomas's writing of poetry, compared with his twenty years as a prose writer, is misleading, for that experience included years as a critic of modern poetry. His criticism served as his poetical apprenticeship.

Thomas's patriotism derived from his passionate attachment to the land, as he revealed to his secretary, Eleanor Farjeon. When she asked why he was going to the war, he picked up a handful of earth and replied, "For this." Many of his early poems, written between January and May 1915, suggest a pastoral elegiac mode reminiscent of Housman. His "In Memoriam (Easter 1915)" makes the simply described countryside a reminder of soldiers fallen in the war:

> The flowers left thick at nightfall in the wood
> This Eastertide call into mind the men
> Now far from home, who, with their sweethearts, should
> Have gathered them and will do never again.

"The Owl," which he wrote three months before his enlistment, combines description of a walking trip with his growing concern that he should enlist. He begins with sensations of physical weariness and deprivation, qualified by his knowledge that "food, fire, and rest" at the inn will set him right:

> Downhill I came, hungry, and yet not starved;
> Cold, yet had heat within me that was proof
> Against the North wind; tired, yet so that rest
> Had seemed the sweetest thing under a roof.

When the poet recognizes the contrast of "what I escaped / And others could not," his mind turns to the war:

> And salted was my food, and my repose,
> Salted and sobered, too, by the bird's voice
> Speaking for all who lay under the stars,
> Soldiers and poor, unable to rejoice.

In "A Private," resembling Housman's elegies for Shropshire lads, he focuses on the contrast between peace and war. In peace, the "ploughman" who "slept out of doors / Many a frozen night" would never let others know where he had slept. Now he "sleeps / More sound in France—that, too, he secret keeps."

On the day of his enlistment, Thomas wrote "For These," which first seems to express only intense nostalgia for the English countryside. In three stanzas he describes "An acre of land," "A house that shall love me as I love it," and "A garden I need never go beyond." However, in the fourth stanza, the poet shifts to a statement of his own uncertainty:

> For these I ask not, but, neither too late
> Nor yet too early, for what men call content,
> And also that something may be sent
> To be contented with, I ask of fate.

Perhaps Thomas is parodying in himself the same trait which Frost had in mind when he wrote "The Road Not Taken," which pokes fun at Thomas's frequent concern that he had made a wrong choice. Thomas indicates that land, house, and garden will not content him, but he does not indicate what will.

In "Home," he describes a rare moment when he and two other soldiers in training take a ten-mile walk across country. After one of the soldiers mentions "home," the poet reflects on the meaning of the word to the three men:

> Between three counties far apart that lay
> We were divided and looked strangely each
> At the other, and we knew we were not friends
> But fellows in a union that ends
> With the necessity for it, as it ought.

The word *homesick* occurs to the poet, who abruptly represses it:

> If I should ever more admit
> Than the mere word I could not endure it
> For a day longer: this captivity
> Must somehow come to an end, else I should be
> Another man, as often now I seem,
> Or this life be only an evil dream.

The attitudes expressed in these poems form only part of his larger vision. Even in his comparatively nostalgic poems, his concern with the war and with the need for it is implicit.

Since Thomas studied history at Oxford, his awareness of the war's place in a much larger perspective should not be surprising. In his most ambitious poem, "Lob," he attempted to celebrate the English spirit in a much larger context than contemporary developments on the Continent. Combining legend, myth, and history, he presents the archetypal English character Lob, who has overcome past threats to England and continues to persevere in the face of the modern challenge:

> One of the lords of No Man's Land, good Lob,—
> Although he was seen dying at Waterloo,
> Hastings, Agincourt, and Sedgemoor, too,—
> Lives yet.

(Originally the phrase "No Man's Land" was "Unowned waste land," but Thomas altered the line to emphasize Lob's present trials.) Although the poem is by no means a Great War epic in the manner of David Jones's *In Parenthesis*, it places the conflict into a much broader context than the poet's contemporaries attempted.

Addressing Thomas's poetic development, R. George Thomas noted,

> Gradually he seemed to learn two things. The one, that, for him, writing, without some connection with speech or the overtones of speech, was fruitless and inadequate. The other, that merely to record sensitive perceptions of natural events was a futile task compared with the attempt to catch the echo of the world of mystery and significance that opened out before him as he attempted to find words for his own active contemplation of nature, or of human existence in the most natural surroundings. Blessed (or cursed) with an acute visual sense, he had to learn to see through and beyond what he so expertly perceived.[9]

Thomas's attempts to place contemporary events include "February Afternoon," which tries to view the war in terms of its cosmic significance:

> Time swims before me, making as a day
>   A thousand years, while the broad ploughland oak
>   Roars mill-like and men strike and bear the stroke
>   Of war as ever, audacious or resigned,
> And God still sits aloft in the array
>   That we have wrought him, stone-deaf and stone-blind.

After writing *The Life of the Duke of Marlborough* in 1915, Thomas could hardly escape noticing the recurrence of English battles in Flanders, and he frequently focused on the transience of an individual compared with humanity's will to destroy. In "Digging," a soldier encounters a reminder of his personal insignificance when he unearths a relic:

What matter makes my spade for tears or mirth,
Letting down two clay pipes into the earth?
The one I smoked, the other a soldier
Of Blenheim, Ramillies, and Malplaquet
Perhaps. The dead man's immortality
Lies represented lightly with my own.

By citing Marlborough's three major battles on the Continent, Thomas can emphasize the place of the present war in a much broader historical framework.

After a long and heated argument with his father, Thomas wrote "This Is No Case of Petty Right or Wrong" in December 1915. The poem is a remarkable statement of Thomas's motives for enlisting, as well as a dismissal of jingoistic patriotism. Thomas rejects the notion of hating the enemy and articulates his feeling that he must accept his role as a soldier:

I hate not Germans, nor grow hot
With love of Englishmen, to please newspapers.
Beside my hate for one fat patriot
My hatred of the Kaiser is love true:—
A kind of god he is, banging a gong.
But I have not to choose between the two,
Or between justice and injustice.

He rejects the understanding of historical necessity as a necessary part of his patriotism: "Little I know or care if, being dull, / I shall miss something that historians / Can rake out of the ashes." However, he connects defense of country with love for the land:

But with the best and meanest Englishmen
I am one in crying, God save England, lest
We lose what never slaves and cattle blessed.
The ages made her that made us from the dust:
She is all we know and live by, and we trust
She is good and must endure, loving her so:
And as we love ourselves we hate her foe.

This poem anticipates several soldiers' view that the real enemy was the jingoistic civilian at home. Since Thomas was not to see action until more than a year later, his affinity with the trench soldiers' view is surprising.

In later poems, Thomas expressed his sense of the individual's insignificance in the larger perspective. In his "No One Cares Less Than I," a soldier composes words to the bugle's call, deflating Rupert Brooke's conception of a "foreign field":

"No one cares less than I,
Nobody knows but God
Whether I am destined to lie
Under a foreign clod,"
Were the words I made to the bugle call in the morning.

But laughing, storming, scorning,
Only the bugles know
What the bugles say in the morning,
And they do not care, when they blow
The call that I heard and made words to early this morning.

In "Roads," which Thomas wrote on 22 January 1916, Thomas includes a transitional stanza which moves the poem from his celebration of roads to his recognition of their immediate significance for him:

Now all roads lead to France
And heavy is the tread
Of the living; but the dead
Returning lightly dance.

Thomas has successfully placed his individual experience within a greater whole.

"The Trumpet," which some have mistaken for an early call to action, is neither early nor a call. It was written after the middle of 1916 and addresses the effect of war on personal destinies. The trumpet "Chases the dreams of men," compelling them to "Rise up and scatter / The dew that covers / The print of last night's lovers." The second stanza tells men to "Forget . . . everything / On this earth new-born, / Except that it is lovelier / Than any mysteries," and ends with the command, "To the old wars; / Arise, arise!" Significantly, "wars" is plural, placing this war in the context of recurring conflicts. Far from being an attempt to inspire men to enlist, "The Trumpet" presents war as a timeless phenomenon which removes men from all that is good.

In "Lights Out," Thomas offers a gloomy but accurate assessment of his chances for survival. Using sleep as a metaphor for death, he indicates his belief that his end is imminent:

I have come to the borders of sleep,
The unfathomable deep
Forest where all must lose
Their way, however straight,
Or winding, soon or late;
They cannot choose.

After describing death as the end of love, despair, and ambition, he refers to "sleep that is sweeter / Than tasks most noble" and reveals his acceptance of his fate:

> There is not any book
> Or face of dearest look
> That I would not turn from now
> To go into the unknown
> I must enter and leave alone
> I know not how.

Few are capable of viewing their own deaths so dispassionately.

Thomas's best poem of the war is "As the Team's Head Brass," which is among his last poems. Andrew Motion has discussed the poem in terms of its "perception of regeneration in the midst of military oppression and agricultural development" and feels that Thomas's original title for the poem, "The Last Team," indicated "that he realised the rural order, as it is represented by the plough, was shortly to be upset by mechanical developments, and intensifies the menace of his conclusion:

> . . . for the last time
> I watched the clods crumble and topple over
> After the ploughshare and the stumbling team."[10]

The poem reveals an awareness of continuing rhythm and change that characterize the land, as well as an acceptance of the natural order. As a soldier sits on a fallen elm and watches the ploughman at work, he sees lovers disappear into the wood. At the end of each full turn, the ploughman exchanges words with the soldier, "About the weather, next about the war." When the ploughman learns that the soldier has not yet been across the Channel and asks whether he wants to go, the soldier's response reveals his apprehensions:

> "If I could only come back again, I should.
> I could spare an arm. I shouldn't want to lose
> A leg. If I should lose my head, why, so,
> I should want nothing more. . . ."

The soldier learns that one of the ploughman's "mates" died in France on the day the elm fell and that the tree would have been moved had the man remained at home. The soldier reflects that, had the tree been moved, "I should not have sat there. Everything / Would have been different. For it would have been / Another world." The ploughman's ambiguous response suggests acceptance of events: "Ay, and a better, though /If we could see all

all might seem good." The poem moves to its conclusion when the lovers reappear from the wood and the soldier watches the horses "for the last time."

"As the Team's Head Brass," whose ploughman continues to plow and whose lovers continue to disappear into the wood, suggests Hardy's "In Time of 'The Breaking of Nations,' " which also has a ploughman, a pair of lovers, and a horse that "stumbles." Hardy's suggestion is essentially optimistic—"War's annals will cloud into night / Ere their story die"—and one could find similar comfort in Thomas's poem were one to adopt the ploughman's explicit belief that "If we could see all all might seem good." However, to accept this would be to reject the existence of evil in the events of the war. The acceptance of the natural order suffers from the soldier's fears of mutilation and his feeling that he watches "for the last time" (emphasized by its placement at the end of the line). The implication that without the war "it would have been / Another world," "and a better," suggests permanent loss both to man and to the land.

Compared with scores of poets who attempted to write pastoral war poetry, Blunden and Thomas remain superior because both recognized the larger perspective of the conflict, felt genuine passion for the English countryside, and loved the language. Blunden's war poetry did not gain recognition during the war for the simple reason that he published it afterwards, and to contemporaries Thomas's poetry did not seem to bear directly on the war. Thomas has suffered further due to his ironical postwar identification with the Georgian poets, which has obscured the quality of his talent. Thomas's acceptance of the war and his avoidance of topical verse and blatant rhetoric made it difficult to recognize the nature of his patriotism, his pity for the soldier, and his love for the land.

Wilfred Owen

DISCUSSIONS OF WILFRED OWEN (1893–1918) SUFFER FROM SEVERAL DISADvantages. Although Owen planned a volume of poems and drafted a preface and table of contents for the book, he was killed before he could finish the arrangement and editing of his work. As a result the manuscripts, which bear evidence of careful revision, remain resistant to definitive emendation and are also difficult to date. Dominic Hibberd's scheme seems, on the whole, the most reliable. Owen's habit of writing in whatever blank spaces were available often makes it difficult to arrange his revisions, and without him to unravel them the poems remain in an essentially "unfinished" state. Critics addressing the war poets have varied greatly in their estimates of Owen. Supporting his view of Owen as an elegist, Hibberd claims, "If we read Owen as the elegist he aspired to be, we can see the inadequacy or irrelevance of such critical approaches as those by John H. Johnston, . . . who vainly expects him to be a writer of epics, or by Jon Silkin, . . . who strenuously tries to make him a 'political' (i.e. socialist) poet. Epic tends to glorify death in war; politics tempt both reader and poet to shift guilt away from themselves onto someone else. Owen fell into neither trap."[1]

Hibberd also rejects the war as the source of Owen's poetry: "The old view of his poems as products of the war, forced out of an immature and ill-informed mind under the pressure of intense experience, is slow in dying but does not deserve to live; the major poems are the result of long years of training and preparation, finding fruit not in some hasty scribble done on the back of an envelope in the trenches but in the meticulous, protracted labour which went on at Ripon in the spring of 1918."[2] Further difficulties arise from gaps in our knowledge of Owen's life. As Joseph Cohen pointed out, such questions as whether Owen was ever in love, what year he matriculated at London University, and what actually occurred when Owen was withdrawn from the lines in June 1917 lack definite answers. Discussions of Owen's "homoerotic tendencies," particularly in the absence of evidence, frequently border on silliness.

Owen was born at Oswestry, Shropshire, on 18 March 1893, the eldest of four children. His father was a minor railway official, and his mother was strong-willed, puritanical, and dedicated to Wilfred. Owen's father wanted him to pursue a trade, his mother wanted him to enter the church, and he wanted to write poetry, beginning when he was about sixteen and using Keats as an early model. He attended London University and then was a private student and lay-assistant to the Reverend Mr. Herbert Wigan, vicar of Dunsden, near Reading. In 1913, after developing lung trouble, Owen obtained a position at Bordeaux teaching English at the Berlitz School and then worked as a tutor in a private French family.

Although the war began in August 1914, Owen remained in France to honor his contract until September 1915, when he returned to England. He enlisted in the Artists' Rifles in October, spent some time training, and received his commission in the Manchester Regiment on 4 June 1916. By January 1917 he was in the trenches, and in April, after spending some days in a shell hole with fragments of a fellow officer, he developed neurasthenia and went to Craiglockhart, where he met Robert Graves and Siegfried Sassoon, read Barbusse's *Le Feu [Under Fire]*, and began to write his more memorable poems. After his discharge from Craiglockhart in October, he had almost a full year of home duty before returning to the front on 31 August 1918. In October Owen won the MC, and on 4 November, one week before the Armistice, he was machine-gunned while directing efforts to place a temporary bridge over Sambre Canal. He was twenty-five.

Only four of Owen's poems appeared in his lifetime. "Song of Songs" was published in the *Hydra* at Craiglockhart, and "Miners," "Futility," and "Hospital Barge at Cérisy" appeared in the *Nation*. Ironically, although he frequently identified himself as a Georgian, his first major appearance in print was in the opposite camp. Mrs. Owen, after her son's death, sent some of Owen's manuscripts to Edith Sitwell, whose 1919 cycle of *Wheels* included "Strange Meeting," "The Show," "A Terre," "The Sentry," "Disabled," "The Dead-Beat," and "The Chances." Siegfried Sassoon edited an edition of twenty-three poems in 1920, and Edmund Blunden published an edition of fifty-nine poems in 1931.

With the exception of Sir Henry Newbolt and W. B. Yeats, most readers responded favorably to Owen's work without identifying it with a specific poetical school. Newbolt dismissed the trench poets as having "suffered cruelly, but in the nerves and not the heart," while Yeats surprisingly (and with some acerbity) excluded Owen and other war poets from the 1936 edition of the *Oxford Book of Modern Verse*. The majority, however, subscribe to the opinion of Frank Swinnerton, who found in Owen's poetry, "instead of impressionism, a peculiar reflective hatred of war from which hysteria is entirely absent,"[3] and to that of Sassoon, who stated in his introduction to the 1920 edition of Owen's poetry, "He never wrote his poems (as so many war poets did) to make the effect of a personal gesture. He pitied others; he did not pity himself."[4] Part of the comprehensive effect of Owen's poetry is a reflection of his unique response to the war. His verse expresses his journey from comparative indifference to a deep conviction that the war was an unconscionable affront to God and man.

Owen's initial response was not the unrestrained enthusiasm of most of his generation. He was in France, where the public reaction to an impending German invasion lacked romantic idealism. As Dominic Hibberd comments, "He came to the conclusion, and declared it in a rather defensive tone, that a poet was more useful to England alive than dead, . . . He was finally persuaded by several factors, including recruiting propaganda in newspapers sent to him from home, a quotation he encountered in an essay by Belloc ("If any man despairs of becoming a Poet, let him carry his pack and march in the ranks") and an enthusiastic reading of [Flaubert's] *Salammbô*.[5] Dennis Welland quotes a letter from Owen dated 4 January 1917 that reveals Owen's surprisingly insensitive early attitude toward the "other ranks" when he arrived at the front: "The men are just as Bairnsfather has them—expressionless lumps. We feel the weight of them hanging on us."[6] Owen also reveals something of the enthusiasm associated with Rupert Brooke in a letter to his mother: "There is a fine heroic feeling about being in France, and I am in perfect spirits."[7] In an early unfinished poem, Owen even alluded to Brooke: "Not one corner of a foreign field / But a span as wide as Europe. . . ." Two weeks later, however, Owen's attitude toward the fighting had changed considerably: "I can see no excuse for deceiving you about these 4 days. I have suffered seventh hell. I have not been at the front. I have been in front of it."[8]

The abruptness with which the brutality of war forced itself upon Owen placed him in a painful dilemma. On the one hand, despite his rejection of orthodox Christianity, he accepted the teachings of Christ which encouraged pacifism (as did his prewar friendship with Laurent Tailhade). On the other, he recognized and accepted his responsibility to the men under his command and did what he could to function as an efficient and compassionate officer. In the last stanza of "At a Calvary Near the Ancre," dated by Hibberd as written in April 1917, Owen focuses on the discrepancy between church and Christianity:

> The scribes on all the people shove
>   And bawl allegiance to the state,
> But they who love the greater love
>   Lay down their life; they do not hate.

In a letter written in June 1917, Owen stated that "one of Christ's essential commands was: Passivity at any price! Suffer dishonour and disgrace, but never resort to arms. . . . am I not myself a conscientious objector with a very seared conscience? . . . Thus you see how pure Christianity will not fit in with pure patriotism."[9]

Owen found the pull of compassion for his men as strong as that of his pacifism, and he effected his return to the front. His identification of Christ with his men appears frequently in his verse, and in a letter to Osbert Sitwell in July 1918 he made the connection explicit: "For 14 hours yesterday I was at work—teaching Christ to lift his cross by the numbers, and how to adjust his crown; and not to imagine he thirst until after the last halt."[10] As becomes evident from the citation for bravery accompanying his Military Cross, his pacifism was not passivity: "Fonsomme Line, 1/2 October, 1918 . . . For conspicuous gallantry and devotion to duty in the attack. On the company commander becoming a casualty he assumed command and showed fine leadership, and resisted a heavy counter-attack. He personally manipulated a captured enemy machine gun from an isolated position, and inflicted considerable losses on the enemy. Throughout he behaved most gallantly."[11] Torn between adherence to his ideals and support for his men, Owen chose the latter.

Sassoon provided a timely impetus more than he changed Owen's poetical theory or method. Susceptible to fits of depression at his lack of achievement, Owen once complained to his brother Harold, "I must have help, and I just can't get it."[12] Sassoon provided Owen with significant insights into the relationship of poetry and war, and he showed Owen drafts of poems which would appear in Sassoon's *Counter-Attack*. For a brief time, Owen imitated Sassoon. Owen was grateful for Sassoon's help. "I spun round you like a satellite for a month," he wrote to Sassoon, "but I shall swing out soon, a dark star in the orbit where you will blaze."[13] In retrospect, the implications of Owen's metaphor have reversed.

That Owen has achieved almost universal recognition as Sassoon's superior results from his closer allegiance to the "truth" of poetry. In the preface Owen drafted for his projected volume of poems, he declared that "these elegies are to this generation in no sense consolatory. They may be to the next. All a poet can do to-day is warn. That is why the true Poets must be truthful."[14] His view of modern warfare's supplanting of the chivalric tradition resembles Sassoon's, but in the preface Owen goes beyond Sassoon's position by declaring, "Above all I am not concerned with Poetry," rejecting "Poetry" insofar as it attempted to pursue beauty at the expense of truth.

In August 1914, Owen wrote his first war sonnet, "The Seed." There is little in the poem to indicate the direction his later poetry would take. "The Seed," in Arthur E. Lane's words, is "self-consciously 'universal' " but "remarkably restrained, both in imagery and movement."[15] In the octave, after describing the outbreak of war as a "foul tornado, centred at Berlin" and its subsequent passage over Europe, Owen focuses on the war's effect on the civilized pursuits of peace:

> Rent or furled
> Are all Art's ensigns. Verse wails. Now begin

Famines of thought and feeling. Love's wine's thin.
The grain of human Autumn rots, down-hurled.

In the sestet, Owen describes the history of western civilization in a seasonal metaphor, in which Spring is Greece, Summer is Rome, and Autumn is the preceding age. "But now, for us, wild Winter, and the need / Of sowings for new Spring, and blood for seed." One can recognize the beginnings of Owen's "pity" in the last line as well as his use of pastoral imagery close to Blunden's, even in an "abstract" poem, to describe the war.

"Greater Love," written after Owen had suffered shell shock, reveals the extent of the change that experience wrought on his sensibility. Assigned provisionally by Hibberd to April 1917, the poem takes as its text John 15: 13: "Greater love hath no man than this, that a man lay down his life for his friends." The poem reveals a characteristic trait of Owen's imagery. Rather than oppose remembered English scenes to the distorted and destroyed front, as did so many others, Owen contrasts healthy youth and their fallen counterparts. In "Greater Love," Owen's effect depends on the juxtaposition of love imagery with the death and injury he describes, focusing on the lips, eyes, forms, and voices of the fallen. Owen's contrast appears markedly in the first two lines: "Red lips are not so red / As the stained stones kissed by the English dead," and such oppositions continue: wooer's love versus the "love pure" of soldiers, a lover's eyes versus soldiers' blinded eyes, and so on. In the final stanza, Owen's imagery becomes even more striking: "Heart, you were never hot, / Nor large, nor full like hearts made great with shot," and the poem ends with an address to the poet's own emotion: "Weep, you may weep, for you may touch them not."

In "The End," written during the same month, Owen returns to a more consciously "universal" approach to death in battle, even including such time-worn images as the "drums of time" and "titanic tears," the latter of which Yeats cited as sufficient reason for not regarding Owen as a significant poet. The poem is interesting, however, for its questioning of resurrection: "Shall Life renew these bodies? Of a truth / All death will he annul, all tears assuage?—" (Owen's mother, by capitalizing *he* in the second line and eliminating the second question mark, made the lines a statement of affirmation for Owen's tombstone). The last lines of the poem, however, reveal the extent of Owen's doubt: "white Age" refuses to answer the question, and the Earth can only respond in despair:

"My fiery heart shrinks, aching. It is death.
Mine ancient scars shall not be glorified,
Nor my titanic tears, the seas, be dried."

"The End" does show that, while Owen strives to find a perspective into which he can place the war, he has not yet discovered the form his more successful poems would take.

Shortly after meeting Sassoon in August 1917, Owen wrote "The Dead-Beat," introducing a blunt, colloquial style new to Owen's verse. The poem is a case history of a shell-shocked soldier who dies after one night in the infirmary. Owen's poem ends with a phrase from the attending physician that combines the doctor's insensibility with Sassoon's predilection for ironical twists at the end of poems: "That scum you sent last night soon died. Hooray."

In a more successful poem, "Anthem for Doomed Youth," Owen's theme is the inadequacy of traditional responses to death in war. The octave establishes the identity of the soldier as victim, implies civilians' inability to respond except with "mockeries," and establishes that the only appropriate responses must come from the front:

> What passing-bells for these who die as cattle?
>   Only the monstrous anger of the guns.
>   Only the stuttering rifles' rapid rattle
> Can patter out their hasty orisons.
> No mockeries now for them; no prayers nor bells,
>   Nor any voice of mourning save the choirs,—
> The shrill, demented choirs of wailing shells;
>   And bugles calling for them from sad shires.

After indicating the ineffectual responses of traditional ritual, Owen continues in the sestet by contrasting the meaningless trappings of traditional burials of the dead to more worthy and more human responses:

> What candles may be held to speed them all?
>   Not in the hands of boys, but in their eyes
> Shall shine the holy glimmers of good-byes.
>   The pallor of girls' brows shall be their pall;
> Their flowers the tenderness of patient minds,
> And each slow dusk a drawing-down of blinds.

Two poems written in October 1917 reveal Sassoon's influence more directly. "Disabled," resembling Sassoon's "Does It Matter?", makes a similar point without running it into the ground. In Owen's poem, echoes of Housman's "To an Athlete Dying Young" appear in an ironical context. Housman's irony in congratulating the young man for being dead is implicit. Owen's irony is explicit, but there is nothing so heavy-handed as Sassoon's image of hunters returning "To gobble their muffins and eggs." Owen's theme is the painful contrast of a crippled soldier's life to the wholeness of those around him. Instead of distorting by exaggeration, Owen juxtaposes the invalid's present situation with memories of his civilian past. A few short lines in the first stanza establish the situation eloquently: "He sat in a wheeled chair, waiting for dark, / And shivered in his ghastly suit of grey, /

Legless, sewn short at elbow." In contrast, the invalid watches boys playing in the park and recalls how the girls had looked in the evening, "In the old times, before he threw away his knees."

> Now he will never feel again how slim
> Girls' waists are, or how warm their subtle hands;
> All of them touch him like some queer disease.

The third stanza contrasts his former beauty with his premature age; the fourth contrasts his once liking "a blood-smear down his leg" after a match with his reason for enlisting, "to please the giddy jilts," and explores the ease with which, influenced by chivalric images, he entered the ranks by lying about his age. The bitter result appears in three lines in the fifth stanza: "Some cheered him home, but not as crowds cheer Goal. / Only a solemn man who brought him fruits / *Thanked* him; and then inquired about his soul." The final lines emphasize his present helplessness and predict "a few sick years in Institutes." The differences between Owen's "Disabled" and Sassoon's "Does It Matter?" suggest the limit of Sassoon's influence. Sassoon economized to the point of distortion. Owen has adopted a curative purpose and has presented an event from the victim's point of view, but he has been more intent on presenting the whole truth of the invalid's situation than on making one blatant point.

The second poem, "Dulce et Decorum Est," also suggests Sassoon in its curative intent and in its response to one or more public poems. One manuscript version indicates that it addresses Jessie Pope, and there may be another source: in the anthology *Soldier Poets*, which Owen owned, appears Sydney Oswald's "Dulce et Decorum Est Pro Patria Mori," which asserts, in the Horatian tradition, that "Glory is theirs." Owen begins his poem with a realistic description of soldiers at the front, "Bent double, like old beggars under sacks, / Knock-kneed, coughing like hags, we cursed through sludge," and includes descriptions of the men's weariness and exhaustion, obliviousness to the sound of exploding shells, and limping along without boots. In the second stanza, the men fumble for gas masks, but one man does not react quickly enough, and "As under a green sea, I saw him drowning. / In all my dreams, before my helpless sight, / He plunges at me, guttering, choking, drowning." After this accurate picture of the "glory" of the trenches, Owen shifts to a direct address, stating that one who marched behind the wagon bearing the victim "would not tell with such high zest / To children ardent for some desperate glory, / The old Lie: Dulce et decorum est / Pro patria mori." The poem recalls Sassoon's work in its explicit description of reality, its dramatic rendering of the gas attack, and its overtly rhetorical address at the end. In Owen's movement toward his realization of the poetry of pity, this poem marks a transition from emphasis on rich

romantic imagery to the virtual absence of romantic diction or poetic metaphor.

In "Apologia Pro Poemate Meo," written in November or December
1917, one also finds traces of the bitterness of Sassoon's anticivilian verse.
Owen begins by celebrating his involvement in the struggle. In a series of
seven stanzas he notes that "I, too, saw God through mud,— / The mud that
cracked on cheeks when wretches smiled," that "Merry it was to laugh
there— / Where death becomes absurd and life absurder," that he has
overcome his fear, that he has "made fellowships," and that his camaraderie
is not that of lovers whose bonds depend on joy, but that of bonds "wound
with war's hard wire whose stakes are strong." In the pivotal eighth stanza,
Owen describes having "perceived much beauty" at the front, and in the last
two stanzas he shifts to a rejection of civilians that recalls the one in Sassoon's
"Suicide in the Trenches":

> Nevertheless, except you share
>   With them in hell the sorrowful dark of hell,
>   Whose world is but the trembling of a flare,
>   And heaven but as the highway for a shell,
>
> You shall not hear their mirth:
>   You shall not come to think them well content
>   By any jest of mine. These men are worth
>   Your tears. You are not worth their merriment.

Although Owen was not to continue long in this vein and would go beyond
Sassoon's negativism, it is worth noting that at least for a time he assumed
that stance.

In January 1918 Owen's "Miners" signalled a major departure, as well as
receiving some public attention. The poem appeared in the *Nation* on 16
January 1918, only two weeks after the pit explosion that occasioned it.
"Miners" drew attention not only for its topical references to the Stratford
pit explosion and to the war, but also for its use of pararhyme. Owen
compares miners dead in the explosion with soldiers dead on the battlefield
in the sixth stanza:

> I thought of some who worked dark pits
>   Of war, and died
> Digging the rock where Death reputes
>   Peace lies indeed.

In the final stanza, Owen sets both soldier and miner apart from civilian:

> The centuries will burn rich loads
>   With which we groaned,

> Whose warmth shall lull their dreaming lids
>> While songs are crooned.
> But they will not dream of us poor lads
>> Lost in the ground.

Sassoon's influence was waning, however. On 30 December 1917 Owen had remarked of Sassoon, "Poetry with him is become a mere vehicle of propaganda,"[16] and shortly afterwards he began to move in a different direction. He had transferred from Craiglockhart to Scarborough in December 1917, and in March 1918 he went to Ripon, where he rented a cottage room to enable him to write without distraction.

Between March and June 1918, when he returned to Scarborough, Owen's most productive period occurred at Ripon. He wrote no fewer than thirteen of his poems, including his best work, as well as drafting the table of contents and preface for a projected volume of poems. Owen's "Insensibility" (March 1918), in Sassoon's manner, blasts civilians for their insensitivity, but with a difference. In addition to his use of pararhyme, Owen has balanced his "curse" at civilians' coldness by comparing it with the soldiers' blunted senses after long tours in the trenches: "Happy are men who yet before they are killed / Can let their veins run cold." This introduces the despairing situation of men expecting death at any moment, whose insensitivity makes their lot that much easier. In the second stanza, Owen explicitly states that "Dullness best solves/ The tease and doubt of shelling," and in the third stanza he continues this theme:

> Happy are these who lose imagination:
> They have enough to carry with ammunition.
> Their spirit drags no pack,
> Their old wounds, save with cold, can not more ache.

Owen contrasts the lot of the trench soldiers to that of those not yet in the fighting, and then he compares the noncombatants' naîve happiness with the awareness of "We wise, who with a thought besmirch / Blood over all our soul" before he lashes the civilians who would have been Sassoon's sole subject:

> But cursed are dullards whom no cannon stuns,
> That they should be as stones;
> Wretched are they, and mean
> With paucity that never was simplicity.
> By choice they made themselves immune
> To pity and whatever moans in man
> Before the last sea and the hapless stars;
> Whatever mourns when many leave these shores;
> Whatever shares
> The eternal reciprocity of tears.

A similar contrast to Sassoon's verse appears in Owen's "À Terre (Being the Philosophy of Many Soldiers)," a dramatic monologue in the colloquial style of the soldier. Like Sassoon, Owen describes the plight of an invalid, but unlike Sassoon he has the soldier overcome his bitterness. On occasion, Owen takes the opportunity to contrast his soldier's words to traditional poetry. At one point the soldier, "blind, and three parts shell," refers to "My glorious ribbons?—Ripped from my own back / In scarlet shreds. (That's for your poetry book.)" He wonders whether he can teach his son only the arts of destruction and of making money, muses that he would gladly trade his remaining one year in a hospital bed for the lot of the meanest dustman, and then expresses his desire for existence in metaphor:

> Dead men may envy living mites in cheese,
> Or good germs even. Microbes have their joys,
> And subdivide, and never come to death.

He also quotes Shelley, ironically:

> "I shall be one with nature, herb, and stone",
> Shelley would tell me. Shelley would be stunned:
>
> The dullest Tommy hugs that fancy now.
> "Pushing up daisies" is their creed, you know.

The soldier concludes, however, that "I shall be better off with plants that share / More peaceably the meadow and the shower," and his resignation does not seem ironical: "Carry my crying spirit till it's weaned / To do without what blood remained these wounds."

In contrast to these poems, which show the lingering influence of Sassoon, "The Show" suggests a larger perspective for the war, one which Sassoon never caught. Blunden compared the perspective of "The Show" with that of Hardy's *The Dynasts* and Dante's *Inferno*. Owen presents an image of the world in a "dream," reinforced with an epigraph from Yeats. The world has become a decaying head, afflicted with "great pocks and scabs of plagues," over which the armies crawl like vermin:

> Across its beard, that horror of harsh wire,
> There moved thin caterpillars, slowly uncoiled.
> It seemed they pushed themselves to be as plugs
> Of ditches, where they writhed and shrivelled, killed.

The imagery of decomposition continues as "smell came up from those foul openings / As out of mouths, or deep wounds," and from the brown and the gray "strings" as they battle. When Owen imagines himself returning to earth,

> . . . Death fell with me, like a deepening moan.
> And He, picking a manner of worm, which half had hid
> Its bruises in the earth, but crawled no further,
> Showed me its feet, the feet of many men,
> And the fresh-severed head of it, my head.

In its overview of the front, the poem recalls Sorley's "A Hundred Thousand Million Mites We Go."

Owen completed several other poems at Ripon. "Arms and the Boy" is vaguely reminiscent of Sassoon's "The Kiss" in its description of bayonet and bullet, although Owen's verse is not ambiguous. The "malice" of the weaponry contrasts sharply to the boy's nature, and Owen's linking "blind blunt bullet-heads" with the loving desire "to nuzzle in the hearts of lads" makes Owen's attitude toward the weapons clear. "Mental Cases" is truly remarkable for its time. When the prevailing view of shell shock was that expressed ironically in "The Dead-Beat," Owen was able to depict the agony of those suffering mental affliction by describing the outward manifestations of their lack of control:

> Who are these? Why sit they here in twilight?
> Wherefore rock they, purgatorial shadows,
> Drooping tongues from jaws that slob their relish,
> Baring teeth that leer like skulls' teeth wicked?

In the second stanza, Owen identifies these men and their grief:

> —These are men whose minds the Dead have ravished.
> Memory fingers in their hair of murders,
> Multitudinous murders they once witnessed.

Once he has established that these men are tormented by sights they cannot forget, Owen shifts to the issue of responsibility and assumes his own share of the burden in the final lines:

> —Thus their hands are plucking at each other;
> Picking at the rope-knouts of their scourging;
> Snatching after us who smote them, brother,
> Pawing us who dealt them war and madness.

Unlike Sassoon, Owen can identify with his targets.

In "Strange Meeting," Owen's best single attempt to chronicle the war, several aspects of his poetry combine. His dependence on the nineteenth-century poetic tradition appears in his echo of Wordsworth's "Ode on the Intimations of Immortality" (substituting "truths that lie too deep for taint" for Wordsworth's "Thoughts that do often lie too deep for tears"). In addition to continuing the equation of war and hell, Owen imbeds his poetic theory into the verse: "I mean the truth untold, / The pity of war, the pity war distilled." Owen's use of pararhyme throughout reinforces the unexpected quality of the soldiers' conversation in the underworld, and Owen's pity comes through more effectively than in his other poems. The greatness of the poem is not only its merging of the several strains of Owen's vision, which include literary awareness, pararhyme, pity, mastery of language, and capacity for timeless perspective, but also its compatibility with Owen's Christian pacifism.

Like "The Show," "Strange Meeting" is a dream vision:

> It seemed that out of battle I escaped
> Down some profound dull tunnel, long since scooped
> Through granites which titanic wars had groined.

Meeting one of the dead convinces the speaker that "we stood in Hell," and the encountered spirit expresses the philosophy of the soldier poet in his regret for the "undone years" and for the "truth untold." As a result of this poet's silence, "men will go content with what we spoiled, / Or, discontent, boil bloody, and be spilled. / They will be swift with swiftness of the tigress. / None will break ranks, though nations trek from progress." The prediction, even in its imagery, anticipates Yeats's "The Second Coming" and seems to predict the political and economic turmoil to follow the war. At the end of this soldier poet's speech, he identifies himself in terms which transcend the nationalistic hatred that has kept the war alive:

> I am the enemy you killed, my friend.
> I knew you in this dark: for so you frowned
> Yesterday through me as you jabbed and killed.
> I parried; but my hands were loath and cold.
> Let us sleep now. . . .

The uncertainty and disillusionment of mood expressed in this poem receive more support from Owen's pararhymes than do any of his other poems.

The argument of "Futility" is deceptively simple. The sun, whose warmth originally stirred life, should be able to rouse a soldier who has died in the trenches during the winter: "If anything might rouse him now / The kind old sun will know." However, in the second stanza, "futility" operates on several levels, identified by Arthur E. Lane: "Not only is it futile to try to wake the man (futility in the most immediate sense); the complex series of events which have shaped him 'dear-achieved' and 'Full-nerved' have now come to nothing (a more generalized futility); and, as the last three lines suggest, insofar as the man is typical of youth, his destruction represents a victory of chaos over order (futility in the most universal sense)."[17] Owen couches these crucial three lines in the form of questions reminiscent of those in "The End":

Was it for this the clay grew tall?
—O what made fatuous sunbeams toil
To break earth's sleep at all?

Two other poems written at this time indicate some influence of Sassoon. In "The Chances," Owen presents in colloquial fashion a discussion recalling Sassoon's "They" in its catalogue of soldiers' injuries. However, Owen is not attempting to hit so unchallenging a mark as a chauvinistic bishop. The poem is a dramatic monologue presenting a soldier's recollection of a talk among five comrades concerning the dangerous possibilities of a coming battle: "Ye get knocked out; else wounded—bad or cushy; / Scuppered; or nowt except yer feelin' mushy." The five comrades experience these four chances, one "blown to chops," one losing his legs, one captured by the Germans, and the narrator escaping without a scratch. Jimmy, who had summarized the chances, has suffered them all: " 'E's wounded, killed, and pris'ner, all the lot, / The bloody lot all rolled in one. Jim's mad."

"The Parable of the Old Man and the Young," frequently criticized for the "superfluous" last line, presents the story of Abram and Isaac in modern dress. After arriving at the point of sacrifice, "Abram bound the youth with belts and straps, / And builded parapets and trenches there, / And stretchèd forth the knife to slay his son." An angel intervenes to order Abram, "Lay not thy hand upon the lad" and to "Offer the Ram of Pride instead of him." This leads to the disputed ending of the poem, the only rhymed lines:

But the old man would not so, but slew his son,
And half the seed of Europe, one by one.

Although war references—"parapets," "trenches," and "belts and straps"—are explicit, the last line is still necessary. Owen had not only to present the tendency of old men to sacrifice the young, but also to specify the extent of the carnage.

Owen's "Exposure" is particularly difficult to date. Johnston has indicated February 1917 as its probable date, while Hibberd has placed the poem as begun in December 1917 and finished in September 1918. The poem is effective in Owen's successful application of pararhyme to emphasize "painful discords." The first line echoes Keats's "Ode to Melancholy" as Owen establishes the soldiers' suffering from bitter cold (probably of the winter of 1916–17, by all accounts unusually severe). Owen captures the soldiers' physical agony, pained memories, continuous uncertainty, and ironical boredom in the refrain "But nothing happens." In the first stanza, one can appreciate the horrors of winter warfare:

Our brains ache, in the merciless iced east winds that knive us . . .
Wearied we keep awake because the night is silent . . .
Low, drooping flares confuse our memory of the salient . . .
Worried by silence, sentries whisper, curious, nervous,
      But nothing happens.

In the next-to-last stanza, Owen provides the soldiers' reason for enduring such trials:

Since we believe not otherwise can kind fires burn;
Nor ever suns smile true on child, or field, or fruit.
For God's invincible spring our love is made afraid;
Therefore, not loath, we lie out here; therefore were born,
      For love of God seems dying.

This recalls the land-based patriotism of Edward Thomas as well as the acceptance shown in Blunden's line in "Zero," "It's plain we were born for this, naught else." The last stanza shows that such certainty does nothing to mitigate the exposure to the cold:

To-night, His frost will fasten on this mud and us,
Shrivelling many hands, puckering foreheads crisp.
The burying-party, picks and shovels in their shaking grasp,
Pause over half-known faces. All their eyes are ice.
      But nothing happens.

"The Sentry," almost certainly written in September 1918, forms a sharp contrast to "Exposure." Instead of describing the trenches and their afflictions in general terms, "The Sentry" is a specific narrative couched in lines whose rhymes sometimes shift unexpectedly, but which employ frequent rhymed couplets. Owen chronicles an episode he has elsewhere described in letters. While occupying a section of the German trenches, Owen's men came under direct artillery fire. The first of three sections describes the general situation as "shell on frantic shell / Hammered on top, but never quite burst through," and the second moves to the destruction caused by one "whizz-bang" that "found our door at last." Owen describes holding a sentry blinded by the blast and trying to comfort him. "Eyeballs, huge-bulged like squids', / Watch my dreams still; but I forgot him there / In posting Next for duty, and sending a scout / To beg a stretcher some-where. . . ." The third section, typographically separated from the rest of the poem, indicates a shift as the narrator recalls the incident from a remote time and place. The narrator tries "not to remember these things now" but recalls the sentry, who had been told that "if he could see the least blurred light / He was not blind; in time he'd get all right." At the end of the poem, the narrator recalls hearing the sentry "shout / 'I see your lights!' But ours had long died out." The poem combines several of Owen's favorite themes—the harrowing nature of life at the front, pity for the maimed sentry, and the lingering impact of fear and injury on those witnessing them.

"Spring Offensive" is probably Owen's last poem, found among his papers after his death. It masterfully describes the contrast between peaceful interludes and the sudden chaos of battle. The poem employs a regular meter as it combines pastoral setting with ironical overtones:

> Halted against the shade of a last hill,
> They fed, and lying easy, were at ease
> And, finding comfortable chests and knees,
> Carelessly slept. But many there stood still
> To face the stark, blank sky beyond the ridge,
> Knowing their feet had come to the end of the world.

Despite the superficial peace of the setting, men, like animals, "fed" rather than ate, and the references to "a last hill" and "the end of the world" function as reminders that this peace is only temporary. In the fourth stanza, the impending battle is introduced in terms appropriate to modern war: "No alarms / Of bugles, no high flags, no clamorous haste— / Only a lift and flare of eyes that faced / The sun. . . ." As the fighting begins, the calm of nature disappears in the tumult of battle:

> And instantly the whole sky burned
> With fury against them; earth set sudden cups
> In thousands for their blood; and the green slope
> Chasmed and steepened sheer to infinite space.

After describing those who "Leapt to swift unseen bullets, or went up / On the hot blast and fury of hell's upsurge," Owen contrasts them to the survivors,

> who rushed in the body to enter hell,
> And there out-fiending all its fiends and flames
> With superhuman inhumanities,
> Long-famous glories, immemorial shames—
> And crawling slowly back, have by degrees
> Regained cool peaceful air in wonder—
> Why speak not they of comrades that went under?

Included in this contrast are the return of "cool peaceful air," the survivors' thought for fallen comrades, and their awareness that their survival did not depend on their being better, but being somehow worse than the others.

Owen's reputation as a poet rests on major accomplishments. He was something of an innovator in his development of pararhyme. As Dominic

Hibberd has commented, *"He was the first English poet to use pararhyme at the ends of lines throughout a poem.* No one had done that before. Terminal pararhymes are his peculiar contribution to prosody."[18] Owen was by no means the first to use pararhymes. Similar variations in rhyme had appeared in the ancient Welsh bards, modern French poets, and even "a group of half-rhymes marked in Owen's copy of Shelley."[19] However, sustained terminal pararhyme in Owen's poetry enhanced Owen's purposes. Middleton Murry called Owen's use of pararhyme in war poetry "a discovery of genius," but Owen also used the device in lyric poetry, notably in "From My Diary, July 1914."

According to David Daiches, "Owen is claimed by some modern poets as an important influence on their poetry, but it is difficult to see how Owen's poetry can influence those who have so much less to say."[20] Ultimately, what Owen had to say has had more influence than how he said it. Owen's declaration that "The poetry is in the pity," his ability to describe a wide range of personal experiences both subjectively and objectively, his commitment to articulate painful experience at the expense of "Poetry," and his ability to communicate without brutality the brutal sources of painful feeling have made his verse unique among the writings of the war poets.

12

Isaac Rosenberg

ISAAC ROSENBERG (1890–1918) WAS THE ANTITHESIS OF THE CONTEMPORARY romanticized view of the soldier poet. Short of stature, frail, ill-educated, poor, and Jewish, Rosenberg was not in the image of Rupert Brooke. Far from joining the army for patriotic reasons, Rosenberg enlisted despite his belief that this was "the most criminal thing a man can do."[1] His parents were bitterly opposed to any military service. His father had fled Russia to avoid conscription. Unlike the majority of public-school soldiers who became subalterns, Rosenberg served in the ranks and refused his sole opportunity for promotion, to corporal, on the grounds that he would not become part of the military establishment.

Rosenberg's war experience contrasts sharply with that of the other war poets. When Blunden's commanding officer heard that he was a fledgling poet, his colonel transferred him to a job behind the lines, but Rosenberg's officer forbade Rosenberg to mail poems home because he refused to "be bothered with going through such rubbish."[2] Owen, despite his conscientious objection to war, served with distinction and won the Military Cross, but Rosenberg, largely due to "absent-mindedness," frequently found himself performing punishment duties for his ineptitude. The officer poets had frequent respites behind the lines and convalescent leaves to England, but Rosenberg, as a private, spent twenty-two months in France with only one ten-day leave home. The privation which Rosenberg experienced in the ranks becomes even more ironical in view of his motive for enlisting. As he wrote to Edward Marsh in December 1915, "I thought if I'd join there would be the separation allowance for my mother."[3]

Rosenberg's father, Barnett, was an itinerant pedlar, and his mother, Hacha, toiled unremittingly to care for the children and to supplement Barnett's meager income. By 1897, when the family moved to London's East End to a one-room apartment behind a rag-and-bone shop, there were five children and no increase in Barnett's income. Barnett persisted in trying to make a living as a pedlar, preferring travel to staying at home. Despite their mutual lack of affection for one another, Barnett and Hacha were concerned with the well-being of their children. For Barnett, who had earlier hoped to become a rabbi, well-being included religious instruction, so he tried to enroll Isaac in the Jews' Free School. However, the school was filled beyond capacity, so Isaac wound up at the Baker Street School. There he was encouraged by a Mr. Usherwood to pursue interests in art and literature, although his parents' circumstances did not make such pursuits easy. Isaac had to leave school in 1904, at the age of fourteen, to begin an apprenticeship at Carl Hentschel's, an engraving firm in Fleet Street.

As the eldest son of an impoverished family, he might have been expected to work earlier, but his life was not entirely luckless. Against the poverty of his youth one can balance his family's sympathy with and support of his artistic pursuits, despite the Rosenbergs' need for money, as well as some financial assistance from Jewish organizations and patrons. Rosenberg began to take evening classes in painting at Birkbeck College in 1907, and he won a National Book prize in 1908 for a charcoal study. He won the Mason Prize as well, and in 1910 he won the Pocock Prize. In 1911 he met Stephen Winsten, Joseph Leftwich, and John Rodker—later to be known as the "Whitechapel Boys"—and in March he left Hentschel's to devote all his energies to a career in art. Solomon J. Solomon, R. A., had remained indifferent to Rosenberg's requests for help to enter the famous Slade School of painting, but Solomon's sister (Lily Delissa Joseph) and two others agreed to underwrite his studies at the Slade.

Rosenberg won some prizes in his first year and might have continued at the Slade longer were it not for his combination of clumsiness and ill luck. Because he had not completed a painting in time for a competition, one patron, Mrs. Cohen, became convinced that Rosenberg was an idler, although nothing could have been farther from the truth, and determined to withdraw her support. Rosenberg added fuel to this fire when he sent her a letter with a blot on it, which she took as a sign of indifference. Fortunately for Rosenberg, the Jewish Educational Aid Society agreed to finance one more year of study. The Society did not limit its support to tuition. When his health required him to take a fortnight's holiday, the Society paid for that, and it also paid for his trip to Cape Town when his lungs continued to trouble him in the middle of 1914.

While working to develop as a painter, Rosenberg was also pursuing his interests in poetry. In 1912 he corresponded with and then met Laurence Binyon, the first literary man of any note to recognize him. In 1913 Rosenberg also met Edward Marsh and T. E. Hulme, and he began correspondence with Gordon Bottomley (later to edit Rosenberg's poetry), R. C. Trevelyan, and Lascelles Abercrombie. In addition to reading widely to make up for his lack of formal education, Rosenberg spent as much time working on poetry as he did on painting. He published three volumes of poetry at his own expense—*Night and Day* (1912), *Youth* (1915), and *Moses* (1916)—and came to regard himself as more poet than painter. Rosenberg, according to Joseph Cohen, had read widely in English literature and knew well his Shakespeare, Milton, Donne, Blake, Keats and Browning. He was familiar with the work of some of his contemporaries: Flint, Masefield, Brooke, Sassoon, D. H. Lawrence, and Pound. He had read Yeats and Hardy, and found that Shaw's plays were the only ones he enjoyed watching. To Bottomley, Trevelyan, and Abercrombie he attached too much significance, for understandable reasons. Poe, Emerson and Whitman were important to him and he held them in higher esteem than Turgenev, Dostoyevsky and Chekhov. He knew his Ibsen, Flaubert, Balzac, Stendhal, and Baudelaire. He had read the Belgians and the Germans, and was particularly fond of Heine. He knew Eliot by name only; he had no occasion to read his poetry. He apparently did not know of T. E. Lawrence, James Joyce, or Wilfred Owen.[4]

Rosenberg's approach to poetry paralleled his growing understanding of painting. In an early short story entitled "Rudolph," the protagonist expresses an attitude toward painting that reveals Rosenberg's attitude toward poetry as well: "My ideal of a picture is to paint what we cannot see. To create, to imagine. To make tangible and real a figment of the brain. To transport the spectator into other worlds where beauty is the only reality. Rossetti is my ideal."[5] This is relatively early—Rosenberg showed this story to Lily Delissa Joseph in May 1911. In October 1912, writing to Mrs. Cohen to defend himself against her accusations of laxity, he said of painting what he might have said of poetry: "Art is not a plaything, it is blood and tears, it must grow up with one; and I believe I have begun too late."[6] Ironically, few have begun so early. In December 1912 or January 1913, he wrote to Miss Winifred Seaton, a schoolmistress whom he had met in 1910, of "genuine poetry, where the words lose their interest as words and only a living and beautiful idea remains,"[7] revealing his growing distance from purely denotative uses of language.

Rosenberg, who had been in Cape Town since June 1914, returned to England in February 1915. He arranged to have *Youth* printed, met Sydney Schiff (who wrote and translated under the pseudonym "Stephen Hudson"), and managed to publish a couple of poems in Cape Town, but otherwise he accomplished little. His efforts to find work, even at Hentschel's, were not successful, and he wrote a letter (apparently never mailed) to Ezra Pound indicating his mixed feelings concerning enlistment: "I think the world has been terribly damaged by certain poets (in fact any poet) being sacrificed in this stupid business. There is certainly a strong temptation to join when you are making no money."[8] At the end of October he did enlist. His height barred him from any unit except the Bantam Battalion of the 12th Suffolk Regiment. He had written to Schiff that he felt that "more men means more war,—besides the immorality of joining with no patriotic convictions,"[9] but his financial exigencies overcame his scruples. He wrote to Marsh in October that "I have just joined the Bantams and am down here amongst a horrible rabble—Falstaff's scarecrows were nothing to these. Three out of every 4 have been scavengers, the fourth is a ticket of leave [one given a choice between prison and enlistment]."[10] Naïvely assuming that the army would provide for his needs, he took only a comb and a handkerchief in addition to what he wore. Some weeks passed before he had even a towel, and when he received his issue of boots, no one told him that he must soften them with grease, so he became lame from their chafing. The food was insufficient both in quality and quantity, and the combination of his Jewishness, stuttering, and ineptness made him a target for special abuse.

Despite his torments, he sustained himself with ironical observations rather than self-pitying complaints. Early in 1916 he wrote to Schiff, "The authorities are quite aware of the state of things, but as the authorities have not got to eat of our food, their energy in the matter is not too obvious."[11] Occasionally he allowed himself the luxury of expressing his feelings. He wrote to Abercrombie in March 1916 that "the army is the most detestable invention on this earth and nobody but a private in the army knows what it is to be a slave. I wonder whether your muse has been sniffing gunpowder."[12] In fact, Abercrombie wrote no poetry between August 1914 and the Armistice. To Marsh, Rosenberg put a more humorous face on matters: "The king inspected us Thursday. I believe it's the first Bantam Brigade been inspected. He must have waited for us to stand up a good while. At a distance we look like soldiers sitting down, you know, legs so short."[13] Many of the less savory Bantams were weeded out of the battalion, and those remaining were transferred to separate units, so that by March 1916 Rosenberg was in the 11th Battalion, King's Own Royal Lancasters Regiment.

In June 1916 he arrived in France, shortly before the rain turned the Somme Valley into a sea of mud. He spent July 1916 at a desk job, but by the end of August he was in the trenches, where he remained until he became ill in January 1917. The following month he was assigned to the 229th Field Company, Royal Engineers, which removed him from tours of the trenches but which required him to participate in wiring parties in No Man's Land. After ten days' leave in England in September 1917, he returned to trench duty, where he remained (except for one period in hospital for influenza and one brief period of rest) until his death. On 1 April 1918, he was killed while on night patrol and buried in an unmarked grave.

Rosenberg's service in France was unmitigated hell for him. He wrote to Bottomley in February 1918, "No drug could be more stupefying than our work (to me anyway), and this goes on like that old torture of water trickling, drop by drop unendingly, on one's helplessness."[14] His health, never good, became even more uncertain during his prolonged exposure to cold and wet. He had little time to write, composing poems in odd moments when he had both opportunity and light. His writing only alienated him further from the other men. His natural clumsiness had caused him sufficient trouble in civilian life. He had ruined a portrait trying to improve it, had failed to notice King George while Rosenberg was copying a painting at the National Gallery, had ruined a copy of "Philip IV" by carrying it before the varnish had dried, had frequently failed to put the addresses on envelopes he mailed, and had accidentally dropped several paintings and drawings overboard when he departed from Cape Town. In the military he continued to display his penchant for misadventure, which frequently resulted in punishment for failure to carry out orders. He also failed to exploit opportunity. When he learned, for example, that Solomon J. Solomon was the colonel in charge of a camouflage unit, he made no effort to effect a transfer although he knew that Solomon would probably remember him sympathetically.

Despite his misery, he maintained a devotion to poetry that was truly impressive. He wrote to Marsh in June 1916 that "I am aware how fearfully busy you must be, but if poetry at this time is no use it certainly won't be at any other,"[15] and he later wrote to Marsh, "The Homer for this war has yet to be found—Whitman got very near the mark 50 years ago with 'Drum Taps.' "[16] During this time he also wrote to Mrs. Cohen, who had sent a copy of the *Poetry Review.* He criticized some soldier poets and Rupert Brooke for their "common-place" approach to poetry. He felt that poetry "should be approached in a colder way, more abstract, with less of the million feelings everybody feels; or all these should be concentrated in one distinguished emotion."[17] Despite his having to compose poetry at random moments over periods of weeks, depending on the odd fragment of candle to enable him to write after dark, his service to the muse was unflagging.

Equally impressive was Rosenberg's essential optimism in spite of physical and emotional discomfort. Before the war, in a letter to Miss Seaton, he outlined his philosophy: "I believe, however hard one's lot is, one ought to try and accommodate oneself to the conditions; and except in a case of purely physical pain, I think it can be done. Why not make the very utmost of our lives?"[18] In France, he resolved to make the best of his lot. He wrote to Binyon in the fall of 1916 that "I am determined that this war, with all its powers for devastation, shall not master my poeting; that is, if I am lucky enough to come through all right. I will not leave a corner of my consciousness covered up, but saturate myself with the strange and extraordinary new conditions of this life, and it will all refine itself into poetry later on."[19] The unfinished state of many of his poems results from his inability to rework them after the war. In that sense, many of his poems were "notes."

In the view of Denys Harding,

> What most distinguishes Isaac Rosenberg from other English poets who wrote of the last war is the intense significance he saw in the kind of living effort that the war called out, and the way in which his technique enabled him to present both this and the suffering and the waste as

inseparable aspects of life in war. Further, there is in his work, without the least touch of coldness, nevertheless a certain impersonality: he tried to feel in the war a significance for life as such, rather than seeing only its convulsion of the human life he knew.[20]

Bergonzi has commented on the more significant distinction of perspective: "Rosenberg had, above all, a two-fold vision of the war: he was aware both of the human suffering it involved, and the unsurpassed human effort, which he regarded as a kind of absolute value, which it called forth. And this set him apart from traditional patriots and from the poets of anti-war protest."[21] Like Edward Thomas, Rosenberg was less a war poet than a poet at war. Like Thomas, he brought with him a talent which had been developing long before the war began.

Rosenberg's first "war poem" was occasional. He first heard of the war in Cape Town, and in the autumn of 1914 he composed "On Receiving News of the War." Instead of trying to describe the war as a contemporary event, Rosenberg placed it in the context of recurring events that always pass. The poem begins with a seasonal metaphor, presenting the arrival of war as the unasked-for arrival of winter after summer. In the third stanza, the effect of war on man appears in general terms:

> In all men's hearts it is.
> Some spirit old
> Hath turned with malign kiss
> Our lives to mould.

In the next stanza, war wounds God so that He mourns, and in the final lines Rosenberg hopes for regeneration:

> O! ancient crimson curse!
> Corrode, consume.
> Give back this universe
> Its pristine bloom.

Unlike many early efforts, this poem is remarkable for its absence of patriotic sentiment and its refusal to exaggerate the need for an English victory. The poem reveals that, at the outbreak of the war, Rosenberg was already a poet with considerable mastery.

"The Dead Heroes," also written at Cape Town and published there in December 1914, seems commonplace in its expression of patriotic feelings. The poem, unlike "On Receiving News of the War," finds no redemption in the superiority of its imagery. One may assume that its quick publication resulted from its accordance with the public mood:

England, they live in thee,
  In thy proud fame,
They died to keep thee free,
  And thy pure name.

"Lusitania" has similar defects and lapses into a partisan stance. Addressing Chaos, Rosenberg ends the poem, "Now you have got the peace-faring *Lusitania,* / Germany's gift—all earth they would give thee, Chaos," With the exception of "On Receiving News of the War," these reflect little credit on Rosenberg's gift. War poems remained a small fraction of his work before his enlistment a year later.

After enlisting, Rosenberg frequently wrote poems describing aspects of military life. One of the first poems he wrote in the barracks was "The Jew," composed in October or November 1915, inspired by the anti-Semitism he encountered. In one short stanza he identifies himself as sprung from Moses, whose "Ten immutable rules" are "a moon / For mutable lampless men." The second stanza identifies "The blonde, the bronze, the ruddy" who follow Mosaic law and derive from Moses's stock, but who persist in sneering at the Jew. Rosenberg hardly makes his complaint strident. Only in the last line does he introduce anti-Semitism, and then only to pose a contrast between the Gentile's debt to and contempt for the Jew.

In "Marching (As Seen from the Left File)," which he mailed to Marsh in December 1915 and which appeared in Harriet Monroe's *Poetry Magazine* in December 1916, he described his view from the ranks as it would appear to a painter. His descriptive imagery in the opening lines reveals a discriminating eye:

My eyes catch ruddy necks
Sturdily pressed back—
All a red brick moving glint.
Like flaming pendulums, hands
Swing across the khaki—
Mustard-coloured khaki—
To the automatic feet.

He moves from this pictorial description to link the marchers with the "ancient glory," and he also seems aware of the change that mechanism has brought to warfare in his statement that "Not broke is the forge of Mars; / But a subtler brain beats iron" to enable "Blind fingers" to release "immortal darkness / On strong eyes."

"The Troop Ship," written after his crossing to France on 3 June 1916, seems deliberately Imagistic in its attention to vivid depiction. He describes soldiers trying to sleep on the crowded troop ship as "Grotesque and

queerly huddled / Contortionists," and his description ends with the evocative reminder that, "should you drop to a doze, / Winds' fumble or men's
feet / Are on your face." When describing the realities of military life,
Rosenberg refuses to sermonize or moralize on their brutality or nature. He
is primarily concerned with recording what he sees.

Rosenberg arrived in France in June 1916. He did not begin to experience
the rigors of life in the trenches until the end of August, but his proximity to
the fighting sufficiently acquainted him with the devastation of modern
warfare, and he wrote some poems which attempted to convey his new sense
of destruction. In "Spring 1916," Rosenberg describes Spring in somber
terms:

> Slow, rigid, is this masquerade
> That passes as through a difficult air;
> Heavily—heavily passes.
> What has she fed on?

He wonders what "forbidden fare" has ruined Spring (using the Persephone
myth), recalls former seasons, and wonders how Spring has become "So
ghastly." His conclusion recalls the end of "On Receiving News of the War":
"Where are the strong men who made these their loves? / Spring! God pity
your mood."

In "From France," written early in 1916, Rosenberg considers the ironical
associations that the war has given to the phrase "Life in France." After the
first stanza recalls the prewar mood, the second ends with men who "groan
to broken men, / 'This is not Life in France.'" The final stanza confines itself
to describing the current reality rather than commenting further:

> Heaped stones and a charred signboard shows
> With grass between and dead folk under,
> And some birds sing, while the spirit takes wing.
> And this is Life in France.

One could imagine Sassoon making this poem the core of a curative diatribe
designed to sober overenthusiastic recruits, or Owen making it into a
compassionate lament for individual victims betrayed by their sense of
patriotism. In Rosenberg's hands it becomes a direct statement of a reality
that he saw.

In "August 1914," which Rosenberg wrote in the summer of 1916, Cohen
finds evidence of an important transition: "Rosenberg had not been in
France long before he developed beyond his earlier loosely-evolved images,
often wrought with extraneous appendages, to the hard, clear images, complete in themselves, shorn of inessentials. With 'August 1914' . . . his emergence as a war poet was complete."[22] Through his imagery, Rosenberg

reveals his mastery of expression as well as his growing awareness of the war's devastation. The poem is a progression of three stanzas, the first of which poses the question of what effect the war has on "our lives." The second declares that each life is three lives—"Iron, honey, gold"—and that only the iron life remains. The third offers hard, precise images which convey the effect of war on land and men:

> Iron are our lives
> Molten right through our youth.
> A burnt space through ripe fields,
> A fair mouth's broken tooth.

Rosenberg composed two "trench poems" before he saw the trenches. "In the Trenches," mailed to Sonia Rodker in June or July 1916 with his comment that the poem was "a bit common-place," attempts to describe the reality of a shell's sudden destruction:

> Down—a shell—O! Christ,
> I am choked . . . safe . . . dust blind, I
> See trench floor poppies
> Strewn. Smashed you lie.

During the summer of 1916 he also wrote "Break of Day in the Trenches," which appeared in *Poetry Magazine* in December 1916 with "Marching (As Seen from the Left File)." The poem is remarkable for its compelling expression of the war's significance. The poem begins as a soldier, at stand-to, sees a "queer sardonic rat" as he plucks a poppy to stick behind his ear. The soldier addresses the rat:

> Droll rat, they would shoot you if they knew
> Your cosmopolitan sympathies.
> Now you have touched this English hand
> You will do the same to a German
> Soon, no doubt, if it be your pleasure
> To cross the sleeping green between.

The roles of the soldier and the rat have become inverted. The rat has dominion, while the soldier fears and starts at sudden noises. At the end of the poem Rosenberg includes a powerful image that exploits the possibilities of poppies in pastoral elegy:

> Poppies whose roots are in man's veins
> Drop, and are ever dropping;
> But mine in my ear is safe—
> Just a little white with the dust.

Rosenberg has managed to convey the enduring significance of the conflict as well as the more mundane aspects of trench warfare, including "torn fields" and the "shrieking iron and flame."

Once assigned to trench duty, Rosenberg had relatively little time for writing poems or letters. In a letter to Marsh, postmarked 27 May 1917, he described the composition of "Daughters of War": "I have written a much finer poem which I've asked my sister to send you. Don't think from this I've time to write. This last poem is only about 70 lines and I started it about October [1916]. It is only when we get a bit of rest and the others might be gambling or squabbling I add a line or two, and continue this way."[23] That he could write at all under those conditions indicates his devotion to verse. That the poetry, "fragmentary" as it sometimes seems, could be so powerful is a tribute to his talent. Since Rosenberg mailed his poetry to his sister Annie so that she could type it, and since he rarely dated his letters (despite a specific request from Schiff to do so), much less his verse, placing the poems in sequence becomes even more difficult than with his earlier verse. Rosenberg wrote on whatever scraps of paper were available to him, leaving as evidence only the postmarks and the infrequent dates of his letters. Even so, as the letter to Marsh reveals, a poem may have been in the works for months before anyone else knew of its existence.

Rosenberg finished his most ambitious war poem, "Dead Man's Dump," before May 1917 (he mailed it to Marsh on 8 May). Marius Bewley, after commenting on the "impersonal and detached" stance and the "hard, almost shocking concreteness and immediacy" of the poem, called attention to the source of the poem's greatness: "no facile, gratuitous commentary on that fate is offered in the whole eighty-six lines of 'Dead Man's Dump.' The poem's strength lies in the composure it maintains when faced by human pain, in its refusal to indulge an easy grief or extend a gala invitation to tears. It shows a sure control of words moving through dangerous emotions at disciplined speeds and leading the reader, by their very restraint and poise, into a fuller understanding of human dignity."[24] Rosenberg begins with a description of the wiring limbers moving toward No Man's Land:

> The plunging limbers over the shattered track
> Racketed with their rusty freight,
> Stuck out like many crowns of thorns,
> And the rusty stakes like sceptres old
> To stay the flood of brutish men
> Upon our brothers dear.

After describing the wagons' lurching over the dead while shells fly over-head, Rosenberg envisions the earth waiting eagerly for men to return to the soil and pictures souls flying out from "their souls' sack." He then turns to

the living and their relationship with the dead, but his attention suddenly
returns to the immediate present:

> A man's brains splattered on
> A stretcher-bearer's face;
> His shook shoulders slipped their load,
> But when they bent to look again
> The drowning soul was sunk too deep
> For human tenderness.

The victim remained "with the older dead."

One of the dying hears the limber's wheels and hopes for life, but Rosenberg crushes the illusory hope of rescue with the stark realism of his
concluding lines:

> Even as the mixed hoofs of the mules,
> The quivering-bellied mules,
> And the rushing wheels all mixed
> With his tortured upturned sight,
> So we crashed round the bend,
> We heard his weak scream,
> We heard his very last sound,
> And our wheels grazed his dead face.

The detachment of the poem is far from indifference. The dispassionate
description of such brutal scenes as the man's splattering brains and the
limber grazing the face of the dead man conveys the horror of the front,
while Rosenberg's musings on the men's departed spirits and his dramatiza-
tion of the yearning of the dead soldier in the last stanza balance the
descriptive features.

"Daughters of War," written before May 1917, reveals an aspect of Rosenberg's poetic vision that had appeared in earlier verses not directly connected
with the war. He inverts the Old Testament story of the "Sons of God and
the Daughters of Men" that D. H. Lawrence frequently employed. In the
poem, the Daughters of War are Amazons who lust after mortals:

> I heard the mighty daughters' giant sighs
> In sleepless passion for the sons of valour,
> And envy of the days of flesh
> Barring their love with mortal boughs across—
> The mortal boughs—the mortal tree of life.
> The old bark burnt with iron wars
> They blow to a live flame
> To char the young green days
> And reach the occult soul; they have no softer lure
> No softer lure than the savage ways of death.

Men, unable to resist, realize that they must be "broken for evermore / So the soul can leap out / Into their huge embraces." There is no mention of parapet, poppy, trench, or shell in the poem, but Rosenberg evokes the very spirit of chaos and destruction in a mystical framework.

Rosenberg's "In War" is less successful because the poet shifts from a restrained description of events to pathos. The restraint endures until the poem's tenth stanza. In the first five, Rosenberg contemplates death in apparently general terms, and in the sixth he shifts suddenly to soldiers on burial detail:

> One day we dug a grave:
> We were vexed
> With the sun's heat.
> We scanned the hooded dead:
> At noon we sat and talked.

The men discuss the battle of three days before, and then Rosenberg summarizes their lot:

> And we whom chance kept whole—
> But haggard,
> Spent—were charged
> To make a place for them who knew
> No pain in any place.

While a priest reads over the dead, the men only vaguely listen, more concerned with their thirst, but in the tenth stanza one soldier suddenly becomes involved: "Sudden my blood ran cold . . . / God! God! it could not be." The next stanza makes clear that the soldier's brother is among the dead. In the last stanza, Rosenberg returns to a more universal perspective:

> What are the great sceptred dooms
> To us, caught
> In the wild wave?
> We break ourselves on them,
> My brother, our hearts and years.

Except for the poem's ending, "In War" presents a "timeless and universal" view of war. However, the recent transfer of his brothers David and Elkon to France appears to have moved Rosenberg to this unrestrained utterance.

Two poems written in the summer of 1917, "A Worm Fed on the Heart of Corinth" and "The Dying Soldier," reveal the extremes of Rosenberg's range. In the first, Rosenberg places the present war into an historical perspective which includes Corinth, Babylon, Rome, and Troy, whose fall was not the result of Helen's abduction but of "this incestuous worm." After

placing falling cities and nations in the context of an eternal impulse toward
chaos and decay, Rosenberg addresses his own country:

> England! famous as Helen
> Is thy betrothal sung
> To him the shadowless,
> More amorous than Solomon.

This perspective approaches the universal. "The Dying Soldier" is at the
opposite extreme, the vivid personal moment. A dying soldier, under artillery fire, gasping, begs water "For one of England's dying sons," but the
dialogue in the final stanza is closer to Sassoon or Gibson than to Newbolt:

> "We cannot give you water,
> Were all England in your breath,"
> "Water!—water!—O water!"
> He moaned and swooned to death.

In "A Worm Fed on the Heart of Corinth," Rosenberg views conflict in a vast
and impersonal perspective. In "The Dying Soldier," he dramatizes conflict
with direct and immediate description.

"The Immortals" and "Louse Hunting," both written in 1917, show
Rosenberg approaching a less widely recognized hazard of the trenches, the
louse. In the first (and probably earlier), he begins by describing a scene of
carnage that could have come from the Old Testament, a slaughter of
thousands which "made my hands red in their gore." Only in the final lines
does the reader discover Rosenberg's irony:

> I used to think the Devil hid
> In women's smiles and wine's carouse.
> I called him Satan, Balzebub.
> But now I call him, dirty louse.

In this poem, as in "Louse Hunting," Rosenberg does not bemoan the
continuing battle with lice but attempts to convey their torments in satiric
whimsy. In "Louse Hunting," he describes soldiers fighting lice in a macabre
revel, and although the poem is laden with irony, there is also appreciation
for the activity that the battle inspires. After describing the naked soldiers
tearing off their clothing to hold it over a candle flame, including such details
as soldiers' oaths, he treats the battle in mock-epic terms:

> Soon like a demons' pantomime
> The place was raging.
> See the silhouettes agape,
> See the gibbering shadows

Mixed with the battled arms on the wall.
See gargantuan hooked fingers
Pluck in supreme flesh
To smutch supreme littleness.

While communicating the antics which the torturing lice have inspired,
Rosenberg refrains from complaint: he is interested not in the men's misery,
but in their frantic energy.

Rosenberg's last important war poem, "Returning, We Hear the Larks,"
written during the summer of 1917, reveals something of his growing uncertainty after months of trench duty. The poem begins with a spirit of foreboding:

Sombre the night is.
And though we have our lives, we know
What sinister threat lurks there.

After describing the return of the weary men to camp, Rosenberg shifts to
the unexpected sound of singing larks, "Music showering our upturned
list'ning faces." The relief is only momentary, however:

Death could drop from the dark
As easily as song—
But song only dropped,
Like a blind man's dreams on the sand
By dangerous tides,
Like a girl's dark hair for she dreams no ruin lies there,
Or her kisses where a serpent hides.

The poem ends as ominously as it began, with veiled threats in the closing
similes. The contrast between the expected shelling and the unexpected song
conveys the continuous sense of uncertainty felt by the men at the front.

Joseph Cohen's biography of Rosenberg includes, as its last chapter, a
review of the slow growth of Rosenberg's reputation. The ill luck that
dogged Rosenberg during his brief life continued to operate on his reputation after his death. Despite the efforts of such editors and critics as Siegfried
Sassoon, Laurence Binyon, Marius Bewley, F. R. Leavis, Denys Harding,
Dennis Silk, and T. S. Eliot, Rosenberg's work never quite caught on. Part of
this, as Cohen has explained, resulted from the timing of the posthumous
editions which seemed to miss the periods of interest in the war and its
poets. As early as March 1920, Eliot cited the neglect of Rosenberg as
evidence that criticism was not performing its proper function. Yeats, however, whose dismissal of Owen aroused indignant reactions in 1936, also
dismissed Rosenberg as "all windy rhetoric" (surely a phrase that would
apply least of all to Rosenberg). Except for the two poems which Harriet

Monroe published in *Poetry Magazine* in 1916, and the "Ah! Koelue!" excerpt from the end of the first scene of *Moses* which appeared (without attribution!) in *Georgian Poetry, 1916–1917*, Rosenberg's publications in his lifetime were printed at his own expense. A plan to include Rosenberg's art in a collection of Georgian painters planned by Edward Marsh failed to materialize when the war made Marsh's project impractical.

Despite this neglect, Rosenberg has left sufficient evidence of his prophetic vision. In a lecture on art, delivered in Cape Town in 1914, Rosenberg indicated his awareness of the precarious position of art and civilization even before the war: "Art is now, as it were, a volcano. Eruptions are continual, and immense cities of culture at its foot are shaken and shivered. The roots of a dead universe are torn up by hands, feverish and consuming with an exuberant vitality—and amid dynamic threatenings we watch the hastening of the corroding doom."[25] This remarkable utterance, eight years before the appearance of *The Waste Land*, seems to anticipate both Eliot's "message" and his imagery. Rosenberg's plight, however, is that of Cassandra, doomed to offer accurate prophecy to deaf ears. As Rosenberg commented in a letter to Schiff in March 1916, "I am afraid my public is still in the womb."[26]

Part IV

Retrospective Views of the Great War

13

Armistice and After

THE ARMISTICE OF 11 NOVEMBER 1918 INSPIRED MANY POEMS WHICH CELE-
brated the end of the war and commented on the war's effects. Thomas
Hardy, whose call to action was among the first of 1914, wrote " 'And There
Was a Great Calm': On the Signing of the Armistice, 11th November 1918."
In nine five-line stanzas, Hardy's broad perspective recalls *The Dynasts* and
might have served him better during the war. In the first four stanzas, Hardy
presents a picture of "years of Passion" during which men discarded the
teachings of their philosophers, suffered untold anguish, became "war-
adept" even as civilians, and watched as "armies fell." In the pivotal fifth
stanza, Hardy indicates his apprehensions of the changes that the war has
brought to the modern consciousness: "So when old hopes that earth was
bettering slowly / Were dead and damned, there sounded 'War is done!' /
One morrow." After describing the winding-down of hostilities, Hardy
ends on an ambiguous note that history would bear out:

> There was peace on earth, and silence in the sky;
> Some could, some could not, shake off misery:
> The Sinister Spirit sneered: "It had to be!"
> And again the Spirit of Pity whispered, "Why?"

He saw enough of the postwar years to convince him of man's essential folly.
In "Christmas: 1924," his assessment is hardly ambiguous: "After two
thousand years of mass / We've got as far as poison-gas."

Fittingly, Siegfried Sassoon expressed the soldier's reaction to the war's
end in a purely lyrical celebration. Written in April 1919, "Everyone Sang"
contrasts sharply with Sassoon's antiwar verse in its optimism and un-
qualified joy. When the soldiers burst into song, "I was filled with such
delight / As prisoned birds must find in freedom." Sassoon includes his
belief that the peace will endure: "O, but Everyone / Was a bird; and the
song was wordless; the singing will never be done."

John Freeman (1880–1929) tried to encompass both civilians' and soldiers'
responses to the Armistice. Although he enjoyed a reputation as a Georgian
poet, critic, and novelist, and won the Hawthornden Prize in 1920, his
income derived from his position as Chief Executive Officer in the Depart-

ment of National Health and Insurance. He somehow contrived to keep his literary and business associates not only separate, but also mutually ignorant of his relationship with the other group. In an early war poem, "Happy Is England Now," Freeman had followed the Georgian pattern of placing the war into a perspective of happy rusticity:

> Happy is England in the brave that die
> For wrongs not hers and wrongs so sternly hers;
> Happy in those that give, give, and endure
> The pain that never the new years may cure;
> Happy in all her dark woods, green fields, towns,
> Her hills and rivers and her chafing sea.

After the realities of the war had rendered his earlier vision obsolete, Freeman wrote "Armistice Day" to communicate mankind's relief that the war was over. He emphasizes that the Armistice has changed nothing in nature—birds sing, hearts beat, blood runs, and birth and death continue—and he states explicitly that "No silent Armistice might stay / Life and Death wrangling in the old way." In the last stanza he contrasts man's momentary relief to the indifference of the universe:

> Earth's pulse still was beating,
> The bright stars circling;
> Only our tongues were hushing.
>   While Time ticked silent on, men drew
> A deeper breath than passion knew.

Freeman conveyed simultaneously his own relief and a more realistic view of the war's significance.

Louis Golding (1895–1956), another Georgian poet, seemed to learn little from the war. In the January 1919 issue of *To-Day* appeared his "November Eleventh," a poem so bad that it seems to parody the worst excesses of the Georgians. The poet expresses his joy at the Armistice by returning to the weekend-cottage nature-view that many trench poets found nauseating. The poem begins with the revelation that sheep no longer walk "ceremonially now in sombre bands," nor do "the cows move their despondent jaws, / As chewing a sour cud." After informing his readers that these creatures have been mourning "cowherds bled in a vain cause" (emphasizing this with the pithy line "Because, alas!"), Golding describes sheep suddenly bounding about euphorically. A change in the cows provides the occasion for a stanza of ludicrous excess:

> And now the cows moo joyously, now the cows
>   Throw back their silly brows,
> And now, great baby things, they whisk their tails,

> And now into bright pails,
> They send sweet milk a-chiming. . . .

Perhaps the implied inability to give milk during the entire 1914–18 conflict explains their sudden exaltation of mood. The animals, "now that men have quenched their thirst / For battles and for boys and blood," can welcome spring with thanksgiving. Golding is hardly representative of the poets who celebrated the Armistice, but he provides convincing evidence that the war by no means ended artificiality of thought, feeling, or expression. Fortunately for Golding, he later discovered that the novel was his literary form.

Lord Dunsany (Edward John Morton Drax Plunkett, 1878–1957) preferred poetry as a youngster but submitted to his father's determination that he become a soldier. He went to Eton and then, after cramming for admissions examinations, entered the Royal Military Academy at Sandhurst. He served at Gibraltar and fought in the Boer War. During the Great War he was a captain in the Royal Inniskilling Fusiliers, assigned to Dublin in 1916 to put down the Easter Uprising. Afterwards he fought on the western front and was wounded during the Somme fighting in 1916. After briefly serving with the American 3rd Army, he held a War Office post until after the Armistice, when he rejoined the Royal Inniskilling Fusiliers. Although he wrote more than seventy books and plays, he published little poetry. G. P. Putnam published his collection of *Fifty Poems* in 1929.

Dunsany's Armistice poem, "A Dirge of Victory," is a Petrarchan sonnet which repudiates the celebrative note. The octave is an apostrophe to Victory to eschew the normal practice of sounding a triumphant call among the survivors,

> But over hollows full of old wire go,
> Where, among dregs of war, the long-dead lie
> . . . .
> There blow thy trumpet that the dead may know,
> Who waited for thy coming, Victory.

In the sestet, Dunsany emphasizes that not the survivors, but the dead who wait where they fell have "deserved thy wreath." His expression of relief is that Victory "hast come to them at last, at last!" Unlike many who celebrated the Armistice, his concern is not peace, but having won the war. His poem, like earlier patriotic effusions, reveals the continuing influence of a chauvinistic tradition.

Herbert Read, whose brother Charles died in action on 5 October 1918, five weeks before the peace, also focuses on the dead in "A Short Poem for Armistice Day." He does not exult in the prospect of victory. He develops an image of Armistice Day poppies, "artificial flowers / of paper tin and metal thread," to establish an extended metaphor: as the speaker can make only artificial flowers with "no sweet scent / no lustre in the petal no increase / from fertilizing flies and bees," so nothing can be done to restore the dead. The flowers do not wither,

> And will not fade though life
> and lustre go in genuine flowers
> and men like flowers are cut
> and wither on a stem

> And will not fade a year or more
> I stuck one in a candlestick
> and there it clings about the socket
> I have no power therefore have patience.

Like Lord Dunsany's "Dirge," Read's poem dwells on the dead, but he takes no false comfort in victory.

Edward de Stein (1887–1965) emphasized an aspect of the war that Read depicted earlier in "My Company." His Armistice poem, "Envoi," recalls the camaraderie of the war in nostalgic tones. Educated at Eton and Oxford, de Stein rose to the rank of major in the King's Royal Rifles on the western front. During the war he published approximately twenty war poems in the *Times, Bystander,* and *Punch,* most of which celebrated trench fellowship and contrasted the men's appalling circumstances with their sense of the ridiculous. His "Envoi" addresses his men, presenting an idealized picture that suggests the abortive attempts of a self-deceiving schoolmaster to be regarded as a chum by his wards. He asks how he can say farewell to men who have taught him to "toil, / Glad in the glory of fellowship, happy in misery. . . . / Facing the world that was not too kind with a jest and a song?" The last line recalls the ending of Owen's "Apologia Pro Poemate Meo": "What can the world hold afterwards worthy of laughter or tears?"

P. H. B. Lyon (b. 1893) indicates that he has not lost sight of his earlier optimism and feeling of life's continuing purpose in his Armistice poem "Now to Be Still and Rest." A schoolmaster educated at Rugby and Oxford, Lyon served as captain in the 6th Durham Light Infantry in France and Flanders. He earned the MC in 1917 and was wounded in 1918. He published *Songs of Youth and War* in 1918 and won the Newdigate Prize in 1919 for his poem "France." First published in the *Spectator,* "Now to Be Still and Rest" begins with the relief of the survivor, returning to what was "learned and loved in the days long past" and "Glad to have come to the long way's end at last." In three stanzas Lyon anticipates the joy of awakening each day, of returning to "the well-loved paths," and of rejoining loved ones. In the last lines, he indicates his belief that mankind will work to improve the world:

Then—with a new-born strength, the sweet rest over,
  Gladly to follow the great white road once more,
To work with a song on our lips and the heart of a lover,
  Building a city of peace on the wastes of war.

Lyon, like many of the survivors, lived to see the cycle of war repeat itself within two decades after the initial optimism of the Armistice.

The "Sinister Spirit" which sneered in Hardy's " 'And There Was a Great Calm' " quickly found a spokesman. Osbert Sitwell's chillingly accurate parable of prophecy, "The Next War (November 1918)," looked ahead to find the miseries of the war "faded" in memory, when "Deaf men became difficult to talk to, / Heroes became bores." The profiteers of the war have aged, but they confer to determine what they should do now. One suggests monuments to those "Who lost all likeness to a living thing, / Or were blown to bleeding patches of flesh / For our sakes," in the hope that the profiteers can "educate" a new generation. However, the richest, displaying the genius which has brought him gain, finds a more profitable and cost-effective method:

"But it seems to me
That the cause for which we fought
Is again endangered.
What more fitting memorial for the fallen
Than that their children
Should fall for the same cause?"

When the profiteers ask "Will you sacrifice / Through your lethargy / What your fathers died to gain?" the victims of a new generation respond willingly. Even the profiteers' slogan—"The world *must* be made safe for the young!"—parodies Woodrow Wilson's call, "The world *must* be made safe for democracy."

Equally sinister was the view of Hugh MacDiarmid (1892–1978), whose tempestuous career suggests a bundle of contradictions. He was expelled from the Scottish Nationalist Party as a communist in 1934 and from the Communist Party for "nationalist deviation" in 1938. He has achieved recognition for fostering the Scottish movement with his editorship of *Northern Numbers* and other periodicals in the early 1920s. His most important work was *A Drunk Man Looks at the Thistle* (1926), analogous in Scottish literature to *The Waste Land* in English literature since the two poems share a wealth of literary, political, historical, and philosophical influences as well as parodying and satirizing literary traditions.

MacDiarmid enlisted in 1915, serving in the RAMC (Royal Army Medical Corps) in Salonika, Italy, and France. He was definitely not inspired by English patriotism. In *To Circumjack Cencrastus* (1930), he commented that the distance to the stars was "a less distance than I'll drive betwixt / England and Scotland yet." During World War II, however, he served as first engineer on a ship in the Merchant Service. That he recognized the futility of war in general and despised any attempt to glorify the war is evident in his poem "Another Epitaph on an Army of Mercenaries," a response to A. E. Housman's "Epitaph on an Army of Mercenaries":

> It is a God-damned lie to say that these
> Saved, or knew, anything worth any man's pride.
> They were professional murderers and they took
> Their blood money and impious risks and died.
> In spite of all their kind some elements of worth
> With difficulty persist here and there on earth.

MacDiarmid was willing to participate in a noncombatant capacity, but he refused to justify conflict by suggesting a worthy purpose for or result of the war.

Alan Patrick Herbert, whose "After the Battle" distinguished the suffering of the troops from the bombastic self-serving rhetoric of the staff, had seen enough of the German war machine by 20 September 1939. Perhaps his having been wounded by shrapnel in an "unmentionable place" inspired Herbert to direct his attention to the continuing menace of German aspirations for conquest. His "No Quarrel," written at the beginning of World War II, starts five of its six stanzas with the phrase "We have no quarrel with the German nation" before undermining that statement. After stating that the Germans tend to follow the worst leaders blindly and to upset the Continent, Herbert recalls the Great War:

> We had no quarrel with the German nation
>   When Wilhelm was the madman off the chain;
> We helped along their rehabilitation—
>   And now, my hat, they do it all again!

He then suggests that perhaps Germans had best not breed, and that "some major operation / (On head and heart) may be the only way" to curb Teutonic barbarism. Despite his experience in the war, Herbert views the prospect of another European conflict as solely the result of the German character. His tone resembles that which he applied to noncombatants in "After the Battle" and suggests that he was most effective when he had a specific target for satire, but his poem recalls the welter of propagandistic anti-German poems one could find in popular periodicals during the years of World War I.

In "To a Conscript of 1940," Herbert Read indicates the changes that the

Great War brought to concepts of heroism and battle, beginning with an epigraph from Georges Bernanos that translates, "He who has never once given up hope will never be a hero." Read's poem develops this philosophy as a soldier/narrator, veteran of the 1914–18 war, meets his World War II counterpart. The narrator identifies himself as "one of the many who never returned, / Of the many who returned and yet were dead," and after he informs the younger soldier that he has experienced the rain and mud, the narrator summarizes the dashed hopes of the between-the-wars years:

> "We think we gave in vain. The world was not renewed.
> There was hope in the homestead and anger in the streets
> But the old world was restored and we returned
> To the dreary field and workshop, and the immemorial feud
>
> Of rich and poor. Our victory was our defeat."

From the narrator's point of view, the abusers of power retained their offices, and the 1914 generation bore the burden of the war's aftermath. However, he claims that his generation learned of the sham behind conventional notions of heroism. Those expecting garlands have only "the hollow victory. They are deceived."

However, there remains one way to attain honor:

> "But you, my brother and my ghost, if you can go
> Knowing that there is no reward, no certain use
> In all your sacrifice, then honour is reprieved.
> To fight without hope is to fight with grace,
> The self reconstructed, the false heart repaired."

When the younger soldier returns the narrator's salute after these words, he accepts this cynical philosophy. Read's approach to World War II oddly resembles Hardy's "Men Who March Away" in that he does not concern himself with notions of political right and wrong, but with the frame of mind of the departing troops. He also recalls Edward Thomas's acceptance of duty without fanfare. Unlike Herbert, who lashed Germany for her tendency to embroil Europe in hostilities, or other war poets who shifted radically to address "Hitler's war," Read retains and expresses the philosophy that the Great War thrust upon the modern consciousness.

In "To a Conscript of 1940," Read addressed a soldier of World War II in terms of the frustrated hopes of the 1914 generation and tried to refine the concept of heroism to apply to a modern war. Earlier, in 1933, Read had published his most ambitious war poem, *The End of a War*. The work stands apart from most war poems, and Yeats included it in his controversial 1936 anthology of modern poetry. *The End of a War* focuses on the universal aspects of the struggle by presenting the contemplations of three persons involved in a central incident: a German officer, a French girl, and an English officer identified as Lieutenant S—.

Read does not attempt to unify this triptych into a narrative or dramatic framework, but he provides an Argument that renders the central incident and makes the meditations comprehensible. On 10 November 1918, as English soldiers approach a village, a wounded German officer assures them that the Germans have left the village undefended. When the English enter the village square, however, heavy machine-gun fire leaves a hundred dead or wounded. A surviving corporal returns to kill the German officer who has tricked the English, and the English discover the body of a young girl whom the Germans have tortured and killed. Lieutenant S—, exhausted by the day's events, sleeps. He awakens the next morning to hear bells signaling the Armistice.

Against this tableau the poem presents three contemplative monologues—"Meditation of the Dying German Officer," "Dialogue Between the Body and the Soul of the Murdered Girl," and "Meditation of the Waking English Officer." The German officer, who met his death at the corporal's hands impassively, exults in battle:

> I fought with gladness. When others cursed the day
> this stress was loosed
> and men were driven into camps, to follow
> with wonder, woe, or base delirium
> the voiceless yet incessant surge
> then I exulted . . .

Rejecting Christianity, the German officer finds a basis for his values in love of the Fatherland:

> Faith in self comes first, from self we build
> the web of friendship, from friends to confederates
> and so to the State.

At the point of death, the officer finds all is "Nichts."

The "Dialogue Between the Body and the Soul of the Murdered Girl" addresses a different kind of patriotism. The French girl, killed because she was caught spying on the Germans, has become a martyr to her love for her country, but her patriotism is like Edward Thomas's love for England rather than the German officer's political and military idealism. The discussion between Body and Soul develops a conflict between narrow and general views of martyrdom. The Body, aware of its sacrifice and trusting in its faith, demands that martyrdom require belief. The Soul counsels a wider view, cautioning the Body against pride. Partly because his purpose is to introduce the complexities implicit in the varying views of those who acted in the struggle, Read does not attempt to resolve this ambiguity.

"Meditation of the Waking English Officer" presents the moral and philosophical uncertainty of the war's survivor. Even as he realizes that the war has ended, the officer indicates that he has fought without conviction: "I answered no call / there was no call to answer. I felt no hate / only the anguish of an unknown fate. . . ." He lacks the sense of conviction that inspired the German officer to fight as well as the faith of the French girl in her martyrdom. After the English officer questions the existence of God, of self, and of meaning in human life, approaching the negativism expressed by the German officer, he encounters a paradox:

> Now I see, either the world is mechanic force
> and this the last tragic act, portending
> endless hate and blind reversion
> back to the tents and healthy lusts
> of animal men: or we act
> God's purpose in an obscure way.

The English officer's need to order his life forces him to reject spiritual negativism, and his meditation ends with his expression of hope. In his postscript to the poem, Read identified his purpose: "It is not my business as a poet to condemn war (or, to be more exact, modern warfare). I only wish to present the universal aspects of a particular event. Judgment may follow, but should never precede or become embroiled with the act of poetry. . . ."[1] Nevertheless, that judgment does appear, both in the poet's selection of and in the reader's response to the diverse philosophies of the three figures, regardless of the poet's desire to capture universal responses from poetic events that the reader, in fact, cannot avoid judging.

Leonard Barnes (1895–1977) sought meaning behind his experiences in the Great War by beginning with a personal response that he could place into an historical perspective. He was educated at St. Paul's and served with distinction in the King's Royal Rifle Corps from 1915 to 1918 on the western front. Twice wounded, Barnes earned the MC with bar. When the war ended, he "emerged . . . [with] a left leg shattered by shrapnel and a mind profoundly affected by the slaughter he had witnessed."[2] He had not expected to survive the conflict, and he spent much of his life trying to come to terms with a "deeply felt sense of guilt that for no special reason he had survived whereas so many of his friends had not."[3] In 1919 he entered University College, Oxford, where he earned distinction in a shortened two-year course in "Greats" (classics). He then placed first in the Civil Service examination and entered the Colonial Office, as his father had before him. After three years of office routine in London, which left him restless, he went to Natal, South Africa, to farm under a government scheme for ex-servicemen. When this

proved financially unsuccessful, he entered journalism as leader-writer, first
for the *Cape Times* and then for the Johannesburg *Star*. In his newspaper
articles during the 1920s, he exposed and opposed South Africa's racist
policies.

When he returned to England in 1932 as a free-lance journalist, he became
known as the most outspoken critic of Britain's colonial policies in Africa
and Asia. His books on Britain's role in the affairs of her former colonies
include *Caliban in Africa* (1930), *The New Boer War* (1932), *Duty of Empire*
(1935), *The Future of the Colonies* (1936), and *Empire or Democracy?* (1939).
From 1936 to 1945 Barnes was Senior Lecturer in Education at Liverpool
University, and from 1945 until 1962 he was Head of the Department of
Social and Administrative Studies at Oxford. After his retirement, the
United Nations Economic Commission for Africa asked him "to conduct a
five-year research project on the social, economic and political forces at
work in post-colonial Africa."[4] He also published *African Renaissance*
(1969) and *Africa in Eclipse* (1971). In retrospect, his public career was that
of an indefatigable reformer who did not flinch from supporting unpopular
causes, as when he vehemently opposed the policy of appeasing Hitler
during the 1930s. In the words of Anthony McAdam, "Leonard Barnes was
an extraordinary man by any measure. He was a poet, philosopher and
humanist and a man who participated in the great historical dramas of his
time with courage, decency and, not least, a sense of style and grace that has
long since gone out of fashion."[5]

In 1933, Barnes published *Youth at Arms*, a volume of poems dedicated to
Denis Oliver Barnett, who fell at Hooge. The book captures both the
immediacy of the trenches and the personal response of the young officer
who functions as narrator in forty-four poems of varying length in a four-
section sequence. The first section, "Spring," includes the initial shock of the
trenches in 11:

> A fit name, No Man's Land, for this back-taste
> Of some remotest mesozoic time,
> Where algae of barbed wire infest a waste,
> Rotting and featureless, of drying slime,
> And even the quaint anachronism, man,
> Reverts to reptile ere he visits it.

In 13, the last poem of "Spring," the battalion has received orders to battle,
and Barnes records the exultation of the men: "Sing and be glad; however
soon we die, / We're up and doing, and the light is sweet."

"Summer" continues in this mood for a space. In 17, the officer tells
himself "All's well, old fellow, / To-day you are good for whatever is up to
you." This gives way, in 18, to the reality of trench warfare described in the
context of classical myth: "Shrieking salvoes of whizzbangs, / Fouler Eu-

menides than ever hounded / The cloudy spirit of Agamemnon's son / . . . / They are costing me a dozen men an hour." By "Autumn," few traces of exaltation remain, although the men retain their sense of purpose, as revealed in 29. At first,

> Not till we're dead, more likely, will war end;
> How tired are we, and how long ways from home!
> War earth's coeval seems. Yet end will come.
> Then we'll be made a cautionary legend.

There are some traces of Sassoon-like resentment:

>   the flatulent press
> Will splash THE TRUTH about us in the news,
> As atoms chased to aimless doom by crime
> Of imbecile commanders.

Yet the sense of purpose has not changed: "Aftertime / One sole fact will recall—We did not lose."

By "Winter," Barnes looks to the human cost of the war. In 37, he addresses the sorrow of the survivor:

> Death has covered their brave eyes
>   With immortality;
> But shots that brought God's peace to them
>   Bring only wounds to me.

In 39, peace brings further resentment:

> Now our mean epicures of vengeance crow
> Upon their dungheap, twist the soldiers' toil
> To this base insult to a gallant foe,
> And war's close-guarded honour vilely soil.

In the last poems of the volume, Barnes expresses disgust for the postwar fruits of civilian opportunism. In 40,

> In England now the glory and the power
> Are wielded by the pitying sly smirk
> Of those who ran to cover in the hour
> When things looked rough; the skill they used to shirk
> Comes in most handy for the statesman's ends.

Barnes notes an irony similar to that expressed in earlier poems of protest: "Sternly pacific while the guns do fire, / Adventurously bellicose in peace." In *Youth at Arms*, Barnes chronicles the soldiers' change in viewpoint from earlier idealism to the bitter recognition that came after the Armistice. He does not reject the concept of heroism so much as he resents the exploitation of the soldiers' courage.

Barnes placed the Great War into the context of his entire adult experience in *The Glory of the World Sonnets* (1979), published posthumously. The fifty sonnets concern the events and experiences of Barnes's life, divided into four sections: "Hope (1919)," "Downward Anguish (1920–1945)," "Rescue Bird (1945–1975)," and "Fiasco (1975 +)." The seven sonnets of "Hope (1919)" develop themes that appeared in many poems during the war, including the notion of Owen's "greater love," the brutal reality of the trenches, the soldiers' hatred for the war, the distinction between a worthy combatant and an unworthy noncombatant, the need to make civilians recognize the horrors of modern warfare, and the hope that the disaster of the war will help to redeem man's future. Unifying these sonnets is Barnes's perspective of the trench soldier and survivor who feels compelled to advance the earlier idealism of the fallen. In "The Dead Speak," he affirms his purpose through the voices of those "by war cruelly slain." The dead absolve Barnes of the "guilt" of survival and then confirm his postwar resolve:

> Now step forth one who worthily served with us,
> But cannot understand why he still lives.
> Let him make others see what we have seen,
> And know what we have known; the cry he gives
> Will echo down the ages; the unclean
> Hearing it shall take heart and turn to us.

Almost half the eighteen sonnets of "Downward Anguish (1920–1945)" express the belied hopes of Great War veterans before the next war looms ominously. By the end of the section, the fond hope that man would learn from the war has fallen before the profiteer's desire to promote conflict for profit and the majority's refusal to look beyond immediate self-gratification. The third section, "Rescue Bird (1945–1975)," suggests various solutions to modern problems in eighteen sonnets. In "Life Lost and Saved" Barnes advocates the Tao as a cure for man's "hate-addictions," in "The Bond" he offers the strength of the "collective bond" as the means for "running the cosmic estate" and becoming the master of destiny, and in "The Common Task" he stresses the need for selflessness in the service of a "common vision" to transform the soul. The final sonnet of the section, "Worship," expresses the spirit of the whole that "Rescue Bird" offers:

> This God of ours
> Pays his worship in masterly uptake
> Whereby all conscious energies and powers
> Are gathered and deployed for the whole's sake,

Striving to interanimate the blind
World's matter-energy with sighted mind.

Barnes's solution to the modern blight combines an awareness of the inherent interdependence of all elements of the cosmos with his belief that man
has the power, at least collectively, to maintain order and to improve mankind. After the resolve to "sow compassion" which grew from his experience of the Great War, and the "Downward Anguish" which epitomizes the
between-the-wars disillusionment, "Rescue Bird" appears to offer hope that
man's efforts to overcome irrationality and destructiveness could succeed,
given proper direction.

The concluding seven sonnets of "Fiasco (1975 +)" form an ironical
contrast to the three parts which have gone before by emphasizing the
frivolous and irrational nature of man's response to his greatest challenge. In
"Demission," Barnes reiterates his resolve formed almost six decades earlier:

My task was to bring round a folk numb-cold
From shock and rough exposure to self-hate,
Able no more to manage its affairs.
Now that I go off duty, spent and old,
And the life-vow I made you nears its date,
Have I, discharging it, shown the right cares?

He asks this question of "You, slaughtered friends, and our great ancestors,"
and then proceeds to evaluate the changes he observes in modern life. In
"Failed Humans" he asks, "How can man win security from men?" and then
indicts humanity for failing to learn from history, deliberately turning away
from the teachings of philosophy. His apostrophe to modernity is his
Jeremiad:

Woe unto you, failed humans, dim washouts,
Whose temper ever since the tribe's first youth
Has been a murderous envy of your peers;
Woe, planet-polluters, fratricidal louts,
Quite without eyes to see the thread of truth
Or gumption even to listen to the seers.

He then views contemporary actions which define modern man: pollution,
ecological imbalance, destruction of the ozone with aerosol sprays, and
government-induced inflation. The final poem of the sequence, "Finistère,"
presents a second "Noah's ark" floating on a "shoreless sea" while mankind
drowns "Beneath untreated sewage and raw slops." The "ghost of Cain" in
the ark rages against

" . . . bowels and bladders and their fruit,
Themselves the fruit of all those teeming wombs
That damned replacements endlessly recruit . . ."

When the waters refuse to recede, Cain "tests the noisome fluid with his toe," realizes that he must swim to shore through the noxious effluvia, and holds his nose as he leaps into the sewage.

Although the sonnets of the volume are not always individually impressive, in their whole they represent one man's lifelong struggle to place the Great War into a perspective of modern experience and observation. Some poets have implied the futility of the war generation's sacrifice, but none has managed to place that sacrifice into the historical framework of postwar disillusionment and absurdity that Barnes envisioned. From his point of view, the war may not have served a specific political or ideological cause well, but it did provide an opportunity to evaluate the ill effects of "progress" on modern life. That man refused to learn from the experience, that men responded to the soldiers' idealistic sacrifice with indifference, that those in power continued to place personal desire for lucre and power before the common good, that the majority refused to learn from their philosophers and social historians to avoid another war, and that even then man seemed perversely inspired to destroy his world—these lessons form the basis for Barnes's conviction that refusal to learn from the Great War has wrought a modern world that is tragic in the classical sense. Barnes's retrospective view of the war and its failure to improve modern life by its bloody example led him, as it has led other thinkers and satirists, to frustration with man's irrational behavior.

14

The Great War Epic

AFTER THE ARMISTICE, FEW POETS USED THE CONVENTIONS OF THE EPIC TO describe the war. Sydney Walter Powell, whose *One-Way Street and Other Poems* appeared in 1934, published one heroic treatment entitled "Gallipoli" in the *Poetry Review* in 1933. The poem does not conform strictly to the conventions of heroic or epic poetry (the meter, for example, is irregular), but it does attempt to depict contemporary events in epic proportions. Powell begins with a prelude invoking gods of the Egyptian pantheon and announcing his intent to sing to them "Of the earth in these days." Beginning *in medias res* as tramping soldiers march to their ship, the poet sings of their heroism and willing sacrifice: "Gladly we made them the gift, for proud men are we, / Free givers. We were besought and we gave. / Let all men know that we cared not but to give princely, / Yet valuing this that we gave." Powell's descriptions of nature embellish his heroic theme with epic imagery: The day "With a wipe . . . has burnished the sea's dull armour." Modern battle frequently suggests modern imagery, as in Powell's description of a destroyed ship: "How funnily its ends tossed, / Closing like a pair of scissors / And spilling its passengers." Later, "There goes another boat. / This shuts up like a jack-knife, the blade upon the handle, / And disrupts, leaving a dark molecular blobbing residue."

In the process of attempting heroic treatment, Powell also records the "ugly reality" of individual death and voices the apprehensions of the men: "We did not come here to drown. It was not in our bargain." His apostrophe to the dead moves the atmosphere closer to war's reality:

Who are these upon the beach
Laid in an orderly row in the sunshine,
Head to the hills, feet to the sea?
Their eyes are wide, but they blink not.
The sun roasts them, but they sweat not.
He scorches them, but they do not redden.
Their colour is clay, for clay are they.

However, the appearance of "Very dark, very dirty men . . . who have *fought*" revives the heroic spirit, and when the moment of battle arrives, traditional blood-lust appears:

Thus in the past a thousand times we fell upon our enemies
With claw, with club, with spear.
Their eyes flinch, they would flee.
It is too late for them.
They would drop their guns and fling up their arms.
It is too late for them.
The madness of undrawn blood is upon us.

We kill.

. . . .
It was an orgie. I will not remember it.
(But I am gladder than I was.)
Wipe off the mess upon your steel.

The final lines establish that "the day [is] delivered of its purpose. / Now is all made clear. / And now the hour of the gift's deliverance / Too is near." The narrator of the poem realizes that he no longer fears, and that "they who buy me shall pay dear!", but the poem ends on an ambiguous note—the birds sing "Good has been our short spring day!" but the sound "drifts" and "dies away," leaving one uncertain of the permanence of the outcome.

Powell departs from heroic tradition to reveal his own retrospective uncertainty regarding the nature of the victory, the long-range utility of the battle, and the soldier's role in the aftermath. He can claim that "All is over. / Death is slain," but the ultimate achievement of the victors remains in doubt. Significantly, Powell chose not to attempt to ennoble the fighting on the western front, perhaps realizing the difficulties inherent in elevating the experiences substantially recorded by Sassoon, Graves, Owen, and others who communicated the ignoble realities of the trenches. His ambiguity seems to result from his inability to reconcile his perceptions with an epic view.

The Great War came closest to inspiring an epic in *In Parenthesis* by David Jones (1895–1974). The antithesis of Leonard Barnes, Jones withdrew from the sphere of social upheaval as soon as he could. "René Hague, who shared his ideals if not all his ideas, gives shrewd hints to some of his weaknesses. One was a valetudinarian husbanding of his energy, a hatred of upheaval. He once postponed going home on leave from the trenches because his parents were moving house. In later years he rarely went out, except to Mass."[1] Born in Southeast London to a Welsh-speaking father and an English mother, Jones early found a vocation in art and entered the Camberwell Art School in 1910, where he studied until 1914. Although his early attempts to enlist failed, he eventually became a private in the Royal Welch Fusiliers on 2 January 1915, and in December 1915 he embarked for France, where he served until March 1918. During the Somme Offensive he was wounded in an attack on Mametz Wood on 11 July 1916. After convalescence in England he returned to France, but after he contracted trench fever he received a transfer to Limerick, where he remained until his demobilization shortly after the Armistice. The effect of military experience on his consciousness suggests itself in his keeping secret for decades an event which occurred at the demobilization center. Carelessly leaving his rifle outside while using a latrine, he returned to discover the weapon missing, and, knowing the military consequences, filched another from an unguarded pile of discarded rifles. Confiding this secret to his friend Peter Orr years later, he asked Orr not to repeat the story lest the military authorities take some action against him even at that late date.

After the war, Jones used a government grant to attend the Westminster School of Art in 1919, and in 1921, after being received into the Roman Catholic Church, he joined Eric Gill in a community of artists and craftsmen, where he divided his energies among painting, poetry, and lettering, as well as working as an illustrator for private presses. In 1927 he began his "war book," *In Parenthesis,* which Faber & Faber published in 1937. *In Parenthesis* won the Hawthornden Prize in 1938, although public recognition of the work was slow to arrive. He published *The Anathemata* in 1951, received a CBE in 1955, and became a Companion of Honour in 1974. In 1971 he became a patient at the Calvary Nursing Home, where he resided until his death, but during his last four years he remained an active correspondent and continued to exhibit his art.

In Parenthesis is a truly original work, both in form and content. Evelyn Waugh called it "Not a novel" so much as a "piece of reporting interrupted by choruses . . . as though Mr T. S. Eliot had written *The Better 'Ole*."[2] Explaining the title of the work, Jones wrote in his preface that he had "written it in a kind of space between—I don't know between quite what— but as you turn aside to do something," that for soldiers the war was a parenthesis, and that "our curious type of existence here is altogether in parenthesis."[3] The between-the-wars period later suggested another parenthesis, and the book is in a parenthesis between poetry and prose. Jones carefully avoided identifying his book by topic or by form: "I did not intend this as a 'War Book'—it happens to be concerned with war,"[4] and he refers to the work as "this writing" throughout his preface, refusing to call it a novel, a long poem, or even a mixture.

He does, however, comment on the unconventional typography of the work in terms of form and meaning, and he indicates that the mixture of lyrical and narrative elements disturbed him. "I have only tried to make a shape in words, using as data the complex of sights, sounds, fears, hopes, apprehensions, smells, things exterior and interior, the landscape and paraphernalia of that singular time and of those particular men. I have attempted to appreciate some things, which, at the time of suffering, the flesh was too weak to appraise. There are passages which I would exclude, as not having the form I desire—but they seem necessary to the understanding of the whole."[5] He addresses his apparent shifts from prose to poetry (without calling them that) as a problem of making his writing intelligible:

> I frequently rely on a pause at the end of a line to aid the sense and form. A new line, which the typography would not otherwise demand, is used to indicate some change, inflexion, or emphasis. I have tried to indicate the sound of certain sentences by giving a bare hint of who is speaking, of the influences operating to make the particular sound I want in a particular instance, by perhaps altering a single vowel in one word. I have only used the notes of exclamation, interrogation, etc., when the omission of such signs would completely obscure the sense.[6]

One reading *In Parenthesis* for the first time will recognize affinities with Eliot's *The Waste Land*, Joyce's *A Portrait of the Artist as a Young Man*, and Pound's *Cantos*, as well as an Imagistic approach to the "data" of the world. Such affinities include Jones's juxtaposition of past and present, his eclectic use of literary forms, his exploitation of myth and epic traditions, and his presentation of sensory experience with a minimum of narrative explanation. His use of epic devices in his work has enabled him to combine "two separate conceptions of the World War I infantry soldier: the heroic conception and the sacrificial conception,"[7] but Jones's allusiveness and his refusal to narrate conventionally have caused some readers, including Paul Fussell, difficulty:

> As readers, we don't always know who's speaking, and to whom. The thirty-four pages of rather pedantic notes at the end bespeak the literary insecurity of the autodidact; they sometimes prop up the text where the author suspects the poetry has miscarried. Some of the poem is badly overwritten, just as the frontispiece drawing by Jones is too crowded with everything he can recall as relevant: a dead body, wire-pickets, rats, barbed wire, a tunic, a steel helmet, an ammunition belt, sandbags, blasted trees, mules, carrying parties, bully-beef tins, shattered houses, chicken-wire netting, and an entrenching tool. Too much. It is the visual equivalent of diction like *millesimal, brumous, pernitric, inutile.*[8]

Jones draws most frequently from Aneirin's *Y Gododdin*, a sixth-century Welsh heroic poem describing a glorious defeat like that of *The Battle of Maldon*. In *Y Gododdin*, three hundred Welshmen who raided England fell at Catraeth, with the exception of three survivors, including Aneirin, who tells the tale. The significance of the analogy between Jones's work and *Y Gododdin* is that both present the inevitable destruction of a unit. That Jones deliberately chose to describe the earlier years of the war, when a continuation of the heroic pattern seemed discernible, suggests that Jones could not frame a war epic that would include the war in its entirety. In his preface he indicates that the action ends in 1916, which roughly marks a change in the character of our lives in the Infantry on the West Front. From then onward things hardened into a more relentless, mechanical affair, took on a more sinister aspect. The wholesale slaughter of the later years, the conscripted levies filling the gaps in every file of four, knocked the bottom out of the intimate, continuing, domestic life of small contingents of men, within whose structure Roland could find, and, for a reasonable while, enjoy, his Oliver. In the earlier months there was a certain attractive amateurishness, and elbow-room for idiosyncrasy that connected one with a less exacting past. The period of the individual rifle-man, of the "old sweat" of the Boer campaign, the "Bairnsfather" war, seemed to terminate with the Somme battle.[9]

He recognized the unheroic aspects of the war and indicated clearly that his purpose was not to ennoble the conflict, but to record the final moments of heroism "in a fresh mythic perspective."[10] The contrast between epic values and Jones's modern perspective reveals how far removed nobility has become from modern war. The Great War had precious little to offer for an epic celebration.

In Parenthesis describes, in seven parts, the movements of an infantry platoon from its embarkation point to its annihilation at Mametz Wood during the Somme Offensive. In Part 7, the men fall one by one, leaving the wounded Private John Ball as the sole survivor. Despite its modern origins and terminology, the work contains several parallels to (and most "requirements" of) epic poetry. Like the epic, *In Parenthesis* is a long narrative poem, concerns itself with history rather than with an invented story, follows a loose and episodic structure, begins *in medias res*, and includes devices commonly associated with battle epics—birds of prey circle the battlefield before the final encounter between the contending factions, Dai Greatcoat utters a long boast before the soldiers move into battle, weapons have personalities, and a soldier's honor includes protecting his weapon. However, epic devices in the work function as analogies rather than as identities, forming a contrast between past and present ideals.

In Joe Donkin, Jones provides the modern equivalent of an epic hero. Joe, a replacement who has joined the regiment at the previous Divisional Rest, breaks his long silence in Part 6 to divulge his attitude toward battle:

Joe looked more set up than ever previous and said outright and before them all that this is what he had 'listed for and how he would most certainly avenge his five brethren from the same womb as himself on these miscreant bastard square-heads and sons of bitches who in a '15 show in these parts so he declared had shamefully done four of them to death in some Jock reg'ment it seemed and the youngest of all six was at this same hour when he Joe Donkin sat and spoke with them going near skelington in Jerry concentration camp back there. Private Float joking and unadvised and because of his inherent inability to get the hang of this man's sensitivity said it serves 'em right for 'listing in a crush like that and how the kilties always got it in the neck if they didn't beat it soon enough which they more generally did and got his arse kicked by this Joe who was in no jocund mood but singly resolved and fore-arming himself in the inward man to be the better and more wholly addressed toward this enterprise of making expiation life for life if by any means he might for the gassing before Fricourt on the same day of the four brothers Donkin all good men of their hands.

In this passage one can recognize parallels in diction and tone to Malory and other recorders of epic and myth, indications of the heroic attitude which combines desire for revenge with eagerness for battle, and even narration of events not explicitly presented. At the same time, the reader sees in Joe Donkin a modern warrior, of low origins, whose attitudes may be heroic but who would not earn mention in a traditional epic and whose desire for vengeance is patently futile.

A similar mixture of heroic attitude with modern reality appears in an-other "hero" who is capable of rising to an occasion but limited in his ability to change the situation:

> But for the better discipline of the living,
> a green-gilled corporal,
> returned to company last Wednesday
> from some Corps sinecure,
> who'd lost his new tin-hat, his mousey hair and pendulous
> red ears like the grocery bloke at the Dry
> said his sentences.
> His words cut away smartly, with attention to the prescribed form, so that when he said do this they bloody did it, for all his back-area breeze-up high.
>> For Christ knows he must persuade old sweats with more than sewn-on chevrons or pocket his legatine prestige and lie doggo.
>> But he'd got them into line at the prone, and loosing off with economy; and he himself knelt at the further beech bole to control their fire.

Gods as well as men appear in this work, as in the traditional epic, although only allusively. At various points references are made to Mars, Balder, and others, including the Queen of the Woods, who brings honor to the men of the platoon who have fallen. In the midst of the description of carnage in Part 7, Jones presents Death in a distinctly timeless perspective:

> But sweet sister death has gone debauched today and stalks on this high ground with strumpet confidence, makes no coy veiling of her appetite but leers from you to me with all her parts discovered.

By one and one the line gaps, where her fancy will—
howsoever they may howl for their virginity
she holds them—who impinge less on space
sink limply to a heap
nourish a lesser category of being
like those other who fructify the land
like Tristram
Lamorak de Galis
Alisand le Orphelin
Beaumains who was youngest
or all of them in shaft-shade
at strait Thermopylae
or the sweet brothers Balin and Balan
embraced beneath their single monument.

The contrast between Jones's work and the traditional epic appears in the contents of epic lists. At one point, Jones combines an epic device with modern content when he lists the items in a storeroom, including "Picks, shovels, dredging-ladles, carriers, containers, gas-rattles," and sundry other items. During the deaths of Part 7 comes another list, this time of the origins of the men of the platoon:

but we are rash levied
from Islington and Hackney
and the purlieus of Walworth
flashers from Surbiton
men of the stock of Abraham
from Bromley-by-Bow
Anglo-Welsh from Queens Ferry
rosary-wallahs from Pembrey Dock
lighterman with a Norway darling
from Greenland Stairs
and two lovers from Ebury Bridge,
Bates and Coldpepper
that men called the Lily-white boys.

In addition to references to Arthur's descent into hell, Jones provides many scenes of battle in both general and particular perspectives. One general view appears in the brief comment in Part 4: "Two armies face and hold their crumbling *limites* intact. They're worthy of an intelligent song for all the stupidity of their contest."

A more particular view comes from the perspective of Private Ball, whose chewing-out by Sergeant Snell in Part 2 is interrupted by an incoming shell:

He stood alone on the stones, his mess-tin spilled at his feet. Out of the vortex, rifling the air it came—bright, brass-shod, Pandoran; with all-filling screaming the howling crescendo's up-piling snapt. The universal world, breath held, one half second, a bludgeoned stillness. Then the pent violence released a consummation of all burstings out; all sudden up-rendings and rivings-through—all taking-out of vents—all barrier-breaking—all unmaking. Pernitric begetting—the dissolving and splitting of solid things. In which unearthing aftermath, John Ball picked up his mess-tin and hurried within; ashen, huddled, waited in the dismal straw. Behind "E" Battery, fifty yards down the road, a great many mangolds, uprooted, pulped, congealed with chemical earth, spattered and made slippery the rigid boards leading to the emplacement. The sap of vegetables slobbered the spotless breech-block of No. 3 gun.

Jones also frequently provides modern equivalents of epic similes, as well as similes which are an admixture of traditional technique and modern content: "Occasionally a rifle bullet raw snapt like tenuous hide whip by spiteful ostler handled."

Jones, choosing a form between poetry and prose, attempted to combine epic devices with particularized glimpses of modern war, thus identifying the Great War as part of a tradition without ennobling the struggle. Jones's most enduring achievement, analogous to Eliot's in *The Waste Land*, was to find a form capable of expressing the contradictory impulses that the war and the modern age have inspired. However, despite Jones's care to dress his work with the trappings of heroic poetry, the final effect of *In Parenthesis* is unsatisfying because the Great War was not a subject for epic celebration. The attempt to provide an epic treatment of the last moment of heroism fails precisely because that heroism served no worthy purpose. Jones fell between two stools—his admiration for the British soldier and his awareness of modern war's brutality. In the end, far from reconciling the two, *In Parenthesis* makes one appreciate the efforts of the war poets who tried to communicate their despair in shorter narrative and lyrical forms.

Appendix
Chronology of Selected Great War Publications

1914   POETRY: Maurice Hewlett, *Singsongs of the War*
       ANTHOLOGIES: *Des Imagistes, Songs and Sonnets for England in War Time*
       OTHER: Bernard Shaw, *Common Sense About the War*; H. G. Wells, *The War That Will End War*

1915   POETRY: Richard Aldington, *Images Old and New*; Rupert Brooke, *1914 and Other Poems*; W. W. Gibson, *Battle*; Julian Grenfell, *Battle*; Robert Nichols, *Invocation: War Poems and Others*; Jessie Pope, *War Poems*; Frank Sidgwick, *Some Verse*; Katharine Tynan, *Flower of Youth*
       ANTHOLOGIES: *Georgian Poetry, 1913–1915*; *Some Imagist Poets, 1915*
       FICTION: Ian Hay, *The First Hundred Thousand*

1916   POETRY: Gilbert Frankau, *The Guns*; Robert Graves, *Over the Brazier*; F. W. Harvey, *A Gloucestershire Lad at Home and Abroad*; W. N. Hodgson, *Verse and Prose in Peace and War*; Patrick MacGill, *Soldier Songs*; E. A. Mackintosh, *A Highland Regiment*; John Masefield, *Gallipoli*; H. Smalley Sarson, *From Field and Hospital*; Cicely Fox Smith, *Fighting Men*; Charles Hamilton Sorley, *Marlborough and Other Poems*; J. C. Squire, *Survival of the Fittest*; W. J. Turner, *The Hunter and Other Poems*; Willoughby Weaving, *The Star Fields and Other Poems*
       ANTHOLOGIES: *Soldier Poets* (ed. G. Kyle); *Some Imagist Poets, 1916*; *Wheels, 1st Cycle*
       FICTION: H. G. Wells, *Mr. Britling Sees It Through*
       OTHER: Edmund Gosse, *Inter Arma: Being Essays Written in Time of War*; Patrick MacGill, *The Great Push: An Episode of the Great War*; Charles Hamilton Sorley, *Letters from Germany*

1917   POETRY: Herbert Asquith, *The Volunteer and Other Poems*; Laurence Binyon, *The Cause: Poems of the War* and *For the Fallen*;

Leslie Coulson, *From an Outpost and Other Poems;* W. N. Ewer, *Five Souls and Other Wartime Verses;* Gilbert Frankau, *The City of Fear and Other Poems;* Lord Gorell, *Days of Destiny: War Poems at Home and Abroad;* Robert Graves, *Fairies and Fusiliers;* Ivor Gurney, *Severn and Somme;* F. W. Harvey, *Gloucestershire Friends: Poems from a German Prison Camp;* Francis Ledwidge, *Last Poems;* Henry Newbolt, *Poems: New and Old;* Robert Nichols, *Ardours and Endurances;* Siegfried Sassoon, *The Old Huntsman and Other Poems;* John W. Streets, *The Undying Splendour;* R. E. Vernède, *War Poems and Other Verses;* Francis Brett Young, *Five Degrees South*

ANTHOLOGIES: *Georgian Poetry, 1916–1917; The Muse in Arms* (ed. E. B. Osborn); *Some Imagist Poets, 1917; A Treasury of War Poetry, First Series* (ed. G. H. Clarke); *Wheels, 2nd Cycle*

OTHER: Francis Brett Young, *Marching on Tanga;* Alec Waugh, *The Loom of Youth*

BIOGRAPHY & CRITICISM: Viola Meynell, *Julian Grenfell*

1918 POETRY: Paul Bewsher, *Bombing of Bruges;* Vera Brittain, *Verses of a VAD;* Ford Madox Ford, *On Heaven and Poems Written on Active Service;* Gilbert Frankau, *The Judgement of Valhalla;* P. H. B. Lyon, *Songs of Youth and War;* E. A. Mackintosh, *War the Liberator and Other Pieces;* Siegfried Sassoon, *Counter-Attack and Other Poems;* Edward Thomas, *Last Poems;* Katharine Tynan, *Herb o' Grace;* Alec Waugh, *Resentment*

ANTHOLOGY: *Wheels, 3rd Cycle*

FICTION: Lord Dunsany, *Tales of War*

OTHER: Arthur Graeme West, *The Diary of a Dead Officer*

BIOGRAPHY & CRITICISM: A. S. J. Adcock, *For Remembrance: Soldier Poets Who Have Fallen in the War;* Edward Marsh, *Rupert Brooke: A Memoir;* William Lyon Phelps, *The Advance of English Poetry in the Twentieth Century*

1919 POETRY: Richard Aldington, *Images of War;* Maurice Baring, *Poems, 1914–1919;* Laurence Binyon, *The Four Years: War Poems;* Edward de Stein, *Picardy and Other Poems;* Ivor Gurney, *War's Embers and Other Verses;* F. W. Harvey, *Ducks and Other Verses;* A. P. Herbert, *The Bomber Gypsy;* D. H. Lawrence, *Bay;* Francis Ledwidge, *Complete Poems;* D. S. MacColl, *Bull and Other Verses;* John McCrae, *In Flanders Fields and Other Poems;* Herbert Read, *Naked Warriors;* Siegfried Sassoon, *The War Poems;* Osbert Sitwell, *Argonaut and Juggernaut;* T. P. Cameron Wilson, *Magpies in Picardy;* Francis Brett Young, *Poems 1916–1918*

ANTHOLOGIES: *Georgian Poetry, 1918–1919; A Treasury of War Po-etry, Second Series* (ed. G. H. Clarke); *Wheels, 4th Cycle*
OTHER: A. P. Herbert, *The Secret Battle;* Charles Hamilton Sorley, *The Letters of Charles Hamilton Sorley;* Alec Waugh, *The Prisoners of Mainz*
BIOGRAPHY & CRITICISM: T. Sturge Moore, *Some Soldier Poets;* Arthur Waugh, *Tradition and Change: Studies in Contemporary Literature*

1920   POETRY: Edmund Blunden, *The Waggoner and Other Poems;* Walter de la Mare, *Collected Poems;* Wilfred Owen, *Poems* (ed. Siegfried Sassoon); Ezra Pound, *Hugh Selwyn Mauberley;* Edward Thomas, *Collected Poems*
ANTHOLOGIES: *Valour and Vision: Poems of the War* (ed. J. T. Trot-ter); *Wheels, 5th Cycle*
FICTION: Jaroslav Hašek, *The Good Soldier Švejk*
BIOGRAPHY & CRITICISM: Edmund Gosse, *Some Diversions of a Man of Letters;* J. Middleton Murry, *The Evolution of an Intellectual* and *Aspects of Literature*

1921   POETRY: Edgell Rickword, *Behind the Eyes;* Frank Sidgwick, *More Verse;* J. C. Squire, *Collected Parodies*
ANTHOLOGY: *Wheels, 6th Cycle*

1922   POETRY: Edmund Blunden, *The Shepherd and Other Poems of Peace and War;* F. V. Branford, *Titans and Gods;* T. S. Eliot, *The Waste Land;* A. E. Housman, *Last Poems;* Isaac Rosenberg, *Poems* (ed. G. Bottomley); R. H. Sauter, *Songs in Captivity*
ANTHOLOGY: *Georgian Poetry, 1920–1922*

1923   POETRY: John Drinkwater, *Collected Poems*
FICTION: D. H. Lawrence, *Kangaroo*

1924   FICTION: Ford Madox Ford, *Some Do Not . . .*
OTHER: T. E. Hulme, *Speculations* (ed. Herbert Read)

1925   POETRY: Humbert Wolfe, *Lampoons*
FICTION: Ford Madox Ford, *No More Parades;* Herbert Read, *In Retreat*

1926   POETRY: W. W. Gibson, *Collected Poems, 1905–1925;* Herbert Read, *Collected Poems, 1913–1925*
FICTION: Ford Madox Ford, *A Man Could Stand Up—*

1927 POETRY: Robert Graves, *Poems, 1914–1926;* Humbert Wolfe, *Requiem*
ANTHOLOGY: *Armistice Day* (ed. A. P. Sanford and R. H. Schauffler)
FICTION: R. H. Mottram, *The Spanish Farm Trilogy 1914–18*

1928 POETRY: Thomas Hardy, *Winter Words in Various Moods and Metres*
FICTION: Ford Madox Ford, *Last Post*
OTHER: Edmund Blunden, *Undertones of War;* Siegfried Sassoon, *Memoirs of a Fox-Hunting Man*

1929 POETRY: Lord Dunsany, *Fifty Poems*
FICTION: Richard Aldington, *Death of a Hero;* Ernest Hemingway, *A Farewell to Arms;* E. M. Remarque, *All Quiet on the Western Front*
OTHER: Robert Graves, *Goodbye to All That*
BIOGRAPHY & CRITICISM: Stephen Gwynn, *The Letters and Friendships of Cecil Spring-Rice: A Record*

1930 POETRY: Edmund Blunden, *Poems, 1914–1930*
ANTHOLOGY: *An Anthology of War Poems* (ed. F. Brereton)
FICTION: Private 19022 (Frederic Manning), *Her Privates We;* H. M. Tomlinson, *All Our Yesterdays;* Henry Williamson, *The Patriot's Progress*
OTHER: Siegfried Sassoon, *Memoirs of an Infantry Officer*
BIOGRAPHY & CRITICISM: Cyril Falls, *War Books: A Critical Guide;* Douglas Jerrold, *The Lie About the War: A Note on Some Contemporary War Books*

1931 POETRY: Wilfred Owen, *The Poems* (ed. Edmund Blunden); Humbert Wolfe, *Early Poems*
BIOGRAPHY & CRITICISM: J. Harvey Darton, *From Surtees to Sassoon: Some English Contrasts*

1932 POETRY: Colin Ellis, *Mournful Numbers, Verses and Epigrams*
CRITICISM: F. R. Leavis, *New Bearings in English Poetry*

1933 POETRY: Leonard Barnes, *Youth at Arms;* Herbert Read, *The End of a War;* Edward Shanks, *Poems 1912–1932*
OTHER: Vera Brittain, *Testament of Youth: An Autobiographical Study of the Years 1900–1925*

1934 POETRY: Herbert Asquith, *Poems 1912–1933;* Vera Brittain, *Poems of the War and After;* S. W. Powell, *One-Way Street and Other Poems*

1935 OTHER: J. C. Squire, *British Propaganda: 1914–1917;* H. M. Tomlinson, *Mars His Idiot*
      BIOGRAPHY & CRITICISM: Frank Swinnerton, *The Georgian Literary Scene, 1910–1935;* E. G. Twitchett, *Francis Brett Young*

1936 POETRY: A. E. Housman, *More Poems*
      OTHER: Siegfried Sassoon, *Sherston's Progress*

1937 POETRY: David Jones, *In Parenthesis;* Isaac Rosenberg, *Collected Works* (ed. G. Bottomley & D. Harding)
      OTHER: Siegfried Sassoon, *The Complete Memoirs of George Sherston*
      BIOGRAPHY & CRITICISM: Robert P. Eckert, *Edward Thomas: A Biography and a Bibliography*

1938 POETRY: G. K. Chesterton, *Collected Poems*
      BIOGRAPHY & CRITICISM: Amiya Chakravarty, *The Dynasts and the Post-War Age in Poetry;* Ethel Smyth, *Maurice Baring*

1939 BIOGRAPHY & CRITICISM: John Moore, *The Life and Letters of Edward Thomas*

1940 POETRY: *Rudyard Kipling's Verse: The Definitive Edition*
      CRITICISM: David Daiches, *Poetry and the Modern World*

1941 OTHER: Richard Aldington, *Life for Life's Sake*

1943 ANTHOLOGY: *Anthology of War Poetry 1914–1918* (ed. Robert Nichols)

1945 ANTHOLOGY: *Soldiers' Verse* (ed. Patric Dickinson)
      OTHER: Siegfried Sassoon, *Siegfried's Journey, 1916–1920*

1946 POETRY: *The Poetical Works of Rupert Brooke* (ed. G. L. Keynes); Siegfried Sassoon, *Collected Poems*

1947 POETRY: Edgell Rickword, *Collected Poems*

1948 POETRY: Richard Aldington, *The Complete Poems*
      BIOGRAPHY & CRITICISM: A. J. A. Stringer, *Red Wine of Youth: A Life of Rupert Brooke*

1949 POETRY: Isaac Rosenberg, *Collected Poems* (ed. G. Bottomley & D. Harding)

1951 CRITICISM: Vivian de Sola Pinto, *Crisis in English Poetry, 1880–1940*

1953 BIOGRAPHY & CRITICISM: Francis Berry, *Herbert Read*

1954 POETRY: Ivor Gurney, *Poems* (ed. Edmund Blunden)

1956 BIOGRAPHY & CRITICISM: H. Coombes, *Edward Thomas*

1958 BIOGRAPHY & CRITICISM: Edmund Blunden, *War Poets 1914–1918*; Eleanor Farjeon, *Edward Thomas: The Last Four Years*; Alec M. Hardie, *Edmund Blunden*

1960 BIOGRAPHY & CRITICISM: D. S. R. Welland, *Wilfred Owen: A Critical Study*; *Stand* 4, no. 3 (War Poets Issue)

1961 POETRY: Siegfried Sassoon, *Collected Poems, 1908–1956*
ANTHOLOGY: *The Pelican Guide to English Literature, vol. 7: The Modern Age* (ed. D. J. Enright)

1963 POETRY: Wilfred Owen, *The Collected Poems* (ed. C. Day-Lewis)
OTHER: Herbert Read, *The Contrary Experience*
BIOGRAPHY & CRITICISM: Harold Owen, *Journey From Obscurity: Wilfred Owen, 1893–1918*, vol. 1; Vernon Scannell, *Edward Thomas*; Frank Swinnerton, *Figures in the Foreground: Literary Reminiscences 1917–40*

1964 POETRY: D. H. Lawrence, *The Complete Poems*
ANTHOLOGY: *Up the Line to Death: The War Poets, 1914–1918* (ed. Brian Gardner)
BIOGRAPHY & CRITICISM: Christopher Hassall, *Rupert Brooke: A Biography*; John H. Johnston, *English Poetry of the First World War: A Study in the Evolution of Lyric and Narrative Form*; Harold Owen, *Journey From Obscurity*, vol. 2.

1965 ANTHOLOGY: *Men Who March Away: Poems of the First World War* (ed. Ian Parsons)
OTHER: Reginald Pound, *The Lost Generation of 1914*
BIOGRAPHY & CRITICISM: Bernard Bergonzi, *Heroes' Twilight: A Study of the Literature of the Great War*; T. R. Henn, *W. B. Yeats and the Poetry of War*; Harold Owen, *Journey From Obscurity*, vol. 3; Robert H. Ross, *The Georgian Revolt, 1910–1922: Rise and Fall of a Poetic Ideal*; Thomas Burnett Swann, *The Ungirt Runner: Charles Hamilton Sorley, Poet of World War I*

1967   ANTHOLOGY: *Poetry of the First World War* (ed. Maurice Hussey)
       BIOGRAPHY & CRITICISM: Joy Grant, *Harold Monro and the Poetry Bookshop;* Michael Thorpe, *Siegfried Sassoon: A Critical Study*

1968   OTHER: *The Letters of Rupert Brooke* (ed. G. L. Keynes)
       BIOGRAPHY & CRITICISM: George A. Panichas, ed., *Promise of Greatness: The War of 1914–1918* (essays by various hands)

1969   BIOGRAPHY & CRITICISM: Michael Kirkham, *The Poetry of Robert Graves*

1970   POETRY: *Maurice Baring Restored: Selections From His Work* (ed. Paul Horgan)
       ANTHOLOGY: *1914–1918 in Poetry* (ed. E. L. Black)
       BIOGRAPHY & CRITICISM: William Cooke, *Edward Thomas: A Critical Biography 1878–1917*

1971   BIOGRAPHY & CRITICISM: David Blamires, *David Jones: Artist and Writer*

1972   BIOGRAPHY & CRITICISM: Mildred Davidson, *The Poetry Is In the Pity;* Arthur E. Lane, *An Adequate Response: The War Poetry of Wilfred Owen and Siegfried Sassoon;* Jon Silkin, *Out of Battle: The Poetry of the Great War;* R. George Thomas, *Edward Thomas; Poetry Wales* 8, no. 3 (David Jones Number)

1973   POETRY: Ivor Gurney, *Poems of Gurney, 1890–1937* (ed. Edmund Blunden); Wilfred Owen, *War Poems and Others* (ed. Dominic Hibberd)
       BIOGRAPHY & CRITICISM: M. S. Greicus, *Prose Writers of World War I*

1974   BIOGRAPHY & CRITICISM: Jon Stallworthy, *Wilfred Owen; Agenda* 12, no. 1 (David Jones Special Issue)

1975   BIOGRAPHY & CRITICISM: Joseph Cohen, *Journey to the Trenches: The Life of Isaac Rosenberg, 1890–1918;* Paul Fussell, *The Great War and Modern Memory;* René Hague, *David Jones;* Dominic Hibberd, *Wilfred Owen;* Jeremy Hooker, *David Jones*

1976   BIOGRAPHY & CRITICISM: Holger Klein, ed., *The First World War in Fiction: A Collection of Critical Essays;* Harold Orel, *The Final Years of Thomas Hardy, 1912–1928;* David Perkins, *A History of Modern Poetry from the 1890s to the High Modernist Mode*

1977   BIOGRAPHY & CRITICISM: Timothy Rogers, ed., *Georgian Poetry, 1911–1922: The Critical Heritage* (essays by various hands); Jon Stallworthy, *Wilfred Owen: A Biography*

1978   POETRY: Edward Thomas, *The Collected Poems of Edward Thomas* (ed. R. George Thomas)
        BIOGRAPHY & CRITICISM: Paul Delany, *D. H. Lawrence's Nightmare: The Writer and His Circle in the Years of the Great War;* Robert Gittings, *Thomas Hardy's Later Years;* Michael Hurd, *The Ordeal of Ivor Gurney;* Jan Marsh, *Edward Thomas: A Poet for his Country;* Andrew Rutherford, *The Literature of War: Five Studies in Heroic Virtue; Poetry Wales* 13, no. 4 (Edward Thomas Centenary Issue)
        BIBLIOGRAPHY: Catherine W. Reilly, *English Poetry of the First World War: A Bibliography*

1979   POETRY: Leonard Barnes, *The Glory of the World Sonnets;* Isaac Rosenberg, *The Collected Works of Isaac Rosenberg: Poetry, Prose, Letters, Paintings and Drawings* (ed. Ian Parsons)
        ANTHOLOGY: *The Penguin Book of First World War Poetry* (ed. Jon Silkin)

1980   ANTHOLOGY: *Scars Upon My Heart: Women's Poetry and Verse of the First World War* (ed. Catherine W. Reilly)
        BIOGRAPHY & CRITICISM: René Hague, *Dai Greatcoat: A Self-Portrait of David Jones in His Letters;* John Lehmann, *The Strange Destiny of Rupert Brooke*

1981   OTHER: Vera Brittain, *War Diary 1913–1917: Chronicle of Youth* (ed. Alan Bishop with Terry Smart); Siegfried Sassoon, *Diaries 1920–1922* (ed. Rupert Hart-Davis); *A Language Not to Be Betrayed: Selected Prose of Edward Thomas* (ed. Edna Langley)
        BIOGRAPHY & CRITICISM: Mark Girouard, *The Return to Camelot;* Dominic Hibberd, ed., *Poetry of the First World War: A Casebook;* John Lehmann, *The English Poets of the First World War;* Andrew Motion, *The Poetry of Edward Thomas*
        BIBLIOGRAPHY: Philip E. Hagar and Desmond Taylor, *The Novels of World War I: An Annotated Bibliography*

1982   POETRY: Ivor Gurney, *Collected Poems* (ed. P. J. Kavanagh); Siegfried Sassoon, *The War Poems of Siegfried Sassoon* (ed. Rupert Hart-Davis)
        OTHER: *In Broken Images: Selected Letters of Robert Graves, 1914–1946* (ed. Paul O'Prey)

1983 POETRY: Wilfred Owen, *The Complete Poems* (ed. Jon Stallworthy); Siegfried Sassoon, *The War Poems of Siegfried Sassoon* (ed. Rupert Hart-Davis)

OTHER: Ivor Gurney, *The War Letters* (ed. R. K. R. Thornton); *Siegfried Sassoon, Diaries 1915–1918* (ed. Rupert Hart-Davis); *Siegfried Sassoon's Long Journey* (ed. Paul Fussell)

1984 ANTHOLOGY: *The Oxford Book of War Poetry* (ed. Jon Stallworthy)

BIOGRAPHY & CRITICISM: Desmond Graham, *The Truth of War: Owen, Blunden, and Rosenberg;* John Press, *Poets of World War I*

1985 POETRY: Charles Hamilton Sorley, *The Collected Poems* (ed. Jean Moorcroft Wilson)

BIOGRAPHY & CRITICISM: Patrick Bridgwater, *The German Poets of the First World War;* Jean Moorcroft Wilson, *Charles Hamilton Sorley: A Biography*

1986 ANTHOLOGY: *Poetry of the Great War* (ed. Dominic Hibberd and John Onions)

BIOGRAPHY & CRITICISM: Stanley Weintraub, *A Stillness Heard Round the World. The End of the Great War: November 1918; Renascence*, 38, no. 2 (David Jones Issue)

Notes

Preface

1. Samuel Hynes, "The Irony and the Pity," *Times Literary Supplement,* 18 December 1981, p. 1469.
2. Robert H. Ross, *The Georgian Revolt, 1910–1922: Rise and Fall of a Poetic Ideal* (Carbondale, Ill.: Southern Illinois University Press, 1965), p. 144.

Chapter 1. Poetry and the Great War

1. Robert Graves, "The Kaiser's War: A British Point of View" in George A. Panichas, ed., *Promise of Greatness: The War of 1914–1918* (New York: John Day Company, 1968), p. 10.
2. H. M. Tomlinson, *All Our Yesterdays* (New York: Harper & Brothers, 1930), p. 371.
3. J. M. Synge, *Collected Works,* ed. Robin Skelton (London: Oxford University Press, 1962), 1, xxxvi.
4. E. L. Black, ed., *1914–1918 in Poetry: An Anthology* (London: University of London Press, 1970), p. 22.
5. John H. Johnston, *English Poetry of the First World War: A Study in the Evolution of Lyric and Narrative Form* (Princeton, N.J.: Princeton University Press, 1964), pp. 3, 5.
6. Ibid., p. 61.
7. Jon Silkin, *Out of Battle: The Poetry of the Great War* (London: Oxford University Press, 1972), p. 343.
8. Arthur Waugh, "War Poetry (1914–1918)," *Quarterly Review* 280 (October 1918): 381.
9. Philip Hobsbaum, "The Road Not Taken," *Listener* 46 (1961): 863.
10. Johnston, p. 340.
11. Quoted in Andrew Motion, *The Poetry of Edward Thomas* (London: Routledge & Kegan Paul, 1981), pp. 92–93.
12. Quoted in Bernard Bergonzi, *Heroes' Twilight: A Study of the Literature of the Great War* (London: Constable, 1965), pp. 168–69.

Chapter 2. Calls to Action and Enthusiastic Replies

1. Edmund Gosse, *Some Diversions of a Man of Letters* (London: Heinemann, 1920), p. 262.
2. Silkin, p. 44.
3. James Hazen, "Hardy's War Poetry," *Four Decades of Poetry, 1890–1930* 2 (1978): 92.
4. George Orwell, "Rudyard Kipling," *Horizon* 5 (February 1942): 118.
5. Ibid., p. 114.

6. Paul Fussell, *The Great War and Modern Memory* (London: Oxford University Press, 1975), p. 249.

7. Ibid.

8. Ibid., p. 26.

9. Quoted ibid.

10. Bergonzi, p. 123.

11. Gosse, p. 268.

12. London *Times* (26 April 1915), reprinted in Dominic Hibberd, ed., *Poetry of the First World War: A Casebook* (London: Macmillan, 1981), p. 38.

13. Quoted ibid., p. 131.

14. Johnston, p. 4.

15. Bergonzi, p. 42.

16. Fussell, p. 276.

17. Edmund Blunden, *War Poets: 1914–1918*, British Council and National Book League, Writers and Their Work, no. 100 (London: Longmans, Green, 1958), pp. 18, 20.

18. Charles Hamilton Sorley, *Letters from Germany and From the Army* (privately printed, 1916), p. 128.

19. Quoted in Silkin, p. 67.

20. Ibid.

21. John Lehmann, *The Strange Destiny of Rupert Brooke* (New York: Holt, Rinehart & Winston, 1980), p. 135.

22. Ibid., p. 163.

23. Quoted in W. K. Thomas, "The War Sonnets of Rupert Brooke," *English Quarterly* 7 (Spring 1974): 28–29.

24. Ibid., pp. 39–40.

25. Ibid., p. 38.

26. T. Sturge Moore, *Some Soldier Poets* (London: Grant Richards, 1919), p. 47.

Chapter 3. The Clash of Chivalry and Modern War

1. Mark Girouard, "When Chivalry Died," *New Republic*, 30 September 1981, p. 30.

2. Gosse, p. 273.

3. Moore, p. 16.

4. Silkin, p. 73.

5. Quoted by Galloway Kyle in his preface to *The Undying Splendour* by Sgt. J. W. Streets, reprinted in Hibberd, p. 34.

6. Fussell, p. 297.

7. Robert Graves, *Goodbye to All That* (London: Jonathan Cape, 1929; revised, London: Cassell, 1957), p. 261.

8. *In Broken Images: Selected Letters of Robert Graves, 1914–1946*, ed. Paul O'Prey (London: Hutchinson, 1982), p. 319.

9. Gosse, p. 279.

10. Douglas Goldring, "The War and the Poets," reprinted in Hibberd, pp. 41–42.

11. Waugh, pp. 397–98.

Chapter 4. Pastorals and Elegies

1. William Lyon Phelps, *The Advance of English Poetry in the Twentieth Century* (New York: Dodd, Mead, 1918; reprint, London: Kennikat Press, 1970), p. 43.

2. Fussell, p. 56.

3. Quoted in Ian Boyd, "Maurice Baring's Early Writing," *Downside Review* 92 (1974): 170.

4. Gosse, p. 274.

Chapter 5. The Imagists

1. Vivian de Sola Pinto, *Crisis in English Poetry, 1880–1940* (New York: Harper & Row, 1966), pp. 151–52.

2. Richard Aldington, *Life for Life's Sake: A Book of Reminiscences* (New York: Viking, 1941), p. 133.

3. Frank MacShane, *The Life and Work of Ford Madox Ford* (New York: Horizon, 1965), p. 96.

4. Ibid., p. 102.

5. Silkin, p. 194.

6. Bergonzi, p. 139.

7. David Daiches, *Poetry and the Modern World: A Study of Poetry in England Between 1900 and 1939* (New York: Biblo & Tannen, 1969), pp. 53, 83.

8. Aldington, p. 209.

9. Richard Aldington, *Death of a Hero* (Garden City, N.Y.: Garden City Publishing Company, 1929), p. 206.

10. Herbert Read, "The Present State of Poetry," *Kenyon Review* 1 (Autumn 1939): 360.

11. Quoted in Johnston, p. 260.

12. Quoted ibid.

13. From the *Egoist* (July 1919), reprinted in Hibberd, p. 52.

14. Quoted in Fussell, p. 162.

15. Fussell, p. 158.

16. Johnston, p. 257.

17. Andrew Rutherford, *The Literature of War: Five Studies in Heroic Virtue* (New York: Barnes & Noble, 1978), p. 84.

Chapter 6. Searchers for Perspective

1. Sorley, p. 184.

2. Graves, *Goodbye to All That,* p. 149.

3. Sorley, p. 89.

4. Ibid., p. 149.

5. Bergonzi, p. 52.

6. Sorley, p. 116.

7. Ibid., p. 146.

8. Ibid., p. 111.

9. Dennis Welland, "Arthur Graeme West: A Messenger to Job" in G. R. Hibbard, ed., *Renaissance and Modern Essays* (New York: Barnes & Noble, 1966), pp. 175–76.

10. Ibid., p. 176.

11. Quoted ibid., p. 173.

12. John Wilson, "Wilfrid Gibson and the War," *Four Decades of Poetry, 1890–1930* 1 (1976): 132.

13. Waugh, p. 396.

14. Quoted in Johnston, p. 208.

15. T. R. Henn, "W. B. Yeats and the Poetry of War," *Proceedings of the British Academy* 51 (1965): 301–19.

Chapter 7. Comedy and Reality

1. Moore, p. 38.
2. Gosse, pp. 279–80.
3. Graves, *Goodbye to All That*, pp. 154–55.
4. Bergonzi, p. 65.
5. Daniel Hoffman, "Significant Wounds: The Early Poetry of Robert Graves," *Shenandoah* 17 (1966): 22.
6. Gosse, p. 281.
7. Graves, "The Kaiser's War," p. 10.
8. Graves, *Goodbye to All That*, p. 252.
9. Graves, "The Kaiser's War," p. 11.
10. Quoted in Alun R. Jones, "Robert Graves: The Romantic Artificer," *Stand* 4 (1960): 53.
11. Quoted in Robert Wohl, *The Generation of 1914* (Cambridge: Harvard University Press, 1979), p. 107.
12. Graves, *Goodbye to All That*, p. 254.

Chapter 8. Satire and Protest

1. Siegfried Sassoon, *Memoirs of a Fox-Hunting Man* (New York: Coward-McCann, 1929), p. 290.
2. Ibid., pp. 293–94.
3. Ibid., p. 305.
4. Sassoon to Ian Parsons, quoted in Ian Parsons, ed., *Men Who March Away: Poems of the First World War* (London: Chatto & Windus, 1965), p. 17.
5. C. E. Maguire, "Harmony Unheard: The Poetry of Siegfried Sassoon," *Renascence* 11 (Spring 1959): 116.
6. Quoted in Arthur E. Lane, *An Adequate Response: The War Poetry of Wilfred Owen and Siegfried Sassoon* (Detroit: Wayne State University Press, 1972), pp. 90–91.
7. Siegfried Sassoon, *Sherston's Progress* (New York: Book League of America, 1936), p. 162.
8. Sassoon, *Memoirs of a Fox-Hunting Man*, p. 359.
9. Sassoon, *Sherston's Progress*, p. 58.
10. Ibid., p. 43.
11. L. Hugh Moore, Jr., "Siegfried Sassoon and Georgian Realism," *Twentieth Century Literature* 14 (January 1969): 207.
12. John Middleton Murry, *The Evolution of an Intellectual* (London: Richard Cobden-Sanderson, 1920), pp. 71, 78.
13. Ibid.
14. Joseph Cohen, "The Three Roles of Siegfried Sassoon," *Tulane Studies in English* 7 (1957): 171.
15. Sassoon, *Sherston's Progress*, p. 17.
16. Wohl, p. 99n.
17. Frank Swinnerton, *The Georgian Literary Scene, 1910–1935: A Panorama* (London: Hutchinson, 1935; revised, 1954), p. 271.
18. Ibid., p. 226.

Chapter 9. Women and the War

1. Swinnerton, p. 258.
2. Ibid.
3. Vera Brittain, "War Service in Perspective," in Panichas, p. 367.
4. Lane, p. 47.
5. Wohl, p. 111.
6. Brittain, p. 369.
7. Ibid., p. 370.
8. Ibid., p. 375.

Chapter 10. Edmund Blunden and Edward Thomas

1. Bergonzi, p. 68.
2. Hobsbaum, p. 860.
3. Quoted in Motion, p. 137.
4. Quoted ibid., p. 92.
5. Quoted in Fussell, p. 59.
6. Samuel Hynes, *Edwardian Occasions: Essays on English Writing in the Early Twentieth Century* (New York: Oxford University Press, 1972), p. 96.
7. Fussell, p. 254.
8. Paul M. Cubeta, "Robert Frost and Edward Thomas: Two Soldier Poets," *New England Quarterly* 52 (June 1979): 149.
9. R. George Thomas, *Edward Thomas* (Cardiff: University of Wales Press, 1972), pp. 33–34.
10. Motion, p. 111.

Chapter 11. Wilfred Owen

1. Dominic Hibberd, *Wilfred Owen* (London: Longman, 1975), p. 28.
2. Ibid., p. 34.
3. Swinnerton, p. 263.
4. Quoted in Blunden, p. 36.
5. Hibberd, *Wilfred Owen*, pp. 13, 14.
6. Dennis Welland, "Elegies to This Generation" in Hibberd, *Casebook*, p. 140.
7. Quoted in Fussell, p. 81.
8. Ibid.
9. Quoted ibid., pp. 159–60.
10. Quoted ibid., p. 119.
11. Quoted in Joseph Cohen, "The Wilfred Owen War Poetry Collection," *Library Chronicle of the University of Texas* 5 (Spring 1955): 33.
12. Philip Larkin, "The Real Wilfred Owen: Owen's Life and Legends," *Encounter* 44 (March 1975): 76.
13. Quoted in Black, p. 149.
14. Quoted in Joseph Cohen, "Wilfred Owen: Fresher Fields than Flanders," *English Literature in Transition* 7 (March 1964): 4.
15. Lane, p. 123.
16. Quoted in Dominic Hibberd, "Silkin on Owen: Some Other War," *Stand* 21 (1980): 31.
17. Lane, p. 145.

18. Dominic Hibberd, "Wilfred Owen's Rhyming," *Studia Neophilologica* 50 (1978): 208–9.

19. Hibberd, *Wilfred Owen,* p. 11.

20. David Daiches, *New Literary Values: Studies in Modern Literature* (Edinburgh: Oliver and Boyd, 1936; reprint, Freeport, N.Y.: Books for Libraries Press, 1968), p. 64.

Chapter 12. Isaac Rosenberg

1. Quoted in Joseph Cohen, *Journey to the Trenches: The Life of Isaac Rosenberg, 1890–1918* (New York: Basic Books, 1975), p. 118.

2. Rosenberg to Edward Marsh, August 1916, in *The Collected Works of Isaac Rosenberg: Poetry, Prose, Letters, Paintings and Drawings* (New York: Oxford University Press, 1979), p. 242.

3. Rosenberg to Marsh, late December 1915, ibid., p. 227.

4. Cohen, *Journey to the Trenches,* pp. 156–57.

5. Rosenberg, "Rudolph," in *The Collected Works,* p. 277.

6. Rosenberg to Mrs. Cohen, September/October 1912, ibid., p. 193.

7. Rosenberg to Miss Seaton, December/January 1912/13, ibid., p. 198.

8. Rosenberg to Ezra Pound, 1915, ibid., p. 214.

9. Rosenberg to Sydney Schiff, October 1915, ibid., p. 219.

10. Rosenberg to Marsh, October 1915, ibid.

11. Rosenberg to Schiff, early 1916, ibid., pp. 229–30.

12. Rosenberg to Lascelles Abercrombie, 11 March 1916, ibid., p. 230.

13. Rosenberg to Marsh, probably 27 May 1916, ibid., p. 234.

14. Rosenberg to Gordon Bottomley, postmarked 26 February 1918, ibid., p. 268.

15. Rosenberg to Marsh, postmarked 30 June 1916, ibid., p. 237.

16. Rosenberg to Marsh, probably December 1916, ibid., p. 250.

17. Rosenberg to Mrs. Cohen, undated, ibid., p. 237.

18. Rosenberg to Miss Seaton, 1911, ibid., p. 181.

19. Rosenberg to Laurence Binyon, Autumn 1916, ibid., p. 248.

20. D. W. Harding, "Aspects of the Poetry of Isaac Rosenberg," *Scrutiny* 3 (March 1935): 358.

21. Bergonzi, p. 113.

22. Cohen, *Journey to the Trenches,* p. 152.

23. Rosenberg to Marsh, postmarked 27 May 1917, in *The Collected Works,* p. 255.

24. Marius Bewley, "The Poetry of Isaac Rosenberg," *Commentary* 7 (January 1949): 37–38.

25. Rosenberg, "Art," in *The Collected Works,* p. 294.

26. Rosenberg to Schiff, possibly March 1916, ibid, p. 231.

Chapter 13. Armistice and After

1. Quoted in Johnston, p. 269.

2. Anthony McAdam, "Foreword: Leonard Barnes—Poet, Philosopher and Humanist" in Leonard Barnes, *The Glory of the World Sonnets* (Rotterdam: Futile, 1979), p. i.

3. Ibid., pp. i–ii.

4. Ibid., p. ii.

5. Ibid., p. i.

Chapter 14. The Great War Epic

1. Michael Alexander, "On David Jones, Man, Poetry and the BBC," *Agenda* 18–19 (1980/1981): 164.

2. Quoted in Anthony Powell, *To Keep the Ball Rolling: The Memoirs of Anthony Powell,* vol. III: *Faces in My Time* (London: Heinemann, 1980), 77.

3. David Jones, *In Parenthesis* (New York: Viking, 1963), p. xv.

4. Ibid., p. xii.

5. Ibid., p. x.

6. Ibid., pp. xi–xii.

7. Johnston, p. 334.

8. Fussell, p. 154.

9. Jones, p. ix.

10. Bergonzi, p. 200.

Select Bibliography

I HAVE LISTED PRIMARY SOURCES ALPHABETICALLY BY AUTHOR'S SURNAME, INDICA-
TING THOSE WORKS WHICH ARE NOT POETRY. I HAVE MARKED WITH AN ASTERISK
THOSE SECONDARY SOURCES I FOUND PARTICULARLY HELPFUL.

Primary Sources

Aldington, Richard. *The Complete Poems of Richard Aldington.* London: Allen &
Unwin, 1948.

———. *Life for Life's Sake: A Book of Reminiscences.* New York: Viking, 1941.
Autobiography.

Asquith, Herbert. *Poems, 1912–1933.* London: Sidgwick & Jackson, 1934.

Baring, Maurice. *Maurice Baring Restored: Selections from His Work.* Edited by Paul
Horgan. New York: Farrar, Straus & Giroux, 1970.

Barnes, Leonard. *The Glory of the World Sonnets.* Edited by Anthony McAdam.
Rotterdam: Futile, 1979.

———. *Youth at Arms.* London: Davies, 1933.

Bewsher, Paul. *Bombing of Bruges.* London: Hodder & Stoughton, 1918.

Binyon, Laurence. *Laurence Binyon Anthology.* London: Hodder & Stoughton,
1927.

Blunden, Edmund. *Poems, 1914–1930.* London: Cobden-Sanderson, 1930.

———. *Undertones of War.* London: Cobden-Sanderson, 1928. Memoirs.

Branford, F. Victor. *Titans and Gods.* London: Christophers, 1922.

Brittain, Vera. *Poems of the War and After.* New York: Macmillan, 1934.

———. *Testament of Youth: An Autobiographical Study of the Years 1900–1925.*
New York: Macmillan, 1933. Autobiography.

Brooke, Rupert. *Collected Poems of Rupert Brooke.* London: Sidgwick & Jackson,
1918.

———. *The Complete Poems of Rupert Brooke.* London: Sidgwick & Jackson, 1932.

Cannan, May Wedderburn. *In War Time: Poems.* New York: Longmans, Green,
1917.

———. *The Splendid Days: Poems.* New York: Longmans, Green, 1919.

Chesterton, G. K. *The Collected Poems of G. K. Chesterton.* New York: Dodd,
Mead, 1938.

de Stein, Edward. *Picardy and Other Poems.* London: Murray, 1919.

Drinkwater, John. *Collected Poems of John Drinkwater.* London: Sidgwick & Jackson, 1923.

Lord Dunsany [Edward J. M. D. Plunkett]. *Fifty Poems.* London: Curtis Brown,
1929.

Ellis, Colin, *Mournful Numbers, Verses and Epigrams.* London: Macmillan, 1932.

Ewer, William Norman. *Five Souls and Other Wartime Verses.* London: Herald, 1917.

Frankau, Gilbert. *The City of Fear and Other Poems.* London: Chatto & Windus, 1917.

———. *The Judgement of Valhalla.* London: Chatto & Windus, 1918.

Gibson, Wilfrid. *Collected Poems, 1905–1925.* London: Macmillan, 1926.

Lord Gorell [Ronald Gorell Barnes]. *Days of Destiny: War Poems at Home and Abroad.* London: Longman, 1917.

Graves, Robert. *Goodbye to All That.* London: Jonathan Cape, 1929; revised, London: Cassell, 1957. Memoirs.

———. *In Broken Images: Selected Letters of Robert Graves, 1914–1946.* Edited by Paul O'Prey. London: Hutchinson, 1982. Letters.

———. *Poems, 1914–1926.* London: Heinemann, 1927.

Gurney, Ivor. *Poems of Gurney, 1890–1937.* Edited by Edmund Blunden. London: Chatto & Windus, 1973.

———. *War's Embers.* London: Sidgwick & Jackson, 1919.

Hardy, Thomas. *Collected Poems of Thomas Hardy.* London: Macmillan, 1931.

———. *Winter Words in Various Moods and Metres.* London: Macmillan, 1928.

Harvey, F. W. *Comrades in Captivity: A Record of Life in Seven German Prison Camps.* London: Sidgwick & Jackson, 1920. Memoirs.

———. *Gloucestershire Friends.* London: Sidgwick & Jackson, 1917.

Herbert, Alan Patrick. *The Bomber Gipsy.* London: Methuen, 1919.

Hewlett, Maurice. *Singsongs of the War.* London: Poetry Bookshop, 1914.

Hodgson, William Noel. *Verse and Prose in Peace and War.* London: Murray, 1920.

Housman, A. E. *Collected Poems.* London: Cape, 1960.

Jones, David. *In Parenthesis.* New York: Viking, 1963.

Kipling, Rudyard. *Rudyard Kipling's Verse: The Definitive Edition.* New York: Doubleday, 1940.

Lawrence, D. H. *The Complete Poems of D. H. Lawrence.* New York: Viking, 1964.

Ledwidge, Francis. *The Complete Poems of Francis Ledwidge.* New York: Brentano's, 1919.

Leighton, Roland. *Poems.* Newbury, England: Privately printed by David Roland Leighton, the author's nephew, n.d.

Letts, Winifred M. *The Spires of Oxford and Other Poems.* New York: Dutton, 1918.

Lyon, P. H. B. *Songs of Youth and War.* London: Macdonald, 1918.

MacColl, D. S. *Bull and Other War Verses.* London: Constable, 1919.

McCrae, John. *In Flanders Fields and Other Poems.* New York: Putnam's Sons, 1919.

MacDiarmid, Hugh. *Collected Poems of Hugh MacDiarmid.* London: Macmillan, 1962.

MacGill, Patrick. *Soldier Songs.* New York: Dutton, 1917.

Mackintosh, E. A. *A Highland Regiment.* London: John Lane, 1917.

———. *War the Liberator and Other Pieces.* London: John Lane, 1918.

Newbolt, Henry. *Poems: New and Old.* London: Murray, 1917.

Nichols, Robert. *Ardours and Endurances.* London: Chatto & Windus, 1917.

O'Rourke, May. *West Wind Days.* London: Macdonald, 1918.

Owen, Wilfred. *Collected Poems of Wilfred Owen.* Edited by C. Day-Lewis. London: Chatto & Windus, 1963.

————. *Wilfred Owen: War Poems and Others.* Edited by Dominic Hibberd. London: Chatto & Windus, 1973.

Peterson, Margaret. *A Woman's Message, 1915 and Other Poems.* London: Truslove & Hanson, 1915.

Pope, Jessie. *Jessie Pope's War Poems.* London: Grant Richards, 1915.

Read, Herbert. *Collected Poems of Herbert Read.* London: Faber & Faber, 1966.

Rickword, Edgell. *Behind the Eyes.* London: Sidgwick & Jackson, 1921.

————. *Collected Poems.* London: John Lane, 1947.

Rosenberg, Isaac. *The Collected Works of Isaac Rosenberg: Poetry, Prose, Letters, Paintings and Drawings.* Edited by Ian Parsons. New York: Oxford University Press, 1979.

Sarson, H. Smalley. *From Field and Hospital.* London: Macdonald, 1916.

Sassoon, Siegfried. *Collected Poems of Siegfried Sassoon.* New York: Viking, 1946.

————. *Memoirs of a Fox-Hunting Man.* New York: Coward-McCann, 1929. Autobiographical fiction.

————. *Sherston's Progress.* New York: Book League of America, 1936. Autobiographical fiction.

Sauter, R. H. *Songs in Captivity.* London: Heinemann, 1922.

Shanks, Edward. *Poems, 1912–1932.* London: Macmillan, 1933.

Shove, Fredegond. *Poems.* London: Cambridge University Press, 1956.

Sidgwick, Frank. *More Verse.* London: Sidgwick & Jackson, 1921.

Sitwell, Osbert. *Selected Poems Old and New.* London: Duckworth, 1943.

Smith, Cicely Fox. *Songs and Chanties, 1914–1916.* London: Mathews, 1919.

Sorley, Charles H. *The Letters of Charles Hamilton Sorley.* London: Cambridge University Press, 1919. Letters.

————. *Marlborough and Other Poems.* London: Cambridge University Press, 1916; 6th ed., 1932.

Squire, John C. *Collected Poems.* London: Macmillan, 1959.

————. *Survival of the Fittest.* London: Allen & Unwin, 1916; revised, 1919.

Streets, John W. *The Undying Splendour.* London: Macdonald, 1917.

Thomas, Edward. "The Beginning of a Writer." *To-Day* 1 (1917): 104–7. Memoir.

————. "Diary of Edward Thomas." Introduced by R. George Thomas. *Anglo-Welsh Review* 20 (Autumn 1971): 8–32. War diary.

————. *Collected Poems.* London: Faber & Faber, 1944.

————. *The Collected Poems of Edward Thomas.* Edited by R. George Thomas. Oxford: The Clarendon Press, 1978.

Vernède, R. E. *War Poems and Other Verses.* London: Heinemann, 1917.

Watson, William. *The Poems of Sir William Watson, 1878–1935.* London: Harrap, 1936.

Waugh, Alec. *Resentment: Poems.* London: Grant Richards, 1918.

Weaving, Willoughby. *The Star Fields and Other Poems.* Oxford: Blackwell, 1916.

West, Arthur Graeme. *Diary of a Dead Officer.* London: Herald, 1918. Posthumously published diary, including poems.

Wolfe, Humbert. *The Fourth of August.* London: Eyre Methuen, 1935.

Yeats, W. B. *Collected Poems.* London: Macmillan, 1959.

Young, Francis Brett. *Poems, 1916–1918.* London: Collins, 1919.

Secondary Sources

1. ANTHOLOGIES

Adcock, Arthur St. John. *For Remembrance: Soldier Poets Who Have Fallen in the War.* London: Hodder & Stoughton, 1918.

*Black, E. L. *1914–1918 in Poetry: An Anthology.* London: University of London Press, 1970.

Brophy, John and Eric Partridge. *Songs and Slang of the British Soldier, 1914–1918.* 3d ed. London: Eric Partridge, 1931.

*Clark, George H. *A Treasury of War Poetry.* Boston: Houghton Mifflin, 1917.

*———. *A Treasury of War Poetry, Second Series.* Boston: Houghton Mifflin, 1919.

*Dickinson, Patric. *Soldiers' Verse.* London: Frederick Mutter, 1945.

*Gardner, Brian. *Up the Line to Death: The War Poets, 1914–18: An Anthology.* Foreword by Edmund Blunden. London: Methuen, 1964.

*Parsons. I. M. *Men Who March Away: Poems of the First World War.* London: Chatto & Windus, 1965.

Reilly, Catherine W. *Scars Upon My Heart: Women's Poetry and Verse of the First World War.* London: Virago, 1980.

Sanford, A. P. and Robert Haven Schauffler. *Armistice Day.* New York: Dodd, Mead, 1927. Includes both poetry and prose.

*Silkin, Jon. *The Penguin Book of First World War Poetry.* Harmondsworth: Penguin, 1979.

Untermeyer, Louis. *Modern British Poetry: A Critical Anthology.* New York: Harcourt, Brace, 1920; revised, 1925.

Wilkinson, Marguerite. *Contemporary Poetry.* New York: Macmillan, 1924.

Williams, Oscar. *The War Poets: An Anthology of the War Poetry of the 20th Century.* New York: John Day, 1945.

2. BIBLIOGRAPHIES

*Blunden, Edmund, Cyril Falls, H. M. Tomlinson, and R. Wright. *The War: 1914–1918: A Booklist.* London: The Reader, 1929. Entries arranged under "History," "Personal Impressions and Recollections," "Psychological Interpretations," "Fiction," "Poetry," "Drama," and "Divisional and Regimental Histories."

*Kuntz, Joseph M. and Nancy C. Martinez. *Poetry Explication: A Checklist of Interpretation Since 1925 of British and American Poems Past and Present.* Boston: G. K. Hall, 1980. Several helpful secondary sources for individual poets.

*Reilly, Catherine W. *English Poetry of the First World War: A Bibliography.* New York: St. Martin's Press, 1978. List of publications of 2,225 English war poets, gleaned chiefly from anthologies and publication lists.

3. BOOKS

*Bergonzi, Bernard. *Heroes' Twilight: A Study of the Literature of the Great War.* London: Constable, 1965. Discusses poetry and evolving attitudes of Brooke, Grenfell, Sorley, Graves, Blunden, Sassoon, Rosenberg, Owen, and others.

Berry, Francis. *Herbert Read.* London: Longmans, Green, 1953. Critical and biographical monograph for Writers and Their Work Series.

*Blamires, David. *David Jones: Artist and Writer.* Toronto: University of Toronto Press, 1972. Full-length critical biography.

*Blunden, Edmund. *War Poets: 1914–1918.* London: Longmans, Green, 1958. Survey of several trench poets for Writers and Their Work Series.

*Cohen, Joseph. *Journey to the Trenches: The Life of Isaac Rosenberg, 1890–1918.* New York: Basic Books, 1975. Full-length critical biography.

*Cooke, William. *Edward Thomas: A Critical Biography.* London: Faber & Faber, 1970. Full-length critical biography.

*Delany, Paul. *D. H. Lawrence's Nightmare: The Writer and His Circle in the Years of the Great War.* New York: Basic Books, 1978. Biography of Lawrence in England during the war.

*Fussell, Paul. *The Great War and Modern Memory.* London: Oxford University Press, 1975. Discusses the effects of poetry and prose of the war years on contemporary attitudes and language.

Hardie, Alec M. *Edmund Blunden.* London: Longmans, Green, 1958. Critical and biographical monograph for Writers and Their Work Series.

*Hassall, Christopher. *Rupert Brooke: A Biography.* London: Faber & Faber, 1964. Full-length biography.

*Hibberd, Dominic, ed. *Poetry of the First World War: A Casebook.* London: Macmillan, 1981. A compendium of secondary sources for several war poets.

*———. *Wilfred Owen.* London: Longman Group, 1975. Critical and biographical monograph for Writers and Their Work Series.

Hooker, Jeremy. *David Jones: An Exploratory Study of the Writings.* London: Enitharmon, 1975. Full-length critical study.

*Hurd, Michael. *The Ordeal of Ivor Gurney.* Oxford: Oxford University Press, 1978. Full-length biography that stresses that Gurney's madness did not result entirely from his experience of war.

*Johnston, John H. *English Poetry of the First World War: A Study in the Evolution of Lyric and Narrative Form.* Princeton, N.J.: Princeton University Press, 1964. Generic approach to the war poems of Brooke, Grenfell, Nichols, Sorley, Sassoon, Blunden, Owen, Rosenberg, Read, and Jones.

*Kirkham, Michael. *The Poetry of Robert Graves.* New York: Oxford University Press, 1969. Full-length critical study.

*Lane, Arthur E. *An Adequate Response: The War Poetry of Wilfred Owen and Siegfried Sassoon.* Detroit: Wayne State University Press, 1972. Full-length critical study of Owen and Sassoon's poetry.

*MacShane, Frank. *The Life and Work of Ford Madox Ford.* New York: Horizon Press, 1965. Discusses Ford's prose and poetry of the war in the context of his life and literary career.

Marsh, Sir Edward. *Rupert Brooke: A Memoir.* London: Sidgwick & Jackson, 1918. Memoir written shortly after Brooke's death.

Marsh, Jan. *Edward Thomas: A Poet for his Country.* London: Elek, 1978. Full-length critical biography.

*Moore, T. Sturge. *Some Soldier Poets.* London: Grant Richards, 1919. Early view of Grenfell, Brooke, Nichols, Sassoon, Graves, Vernède, Sorley, Ledwidge, Thomas, Harvey, and Aldington.

Morgan, Edwin. *Hugh MacDiarmid.* London: Longman Group, 1976. Critical and biographical monograph for Writers and Their Work Series.

*Motion, Andrew. *The Poetry of Edward Thomas.* London: Routledge & Kegan Paul, 1981. Comprehensive study of Thomas's life and work.

Orel, Harold. *The Final Years of Thomas Hardy, 1912–1928.* Lawrence: University Press of Kansas, 1976. Biography of Hardy during and after the war years.

Owen, Harold. *Journey from Obscurity: Wilfred Owen, 1893–1918.* 3 vols. Oxford: Oxford University Press, 1963–1965. A family memoir.

*Panichas, George A., ed. *Promise of Greatness: The War of 1914–1918.* New York: John Day, 1968. Collection of articles by survivors of the war and others.

*Rogers, Timothy, ed. *Georgian Poetry, 1911–1922: The Critical Heritage.* London: Routledge & Kegan Paul, 1977. Seventy-four collected reviews of the Georgian poetry anthologies and some later articles.

*Ross, Robert H. *The Georgian Revolt: 1910–1922: Rise and Fall of a Poetic Ideal.* Carbondale: Southern Illinois University Press, 1965. Follows the Georgian movement from inception, through the war, to its decline.

*Scannell, Vernon. *Edward Thomas.* New York: Longmans, Green, 1963. Critical and biographical monograph for Writers and Their Work Series.

Seymour-Smith, Martin. *Robert Graves.* London: Longmans, Green, 1956. Critical and biographical monograph for Writers and Their Work Series.

*Silkin, Jon. *Out of Battle: The Poetry of the Great War.* London: Oxford University Press, 1972. Includes discussion of Hardy, Kipling, Brooke, Sorley, Thomas, Blunden, Gurney, Sassoon, Read, Aldington, Ford, Owen, Rosenberg, and Jones.

Sparrow, John. *Robert Bridges.* London: Longmans, Green, 1962. Critical and biographical monograph for Writers and Their Work Series.

*Stallworthy, Jon. *Wilfred Owen.* London: Oxford University Press, 1974. Full-length critical biography.

Sturgeon, Mary C. *Studies of Contemporary Poets.* New York: Dodd, Mead, 1919. Includes chapters on Brooke, de la Mare, Gibson, Ford, Macaulay, Monro, Margaret Woods, Drinkwater, Hardy, Squire, Contemporary Women Poets, and Yeats.

*Swann, Thomas Burnett. *The Ungirt Runner: Charles Hamilton Sorley, Poet of World War I.* Hamden, Conn.: Archon, 1965. Full-length critical biography.

*Thomas, R. George. *Edward Thomas.* Cardiff: University of Wales Press, 1972. Biographical monograph for Writers of Wales Series.

*Thorpe, Michael. *Siegfried Sassoon: A Critical Study.* London: Oxford University Press, 1967. Full-length critical study of Sassoon's poetry.

*Welland, D. S. R. *Wilfred Owen: A Critical Study.* London: Chatto & Windus, 1960. Full-length study of Owen's poetry.

4. PARTS OF BOOKS

Banarjee, A. *Spirit above Wars: A Study of the English Poetry of the Two World Wars,* pp. 16–82. London: Macmillan, 1976. Includes as Chapter 2, "Poetry of the First

World War," which discusses Brooke, Grenfell, Sorley, Sassoon, Owen, and Rosenberg.

Bowra, C. M. *In General and Particular,* pp. 193–222. New York: World, 1964. Chapter entitled "Poetry and the First World War."

*Chakravarty, Amiya. *The Dynasts and the Post-War Age in Poetry,* pp. 136–74. New York: Octagon, 1970. Includes a chapter on "Hardy and 'War Poetry.'"

Connolly, Cyril. *Ideas and Places,* pp. 89–90, 97–98, 105–6. London: Weidenfeld & Nicolson, 1953. Questionnaire responses from Robert Graves, Rose Macaulay, and Herbert Read.

Daiches, David. *New Literary Values: Studies in Modern Literature,* pp. 52–68. Freeport, N.Y.: Books for Libraries Press, 1958. Discussion of Owen's poetry.

*———. *Poetry and the Modern World: A Study of Poetry in England Between 1900 and 1939,* pp. 38–89. New York: Biblo & Tannen, 1969. Includes the chapters "The Georgian Poets" and "War Poetry—The Imagists—Post-War Satire—The Sitwells."

Drinkwater, John. *The Muse in Council,* pp. 224–47, 273–303. New York: Houghton Mifflin, 1925. Discussions of Alice Meynell, Housman, Brooke, and Ledwidge.

Enright, D. J. *Conspirators and Poets,* pp. 77–105. London: Chatto & Windus, 1966. Essays on Brooke, Owen, Lawrence, and Read.

*———. *The Modern Age,* pp. 154–69. London: Penguin, 1961. Includes an overview of changes the war wrought on poetry.

Farrar, L. L., Jr., ed. *War: A Historical, Political, and Social Study,* pp. 247–51. Santa Barbara, Calif.: Clio, 1978. Discusses poetry of Owen, Brooke, Shaw-Stewart, Grenfell, McCrae, Sorley, Coulson, Binyon, and Sassoon.

Gillie, Christopher. *Movements in English Literature: 1900–1940,* pp. 65–89. London: Cambridge University Press, 1975. Brief discussion of Owen, Rosenberg, Housman, Hardy, Thomas, Binyon, Yeats, and T. S. Eliot.

Gittings, Robert. *Thomas Hardy's Later Years,* pp. 93–105. Boston: Little, Brown, 1978. Includes chapter "War at Home and Abroad."

Gosse, Edmund. *Inter Arma: Being Essays Written in Time of War,* pp. 3–38. London: Heinemann, 1916. Discusses early effects of the war on literature in France.

*———. *Some Diversions of a Man of Letters,* pp. 261–85. London: Heinemann, 1920. Provides a survey of about fifteen soldier and civilian war poets.

Grant, Joy. *Harold Monro and the Poetry Bookshop,* pp. 101–8. Berkeley: University of California Press, 1967. Provides the story of the Poetry Bookshop and includes a section on the rejection of Thomas's poetry and the Poetry Bookshop's relationship to Owen's poetry.

Greene, Graham. *Collected Essays,* pp. 135–40, 159–71, 351–58. New York: Viking, 1969. Essays on Chesterton, Ford, and Read.

*Hague, René. *David Jones,* pp. 36-50. Cardiff: University of Wales Press, 1975. Monograph for Writers of Wales Series; Chapter 3, "The Great War and 'In Parenthesis,'" is particularly useful.

Harding, D. W. *Experience into Words,* pp. 91–103. New York: Horizon Press, 1964. Chapter on Rosenberg.

Heaney, Seamus. *Preoccupations: Selected Prose, 1968–1978,* pp. 202–6. New York: Farrar, Straus & Giroux, 1980. Discussion of relationship between Francis Ledwidge and Lord Dunsany.

Hynes, Samuel. *Edwardian Occasions: Essays on English Writing in the Early Twentieth Century,* pp. 91–99, 123–28, 144–52. New York: Oxford University Press, 1972. Chapters on Edward Thomas, T. E. Hulme, and Rupert Brooke.

Klein, Holger, ed. *The First World War in Fiction: A Collection of Critical Essays,* pp. 160–73. London: Macmillan, 1976. Includes Dianne DeBell's "Strategies of Survival: David Jones, *In Parenthesis,* and Robert Graves, *Goodbye to All That.*"

Leavis, F. R. *New Bearings in English Poetry: A Study of the Contemporary Situation,* pp. 27–74. Ann Arbor: University of Michigan Press, 1960. Includes a chapter entitled "The Situation at the End of World War I."

Murry, John Middleton. *The Evolution of an Intellectual,* pp. 71–79. London: Cobden-Sanderson, 1920. Includes chapter entitled "Mr. Sassoon's War Verses."

Perkins, David. *A History of Modern Poetry from the 1890s to the High Modernist Mode,* pp. 416–45. Cambridge, Mass.: Belknap, 1976. Includes chapter entitled "British Poetry After the War, 1918–1928."

*Phelps, William Lyon. *The Advance of English Poetry in the Twentieth Century,* pp. 1–193. New York: Dodd, Mead, 1918; reprint, London: Kennikat Press, 1970. Survey of several prewar and war poets.

*Pinto, Vivian de Sola. *Crisis in English Poetry: 1880–1940,* pp. 36–157. New York: Harper & Row, 1966. Survey of several prewar and war poets.

Rutherford, Andrew. *The Literature of War: Five Studies in Heroic Virtue,* pp. 64–112. New York: Barnes & Noble, 1978. Chapter 4, "The Common Man as Hero: Literature of the Western Front" discusses shifts in the concept of heroism.

*Spender, Stephen. *Love-Hate Relations: English and American Sensibilities,* pp. 133–49, 170–88. New York: Random House, 1974. Includes chapters on the Georgians, Frost and Thomas, and English Poets and the War.

*Swinnerton, Frank. *The Georgian Literary Scene, 1910–1935: A Panorama,* pp. 207–27, 257–72. London: Hutchinson, 1935; revised, 1954. Includes chapter-length studies of prewar Georgian poets and war poets.

Williamson, Henry. *The Linhay on the Downs,* pp. 224–62. London: Faber & Faber, 1934. Discusses the war prose of Blunden, Sassoon, Graves, and others.

*Wohl, Robert. *The Generation of 1914,* pp. 85–121. Cambridge: Harvard University Press, 1979. Discusses Brooke, Sassoon, Owen, Brittain, and others.

5. ARTICLES

"Arma Virumque: The Poetry of Three Wars." *Times Literary Supplement,* 10 March 1966, pp. 186–88. Overview of developing trend of war poetry.

Benkovitz, Miriam J. "Edmund Blunden's Ghosts." *Columbia Library Columns* 27 (1978): 14–22. Compares war experiences in Blunden's poetry with those in his prose.

*Bergonzi, Bernard. "Before 1914: Writers and the Threat of War." *Critical Quarterly* 6 (Summer 1964): 126–34. Survey of prewar unrest in poetry.

*Bewley, Marius. "The Poetry of Isaac Rosenberg." *Commentary* 7 (January 1949): 34–44. Biographical and critical survey of Rosenberg's development.

Blissett, William. "*In Parenthesis* among the War Books." *University of Toronto Quarterly* 42 (Spring 1973): 258–88. Discusses *In Parenthesis* in context of fiction and memoirs of the war.

Brophy, James D. "The War Poetry of Wilfred Owen and Osbert Sitwell: An Instructive Contrast." *Modern Language Studies* 1 (1971): 22–29. Contrasts Owen and Sitwell to conclude that Owen covers greater range of experience while Sitwell more effectively denounces war.

*Buitenhuis, Peter. "Writers at War: Propaganda and Fiction in the Great War." *University of Toronto Quarterly* 45 (Summer 1976): 277–94. Discusses the role of established literary figures in the service of the British propaganda machine at Wellington House.

*Carr, Ian. "Edmund Blunden and the 1914–1918 War." *Stand* 4 (1960): 48–51. Discusses the war's impact on Blunden and his poetry.

Churchill, R. C. "War and the Poet's Responsibility." *Nineteenth Century and After* 137 (April 1945): 155–59. Analysis of the poet's responsibility to approach war with high seriousness.

*Cohen, Joseph. "In Memory of W. B. Yeats—and Wilfred Owen." *Journal of English and Germanic Philology* 58 (October 1959): 637–49. Examines basis of Yeats's animosity toward Owen and suggests a poetical kinship between the two.

———. "Isaac Rosenberg: From Romantic to Classic." *Tulane Studies in English* 10 (1960): 129–42. Rosenberg's development from early romanticism to classical leanings.

*———. "Isaac Rosenberg: The Poet's Progress in Print." *English Literature in Transition* 6 (1963): 142–46. Chronicle of the slow growth of Rosenberg's reputation.

*———. "Owen Agonistes." *English Literature in Transition* 8 (1965): 253–68. Essay on lacunae in biographical accounts of Owen.

———. "The Three Roles of Siegfried Sassoon." *Tulane Studies in English* 7 (1957): 169–85. Discusses Sassoon as "angry prophet," "country gentleman," and "self-effacing hermit."

———. "The War Poet as Archetypal Spokesman." *Stand* 4 (1960): 23–27. Argues that the poet in uniform has superior insight regarding issues of physical and spiritual stress and succor.

*———. "Wilfred Owen: Fresher Fields Than Flanders." *English Literature in Transition* 7 (March 1964): 1–7. Chronicles the development of Owen's literary reputation.

———. "Wilfred Owen in America." *Prairie Schooner* 31 (1957): 339–45. Discusses slower growth of Owen's reputation in the United States.

———. "The Wilfred Owen Poetry Collection." *Library Chronicle of the University of Texas* 5 (Spring 1955): 24–35. Describes the Owen materials held at the University of Texas, Austin.

*Cooke, William. "Edward Thomas, E. M., and the Georgian Anthologies." *Four Decades of Poetry* 2 (1978): 94–100. Discusses Thomas's relationship with the Georgians and his omission from Marsh's anthologies.

*———. "The War Diary of Edward Thomas." *Stand* 19 (1977): 5–9. Discusses Thomas's war diary entries and their relationship to his last poems and days.

*Cubeta, Paul M. "Robert Frost and Edward Thomas: Two Soldier Poets." *New England Quarterly* 52 (June 1979): 147–76. Discusses Thomas's poetry in the context of the war and Frost's friendship.

Dickinson, Patric. "Poets of the First World War." *Listener* 67 (1962): 259–60. General survey of war poets.

———. "War Poets." *The Spectator,* 177 (13 December 1946): 639. Discusses influence of the war poets.

Dollimore, Jonathan. "The Poetry of Hardy and Edward Thomas." *Critical Quarterly* 17 (Autumn 1975): 203–15. Contrasts Hardy's and Thomas's uses of nature in poetry.

Eckert, Robert P., Jr. "Edward Thomas: Soldier-Poet of his Race." *American Book Collector* 4 (July/August 1933): 19–21, 66–69. Survey of Thomas's relationship with Frost and assessment of his value to a book collector.

Gardner, Philip. "Edmund Blunden: War Poet." *University of Toronto Quarterly* 42 (Spring 1973): 218–40. Examination of Blunden's war poetry in the context of his literary career.

*Gemmill, Janet P. *"In Parenthesis:* A Study of Narrative Technique." *Journal of Modern Literature* 1 (March 1971): 311–28. Discusses the problems of narration in *In Parenthesis.*

*Gillet, L. B. "Poets in the War." *North American Review* 209 (June 1919): 822–36. Contemporary survey of several war poets.

*Girouard, Mark. "When Chivalry Died." *The New Republic,* 30 September 1981, pp. 25–30. Analysis of the war's breakdown of the prewar chivalric tradition.

Glover, John. "Owen and Barbusse and Fitzwater Wray." *Stand* 21 (1979): 22–32. Influence of Barbusse's *Le Feu* on Owen.

*Gregory, Horace. "The Isolation of Isaac Rosenberg." *Poetry* 68 (April 1946): 30–39. Isolation as an influence on Rosenberg's work.

Hague, René. "David Jones: A Reconnaissance." *The Twentieth Century* 168 (July 1960): 27–45. *In Parenthesis* and the *Anathemata.*

*Harding, D. W. "Aspects of the Poetry of Isaac Rosenberg." *Scrutiny* 3 (March 1935): 358–69. Rosenberg's treatment of war experience and handling of language.

*Hazen, James. "Hardy's War Poetry." *Four Decades of Poetry* 2 (1978): 76–93. Discussion of Hardy's developing critical attitude toward war.

*Henn. T. R. "W. B. Yeats and the Poetry of War." *Proceedings of the British Academy* 51 (1965): 301–19. Discussion of Yeats's war poems.

*Hibberd, Dominic. "Wilfred Owen and the Georgians." *Review of English Studies* 30 (1979): 28–40. Georgian influence on Owen's early verse.

*———. "Wilfred Owen's Rhyming." *Studia Neophilologica* 50 (1978): 207–14. Owen's pararhymes.

*Hobsbaum, Philip. "The Road Not Taken." *Listener* 46 (1961): 860, 863. Discusses effect of the deaths of Thomas, Rosenberg, and Owen on English poetic tradition.

*Hoffman, Daniel. "Significant Wounds: The Early Poetry of Robert Graves." *Shenandoah* 17 (1966): 21–40. Discusses literary and mythic influences that inform Graves's poems.

*Holbrook, David. "The Poetic Mind of Edgell Rickword." *Essays in Criticism* 12 (1962): 273–91. Discusses role of wit in Rickword's verse.

*Johnston, J. H. "Charles Sorley's 'Bright Promise.'" *West Virginia University Philological Papers* 13 (1961): 65–75. Survey of Sorley's work.

*———. "David Jones: The Heroic Vision." *Review of Politics* 24 (January 1962): 62–87. Discusses how Jones attained a more comprehensive perspective than did most war poets.

Jones, Mary E. "Heroism in Unheroic Warfare." *Poetry Wales* 8 (Winter 1972): 14–21. Jones's success at placing the war into an heroic context.

*Kirkham, Michael. "Edward Thomas and Social Values." *Four Decades of Poetry* 1 (1977): 247–63. Places Thomas's poetry into the context of community.

*Larkin, Philip. "The Real Wilfred: Owen's Life and Legends." *Encounter* 44 (March 1975): 73–81. Survey of biographical writings on Owen.

*McCourt, Edward A. "Rupert Brooke: A Re-Appraisal." *Dalhousie Review* 24 (April 1944): 148–56. Discusses the validity of Brooke's early popularity in terms of lasting value of the *1914* sonnets.

*———. "Thomas Hardy and War." *Dalhousie Review* 20 (1940): 227–34. Discusses reasons for Hardy's writing patriotic poetry during the war.

Mackerness, E. D. "Charles Hamilton Sorley (1895–1915)." *Die Neueren Sprachen* (1961): 330–34. Discusses Sorley's life and work.

*———. "The Poetry of Ivor Gurney." *Review of English Literature* 3 (1962): 68–77. Discusses *Severn and Somme* and *War's Embers*.

Magalaner, Marvin. "Harold Monro: Literary Midwife." *Arizona Quarterly* 5 (1949): 328–38. Monro's role as sponsor and editor of other poets.

Maguire, C. E. "Harmony Unheard: The Poetry of Siegfried Sassoon." *Renascence* 11 (Spring 1959): 115–24. Sassoon's growing control and more harmonious style in his verse.

*Marsh, Jan. "New Numbers." *Four Decades of Poetry* 1 (1976): 109–26. Discusses joint enterprise of Abercrombie, Brooke, Drinkwater, and Gibson to found *New Numbers*.

*Mathias, Roland. "Edward Thomas." *Anglo-Welsh Review* 10 (1960): 23–37. Discusses acceptance in Thomas's poems, his last years, and his influence on later poets.

Matthews, Geoffrey. "Brooke and Owen." *Stand* 4 (1960): 28–34. Concludes that compassion distinguishes Owen's poetry from Brooke's.

*Melada, Ivan. "The Politics of Writers in the Trenches." *Dalhousie Review* 59 (Summer 1979): 338–49. A discussion of attitudes toward war in Ford, Blunden, Aldington, Graves, Sassoon, Macaulay, Owen, and others.

*Moore, L. Hugh, Jr. "Siegfried Sassoon and Georgian Realism." *Twentieth Century Literature* 14 (January 1969): 199–209. Role of Georgian movement in shaping Sassoon's verse.

Murray, Atholl C. C. "In Perspective: A Study of David Jones's *In Parenthesis*." *Critical Quarterly* 16 (Autumn 1974): 254–63. Jones's achievement of discerning order in the war.

Murry, John Middleton. "The Condition of English Literature." *Athenaeum*, 7 May 1920, pp. 597–98. An appraisal of the state of English poetry shortly after the war.

———. "The Condition of English Poetry." *Athenaeum*, 5 December 1919, 1283–85. An appraisal of the state of English poetry shortly after the war.

*Orel, Harold. "Rudyard Kipling and the Establishment: A Humanistic Dilemma." *South Atlantic Quarterly* 81 (Spring 1982): 162–77. Discusses politically inspired deprecation of Kipling by "Establishment Critics."

*Orr, Peter. "Mr. Jones, Your Legs Are Crossed: A Memoir." *Agenda* 15 (Summer/ Autumn 1977): 110–25. A memoir of Jones's last years.

Orwell, George. "Rudyard Kipling." *Horizon* 5 (February 1942): 111–25. Discusses Kipling and the economics of empire.

*Pacey, Philip. "*The Outrage on Nature:* The Landscape of War in the Work of Paul Nash and David Jones." *Anglo-Welsh Review* 22 (Autumn 1973): 13–30. Compares Nash's painting with Jones's literary depictions of nature in *In Parenthesis*.

Parsons, I. M. "The Poems of Wilfred Owen (1893–1918)." *New Criterion* 10 (July 1931): 658–69. Essay on Owen's significance.

*Patrick, John M. "The Great Explosion August, 1914, and the English Poets." *Proceedings of the Utah Academy of Sciences, Arts, and Letters* 42 (1965): 14–22. Discussion of Georgian poets' response to the war.

Pearsall, Robert B. "The Vendible Values of Housman's Soldiery." *Publications of the Modern Language Association* 82 (1967): 85–90. Discusses Housman's view of soldiering as expressed in his poetry.

*Press, John. "Charles Sorley." *Review of English Literature* 7 (April 1966): 43–60. Survey of Sorley's life and work.

*Quinn, Maire A. "The Personal Past in the Poetry of Thomas Hardy and Edward Thomas." *Critical Quarterly* 16 (Spring 1974): 7–28. Contrasts role of personal experience in the poems of Hardy and Thomas.

Sackton, Alexander H. "Two Poems on War: A Critical Exercise." *Studies in English* 31 (1952): 120–24. Compares Sassoon's "Aftermath" with Rosenberg's "Break of Day in the Trenches."

Savage, D. S. "Two Prophetic Poems." *Western Review* 13 (Winter 1949): 67–78. Discusses Yeats's "The Second Coming" and Owen's "Strange Meeting" as prophetic of the postwar years.

*Stallworthy, Jon. "W. B. Yeats and Wilfred Owen." *Critical Quarterly* 11 (Autumn 1969): 199–214. Emphasizes Yeats's inability to recognize Owen's worth.

*Strong, L. A. G. "English Poetry Since Brooke." *American Mercury* 35 (1935): 56–62. Discusses some war poets' later influence.

*Thomas, W. K. "The War Sonnets of Rupert Brooke." *English Quarterly* 7 (Spring 1974): 27–53. Analysis of the *1914* sonnets in the context of Brooke's experience and reading.

*Thomas, William David. "The Impact of World War I on the Early Poetry of Robert Graves." *Malahat Review* 35 (1975): 113–29. Discusses the war's effect on Graves's early poetry.

Waugh, Alec. "Robert Graves." *To-Day* 4 (February 1919): 209–13. Contemporary criticism of Graves's war poetry.

*Waugh, Arthur. "War Poetry (1914–1918)." *The Quarterly Review* 280 (October 1918): 380–400. Early critical survey of several soldier poets.

*Welland, Dennis. "Arthur Graeme West: A Messenger to Job." In *Renaissance and Modern Essays,* edited by G. R. Hibbard, pp. 169–79. New York: Barnes & Noble, 1966. Discussion of West's stance in his war verse.

*———. "Half-Rhyme in Wilfred Owen: Its Derivation and Use." *Review of English Studies* 1 (July 1950): 226–41. Discusses Owen's half-rhymes and attempts of later poets to use them to advantage.

*———. "Wilfred Owen's Manuscripts." *Times Literary Supplement,* 15 June 1956, p. 368; 22 June 1956, p. 384. Problems of editing and interpreting Owen's manuscripts.

*Wilson, John. "Wilfrid Gibson and the War." *Four Decades of Poetry* 1 (1976): 130–40. Discusses Gibson's war poetry.

Index